THE KEY TO THE
HERMETIC SANCTUM

The Key to the
Hermetic Sanctum

EDITED, TRANSLATED, AND ANNOTATED BY

Christer Böke, John Koopmans
& Juan Duc Perez

WITH A PREFACE BY
AARON CHEAK

AUCKLAND · MMXX

The Key to the Hermetic Sanctum
(La Clef du cabinet hermétique)

EDITED, TRANSLATED, AND ANNOTATED BY
Christer Böke, John Koopmans, & Juan Duc Perez
with a Preface by Aaron Cheak

❧

First edition published by

RUBEDO PRESS
AUCKLAND · NEW ZEALAND

© Rubedo Press 2020

ISBN: 978-0-9951245-6-1

❧

Design and typography
by Aaron Cheak

Cover image from Barent Cœnders van Helpen
Escalier des sages ou la philosophie des anciens
Groningen: Charles Pieman, 1686.

SCRIBE SANGUINE QUIA SANGUIS SPIRITUS

CONTENTS

Preface

COMPOSED IN MIDDLE FRENCH AND PRESERVED IN
an eighteenth-century manuscript which strongly influenced
Fulcanelli, *The Key to the Hermetic Sanctum* presents itself
with a singular purpose: to unlock the symbolic philosophy
of the *Emerald Tablet* in order to provide the foundations of
alchemical practice.

Previously unknown apart from some captivating cita-
tions from Fulcanelli, this mysterious text recently surfaced
among the manuscripts of the Gallatins, a family of Swiss
provenance who rose to prominence among the founding
fathers of the United States of America. Originating specifically from the personal collection of Albert H. Gallatin—a
professor of chemistry, geology, and mineralogy who devoted himself to the study of ancient langauges in order to
understand alchemical texts—this manuscript is of singular
interest to scholars of religion, historians of science, and prac-
titioners of the royal art.

Translated into English for the very first time, *The Key
to the Hermetic Sanctum (La Clef du cabinet hermétique)* appears here in a handsome, dual-language edition featuring
a carefully prepared edition of the French text alongside a
clear English translation. This copiously annotated volume
comes with an introduction exploring the figure of Gallatin and his possible connections to Fulcanelli—one of the
twentieth century's most enigmatic alchemists—together

with an appendix clarifying the relationship of this text to other texts known under the same or similar names.

OF CABINETS AND SANCTUMS

At first glance, the title of our manuscript, *La Clef du cabinet hermétique*, appears to lend itself to a fairly straight-forward translation: 'The Key to the Hermetic Cabinet'. This, however, risks falling for the *faux amis du traducteur* (the false friends of the translator), i.e., those words which look or sound similar but which in fact have substantially different meanings. The French term *cabinet* is one such word.

The literal and contextual meaning of *cabinet* in French is essentially a 'chamber or room in which a professional undertakes their activity'. A *cabinet du médecin*, for instance, is a doctor's office; a *cabinet de chimie*, a laboratory. The famous *cabinets des curiosités* (German *Wunderkammern*, 'rooms of wonder'), were museum-like galleries of marvelous art and unusual natural specimens.

The word also accrued further literary and artistic uses: a *cabinet du lecture*, or *cabinet littéraire*, referred to a study, reading room, or library. The meaning of *cabinet* as a place where one conserves precious objects such as manuscripts and books would inform its meaning as a museum. As the appendix to this volume makes clear, there is an early reference to a *cabinet hermétique* which turns out to be a reference to the collection of alchemical texts known as the *Musæum Hermeticum*—'The Hermetic Museum'. But even here it is the archaic meaning of museum that is to be understood—a chamber of study conceived as a place of inspiration. Museums, it should be noted, were originally temples and shrines to the *muses*. Only later did they become repositories of cultural inspiration: libraries and studies at first, and later, museums in the modern sense. The exact translation of the word *cabinet* thus shifts according to context.

The 'chamber of practice' of a Hermetic philosopher is, historically speaking, twofold: oratory and laboratory. This is confirmed by the earliest identifiable alchemist that we have any substanial biographical information on—the fourth century Egyptian artisan-priest, Zosimos of Panopolis.[1] As both theurgist and metallurgist, his chambers of practice were temple and atelier. This dual heritage continued into the European alchemical tradition, where it became embodied in the adage, *ora et labora*, 'pray and work'.

Our manuscript itself explicitly perpetuates this sacred aspect of the tradition. No one, we are told, will be able to unravel the intentionally obfuscated descriptions of the alchemical opus without divine inspiration. Thus, while 'chamber' alone might have been a safe enough translation for ordinary purposes, we have gravitated towards the more evocative 'sanctum'—the sacred enclosure—because it elicits the space in which the alchemists seclude themselves in order to unlock the mystery of the great work.

The decision to translate *cabinet* as sanctum has not been unanimously undertaken, and the publisher takes responsibility for insisting on this usage. Yet it is our view that the predominant meaning of the English word 'cabinet'—a piece of furniture with shelves, cupboards, or drawers used for storing or displaying things—is completely inadequate in this context.[2] While 'sanctum' may take a certain measure of poetic license, it nevertheless evokes the spirit of the word far more effectively than the English word 'cabinet'. On this general

---

1   See especially Shannon Grimes, *Becoming Gold: Zosimos of Panopolis and the Alchemical Arts in Roman Egypt*, Auckland: Rubedo Press, 2018.

2   In the English editions of Fulcanelli's works which reference our manuscript, *cabinet* is given simply as 'cabinet' or 'chest'. Although the English word cabinet does in fact retain an archaic meaning of 'room' or 'chamber' in accordance with its etymology—a diminutive of cabin—this sense is extremely oblique to the modern reader and remains inadequate.

point, the author of our manuscript is himself quite explicit:
'we must not stop at the letter, but only at the meaning of the
thing: not at the sound of words, but what they signify'.

UNLOCKING THE EMERALD TABLET

Regarding the nature of the *cabinet hermétique* as a work of
studied contemplation, divine inspiration, and praxis, the
anonymous author of the manuscript cites Hermes himself
as his guarantor. Specifically, we are told that this treatise 'is
only an explanation or commentary on his *Emerald Tablet*,
in which is contained all the mysteries of this admirable art'.
'This', our author adds, 'is why I entitled it the Key to the Hermetic *Cabinet*'. The chamber that this key unlocks, therefore,
is first and foremost a textual one: the symbolic philosophy
of the *Emerald Tablet*.

Attributed to the thrice-great Hermes, the *Emerald Tablet*, or *Tabula Smaragdina*, comes down to us via Latin translations of medieval Arabic works that appear to reflect Syriac
and perhaps even Greek originals. Its opening lines famous-
ly state: 'that which is above is like that which is below, and
that which is below is like that which is above, to perform the
miracles of the one thing'. Arabic sources ascribe this work to
pseudo-Apollonius of Tyana's *Book of the Secret of Creation*,
or *Book of Causes* (*Kitāb Sirr al-khalīqa,* or *Kitāb al-ʿilal*).
However, the opening formula bears a still deeper identity to
the hieratic art practiced by the Neoplatonic theurgists, who
according to Proclus, saw 'the lowest things in the highest
and the highest in the lowest'.[3]

Among the various ways in which our manuscript un-
packs the *Emerald Tablet*, one point in particular should
be emphasised because it speaks directly to the nature of al-

3   Proclus, *On the Hieratic Art,* 148, cited in Uždavinys, ed., *The Golden
     Chain: An Anthology of Pythagorean and Platonic Philosophy,* Bloo-
     mington, Indiana: World Wisdom, 2004, p. 300.

chemy as a 'divine art', an expression whose provenance also drinks deeply from the Greek and Arabic roots of alchemy. The similitude of above and below is revealed here in its deeper meaning. The alchemical work is a microcosm of the cosmos at large because the alchemist replicates the divine act of cosmogenesis:

> The philosopher must join heaven with the earth, he must draw from the chaos, that is to say from his subject, the luminaries, to separate the light from the darkness, and by the union of the spirit to make a perfect whole, imitating by this act God in the creation of the world.

The divine act of conjoining above and below, of drawing forth two natures from one substance in an almost Daoist dance of darkness and light, thus forms the essence of the alchemical art. Upon this basis, our manuscript opens the gates to the philosophy and practice of the *œuvre*, and ultimately, to the divine aims of alchemy itself—the perfection of metals and mortals through the restoration of their incorruptible natures.

AARON CHEAK, PHD

Editor-in-Chief, Rubedo Press

Introduction

THE KEEN READER OF FULCANELLI IS ALREADY familiar with the multiple references to the alchemical manuscript: *La Clef du cabinet hermétique*. It has been a legendary manuscript in the modern alchemical community ever since it was first mentioned by Fulcanelli. Eagerly sought after for several decades, it came close to becoming yet another manuscript lost to history. It has not been translated into any language—until now.[1]

Fulcanelli quotes extensively from *La Clef du cabinet hermétique* on several occasions, in both of his works: *Le Mystère des cathédrals* (1926) and *Les Demeures philosophales* (1930). In *Le Mystère des cathédrals* (The Mystery of the Cathedrals), he refers to it as a 'precious anonymous manuscript from the eighteenth century'.[2] A footnote from *Les Demeures philosophales* (The Dwellings of the Philosophers) states that this work was 'copied after an original that belonged to M.

---

1 A transcript of the French text of the manuscript was published in January 2018 via Lulu/Philemon Editions; unfortunately, it lacked any editorial presentation and contained several flaws, such as missing words or parts of sentences, as well as erroneous interpretations of the handwritten script. A 2020 edition appeared through the same publisher, but we have not been able to consult this edition at the time of the present publication.

2 Fulcanelli, *Le Mystère des cathédrales et l'interprétation ésotérique des symbols hermétiques du grand œuvre*, Paris: Jean Schmidt, 1926, p. 55 (*Le Mystère des cathédrales*, London: Neville Spearman: 1971, p. 80).

Desaint, doctor, rue Hiacinthe in Paris'.[3] Canseliet leaves us to understand that it was not Fulcanelli who had copied it from this person, but that this information derived from a note in the very copy of the manuscript that Fulcanelli possessed:

> *La Clef du cabinet hermétique*, on paper *vergé bleuté*, copied in 15 days, by an amateur who adds in a note: Mr Desaint, doctor, rue Hiacinthe, porte St-Michel, lent me the manuscript from which I have made the following copy.[4]

There is no doubt that Fulcanelli was very much inspired by this manuscript. He clearly endorses it as a highly revealing text. Without going into too much detail about the suggested alchemical work, it is nevertheless worth emphasising that the only time Fulcanelli describes the alchemical solvent[5] in a liquid form—he usually argued for it as being a solid, crystalline mineral or 'metallic salt'—is in the context of a quote that is drawn from the *La Clef du cabinet hermétique*. This was done while giving his alchemical interpretation of the myth of Zeus and Danæ:

> It is precisely the case of the hermetic solvent, which, after undergoing fermentation in an oak barrel, assumes, upon decantation, the appearance of liquid gold. The anonymous author of an unpublished eighteenth-century manuscript [*La Clef du cabinet hermétique*] writes on the subject: 'If you let this

3   Fulcanelli, *Les Demeures philosophales et le symbolisme hermétique dans ses rapports avec l'art sacré et l'ésotérisme du grand-oeuvre*, Paris: Jean Schmidt, 1930, p. 196 (*The Dwellings of the Philosophers*, Boulder: Archive Press, 1999, p. 303 n. 2).

4   Eugène Canseliet, 'Quelques réflexions alchimiques sur les drogues', in *Les Cahiers de la Tour Saint-Jacques* 1, 1er trim., 1960, p. 22.

5   Fulcanelli referred to this agent *passim* as: 'First mercury', 'Common mercury', 'Universal solvent', and 'Mother of the work'.

water run, you will see with your very eyes the gold shining in its first being with all the colours of the rainbow'.[6]

There is another quote in the *Les Demeures philosophales* which is related to the above, and indirectly taken from the *La Clef du cabinet hermétique*, as the reader will be able to see for themselves, but here Fulcanelli does not mention it explicitly:

> Let us note in passing that the cabalists, with one of the puns for which they were famous, have taught that fermentation had to occur by means of a wooden vessel or better yet, in a cask cut in half to which they applied the qualifier of hollow oak tree.[7]

The theme of the mysterious 'vessel of wooden oak cut in half' also appears in another rather lengthy quote taken directly from the *La Clef du cabinet hermétique*, which Fulcanelli reproduces in his *Le Mystère des cathédrales*:

> Now this is the place to reveal one of the great secrets of this Art, which Philosophers have hidden. This is the vessel, without which you cannot carry out the putrefaction and purification of our elements, any more than one can make wine without fermenting it in a cask. Now, as the barrel is made of oak, so the vessel must be of old oak, rounded inside like a half globe, whose sides are good and stout; failing which, two kegs, one over the other.[8]

So that no one is mistaken: Fulcanelli makes it very clear to the reader that he does not understand the reference to

6   *The Dwellings of the Philosophers*, 1999, p. 303.
7   *The Dwellings of the Philosophers*, 1999, pp. 372–73.
8   *Le Mystère des cathédrales*, 1971, p. 93.

the 'vessel made of oak' in a literal sense. 'The spirit gives light, but the letter kills', as he himself emphasises with regards to the finalisation of the quote. It is of course up to the reader to draw his or her own conclusion upon the matter, and the possible meaning of the 'oak vessel' or the 'hollow oak tree'. Let us note in passing that the concept of a vessel made of oak can be found in many other alchemical texts as well. It is, for example, mentioned by Jean d'Espagnet in his *Arcanum Hermeticæ philosophiæ* (The Secret of Hermetic Philosophy, 1623) and of course by Nicholas Flamel, who is famous for his brief statement in *Le Livre des figures hiéroglyphiques* (Book of the Hieroglyphic Figures, 1612): 'Note this oak'. One could also add that the enigmatic passage in our manuscript quoted by Fulcanelli, in which the vessel of oak is 'rounded inside like a half globe ... two kegs, one over the other',[9] might recall the alchemical symbol for *salt*: $\ominus$. We also know that oak wood was often given preference in the preparation of the salt that was for a long time known as 'fixed alkali', i.e., potassium carbonate.

THE FULCANELLI CONNECTION

As already said, the manuscript *La Clef du cabinet hermétique* does not appear to have been mentioned by anyone before Fulcanelli. The manuscript is therefore a smoking gun.[10] This alone is rather astonishing, given the large number of physical and digital books and catalogues of chymical and alchemical

9 *Le Mystère des cathédrales,* 1971, p. 93.
10 According to the work *Cagliostro: homme de lumière,* by François Ribadeau Dumas, Paris: Éditions philosophiques: 1981, p. 45, it is claimed that Cagliostro worked some true (alchemical) processes out of the 'Key' to the *Cabinet Hermétique,* but no source is given for this statement and, considering that there are some other works that bear a similar title to *La Clef du cabinet hermétique,* it is possible that the author either had another text in mind, or simply used the expression in a rhetorical sense. See the appendix for more information.

manuscripts in existence. In the copy of the manuscript that we managed to rediscover—more about this later—there is an incription bearing the name of the person to whom the manuscript previously belonged: A. H. Gallatin.

This person was not previously familiar to us. However, research soon revealed that the initials A. H. Gallatin stand for a certain Albert Horatio Gallatin (7 March 1839–25 March 1902), an American professor of chemistry. But what struck us the most was the fact that Gallatin was born in the year 1839—the birth year of Fulcanelli according to the classical account given by Canseliet. It might be pure coincidence, but it almost seems a little too good to be true. Could this piece of information somehow have been used or incorporated in the creation of the Fulcanelli mythos? It is beyond the topic of this introduction to go into a detailed discussion of the alleged identity of Fulcanelli. After having carefully followed the research on the subject for the past twenty years, it appears that the most probable scenario is that the Fulcanellian literature derived from the work of Pierre Dujols in collaboration with Jean-Julien Champagne.[11]

With this said, it cannot be considered impossible that Gallatin somehow played a role in the affair. If not directly, then perhaps he, for whatever reason, might have served as an inspiration to the above gentlemen in terms of ideas and content, even though the whereabouts of hypothetical notes or manuscript(s) remains unknown.

Be as it may, we feel that it is of interest to say a few more words concerning Gallatin. In fact, very little has been written about him, and there is no dedicated biography. It is reasonable to assume that Gallatin frequented Europe due to his ancestry, and in this regard, our manuscript also carries a note: 'Paris 1869'. Gallatin belonged to a wealthy family.

11   See Geneviève Dubois, *Fulcanelli devoilé*, Paris: Dervy, 1996 (*Fulcanelli and the Alchemical Revival*, Rochester, Vermont: Destiny, 2006); Jean Artero, *Julien Champagne: Apôtre de la Science Hermétique*, Paris: Grenoble Le Mercure dauphinois, 2014.

His great grandfather, Albert Gallatin (1761–1849), was an extremely influential man who among other prominent titles, carried the title of 'Secretary of the Treasury' under two Presidents: James Madison and Thomas Jefferson.[12]

The Gallatin family originally migrated from Switzerland, so it is reasonable to assume that our Gallatin was brought up speaking several different languages. In the New York Public Library, there is a list of books that formerly belonged to our Gallatin, among which are many alchemical titles in English, French, German, and Latin. From certain private letters that we have obtained copies of, we also know that Gallatin had a vivid interest, from an early age, in alchemical texts. According to one letter, he even picked up the endeavor to learn Arabic:

> I am very busy indeed now, working from sunrise to sunset in my laboratory, and at night writing lectures, and reading scientific works. Fridays, Saturdays, Sundays I spend partially in studying German and Arabic. I thought I would take advantage of the dreamy country hours, to study the tongue in which the adepts in Alchemy wrote many of their masterpieces in the fourteenth and fifteenth centuries and which still lie buried, untranslated in the musty libraries of Spain of all the relics of the ancient civilization which conquered that territory, by far the most interesting to me.[13]

Despite his indisputable passion for alchemy, there is another circumstance that is perhaps the most intriguing aspect,

12   See Gregory May, *Jefferson's Treasure: How Albert Gallatin Saved the New Nation from Debt*, Washington, DC: Regnery History, 2018, as well as Nicholas Dungan, *Gallatin: America's Swiss Founding Father*, New York: NYU Press, 2010.

13   Albert Horatio Gallatin to Horatio Gates Stevens, Wednesday 24 February 1864; *Albert H. Gallatin Letters*, 51750; Norwich University Archives; Kreitzberg Library; Northfield, Vermont. H. G. Stevens (1778–1873) was Gallatin's maternal grandfather.

and which could possibly link Gallatin more directly to the Fulcanelli mythos—if not being Fulcanelli himself. In *The Dwellings of the Philosophers*, Fulcanelli communicates a very personal reflection on an earlier phase of his life:

> We know how costly it is to exchange diplomas, seals, and parchments for the humble mantle of the philosopher. At age of 24 we had to drain this chalice filled with a bitter beverage. Heart-wounded, ashamed of the errors of our young years, we had to burn the books and the notebooks, we had to confess our ignorance, and as a modest neophyte, decipher another science on the benches of another school, and so, it is for those who had the courage to forget everything that we take the trouble to study the symbol and to strip its esoteric veil.[14]

Now, how might the above quotation possibly relate to Albert Horatio Gallatin? We said earlier that he was a Professor. In fact he received the title at a very young age, more specifically, in August 1863, at the age of 24, when he joined the Norwich faculty as a Professor in chemistry, geology, and mineralogy. But yet, for reasons unknown to us, he resigned suddenly in August 1864 after only one year.[15]

All this is rather suggestive, considering the above statement from Fulcanelli. What Gallatin did afterwards is not entirely clear, but even though he does not seem to have quit the academic world, he must have taken a different turn in life. He became a Professor in analytical chemistry at the Cooper Institute, and eventually at the University of New York (which is likely the reason why the Gallatin papers and manuscripts ended up in the New York Public Library).

---

14   *The Dwellings of the Philosophers*, 1999, pp. 141–142.
15   *Guide to the Albert H. Gallatin Letters, 1864*, Norwich University Archives and Special Collections, 2010.

A further piece of circumstantial evidence that might link Gallatin to Fulcanelli is found in another biographical reference from *The Dwellings of the Philosophers*:

> Light—rarified and spiritualized fire—possesses the same chemical virtues and power as elementary crude fire. An experiment, with the object of synthetically creating hydrochloric acid (HCl) from its components, amply demonstrates it. If we put equal volumes of chlorine and hydrogen gas in a glass flask, the two gases will keep their own individuality as long as the flask that contains them is kept in darkness. With some diffused light, they progressively combine. But if we expose the vessel to direct solar rays, it explodes and shatters violently.[16]

Fulcanelli does not present us with any source, but the whole argument comes very close to an article that was published in the *Philosophical Magazine* in November 1857: 'On the influence of light upon chlorine and some remarks on alchemy'. This text was written by John William Draper (1811–1882), a professor of chemistry at New York University—the same university and faculty that Gallatin later belonged to. As the title betrays, it is not only a question of the influence of light upon chlorine, a rather separate subject in itself, but of an outspoken connection to the rather infamous subject of alchemy. In the very beginning of the article we read the following:

> Several years ago I observed that when a mixture of chlorine and hydrogen is exposed to light, union does not occur at once, but that a certain interval must elapse, during which absorption takes place, the combination then proceeding in a uniform manner. It is by the chlorine that this absorptive agency is exercised,

16   *The Dwellings of the Philosophers*, 1999, p. 52.

the indigo ray being chiefly influenced. And not only
is it that ray which is thus absorbed: to it also must be
attributed the subsequent combination.

Except for the obvious reference to light and the combination of chlorine and hydrogen (which further on in the
piece is said to have taken place in equal parts, as in the account of Fulcanelli), the attentive reader might have noticed
the reference to indigo. The subject of indigo was close to an
obsession of René Schwaller de Lubicz, who had a long-term
partnership with his friend Jean-Julien Champagne with regards to the reproduction of the red and blue glass of Char-
tres.[17] Continuing to delve into all these potential correlations
and leads would take us too far away from our current topic.
We will be pleased if we have aroused some inspiration or to
have encouraged future research on Gallatin and his possible
relation to the Fulcanelli affair.

According to a brief obituary in the *Troy Daily Times*,[18]
Gallatin was said to have died of a heart failure in his New
York home at 25 Gramercy Park on 25 March 1902. This is,
of course, a long time before Fulcanelli is said to have appeared on the alchemical scene in Paris, which was around
1914–1915 according to the testimony of Canseliet. But as we
said earlier, there seems to be little evidence for a real, physical Fulcanelli, except for perhaps Jean-Julien Champagne,
who evidently presented himself as this identity, according
to at least two independent persons: Schwaller de Lubicz and
Jules Boucher.[19] Nevertheless, it is still something of a mystery
as to where the ideas and content of the Fulcanellian works

17   André Vandenbroeck, *Al-Kemi: Hermetic, Occult, Political, and Pri-
     vate Aspects of R.A. Schwaller de Lubicz*, Rochester, Vermont: Lin-
     disfarne Press, 1987; Aaron Cheak, *Light Broken through the Prism
     of Life: René Schwaller de Lubicz and the Hermetic Problem of Salt*,
     Dissertation, University of Queensland, 2011.
18   The obituary appeared on Wednesday 26 March 1902.
19   Vandenbroeck, *Al-Kemi*, 1987; Artero, *Julien Champagne*, 2014.

derived from. Pierre Dujols obviously played a great part in it; the similarities between his *L'Hypotypose* (1914) and his manuscript *Le Chrysopée*,[20] along with the inclinations of Ful-canelli, speak for themselves. Some ideas might have derived from Schwaller de Lubicz, probably indirect and through his partnership with Champagne, though we strongly doubt that he was the great mastermind behind *Le Mystère des cathédrales*, as he himself portrayed it through the account of Vandenbroeck.[21] Jean-Julien Champagne, once considered an alchemical illiterate and merely the humble illustrator of the Fulcanellian literature, was definitely a man of his own ideas and knowledge, which recent research has now made perfectly clear.[22] And finally, perhaps is it possible that some of the Fulcanellian content, in some mysterious way, came from Professor Albert Horatio Gallatin. Only time will tell.

THE AUTHORSHIP

It is of course difficult to say much about the author behind *La Clef du cabinet hermétique* when so very little information exists. Again, there is possibly not even a single reference to this text before Fulcanelli. However, there is a certain lead to follow which stands out as a beacon to the readers who are already familiar with the corpus of modern western alche-my. The very beginning of the text is identical to the French translation of another alchemical text—the *Manuductio ad cælum chemicum* (1688) by Jacob Toll.[23] This raises the ques-

---

20   Jean-François Gibert, *Propos sur la Chrysopée, suivi de 'Manuscrit de Pierre Dujols-Fulcanelli traitant de la pratique alchimique'*, Paris: Der-vy, 1995.

21   André Vandenbroeck, *Al-Kemi*, 1987.

22   See Artero, *Julien Champagne*, 2014; Julien Champagne, *La Vie Mi-nérale: Étude de Philosophie Hermétique et d'Ésotérisme Alchimique*, 1908; Amboise: Éditions Les Trois R, 2011; and *Procede de Mr Yard-ley*, 1913; Amboise: Éditions Les Trois R, 2015.

23   Jacobus Tollius, *Manuductio ad caelum chemicum*, Amsterdam: Jans-

tion of whether *La Clef du cabinet hermétique* could possibly have been authored by him: a manuscript that was never published for whatever reason, and for which he reused the introduction for the *Manuductio*? It seems unlikely that someone other than the author himself, would have copied the introduction from Toll and used it as his own, especially considering that the rest of the text has certainly not been plagiarised. Further research into the life of Jacob Toll could perhaps throw additional light on the matter.

Since the manuscript includes numerous references to the *Hermetic Triumph*,[24] which was first published in 1689, it is therefore fairly certain that it could not have been written prior to that year. Interestingly, both *La Clef du cabinet hermétique*, and the French translation of the *Manuductio*, *Le Chemin du ciel chymique*, were written in Middle French. This is unusual, since Middle French is generally considered to have been replaced with Modern French by about 1611. It may be possible that both manuscripts were written by the same hand.

THE DISCOVERY

As mentioned, the search for the manuscript of *La Clef du cabinet hermétique* has been a challenge for many people, the editors included, ever since it was mentioned by Fulcanelli. Our breakthrough came in 2013 when Juan Duc Perez noticed one day that a manuscript with the title *La Clef du cabinet hermétique* had been listed on the website of the

---

sonio-Waesbergios, 1688; Jacob Toll, 'Le Chemin du ciel chymique', in Alexandre-Toussaint de Limojon de Saint Didier, *Lettre d'un philosophe sur le secret du grand oeuvre, écrite au sujet de ce qu'Aristée a laissé par écrit à son fils, touchant le magistère philosophique.* Paris: Laurent d'Houry, 1688.

24   Alexandre-Toussaint de Limojon de St Didier, *Le Triomphe Hermétique ou la pierre philosophale victorieuse.* Amsterdam: Henry Wetstein, 1689.

New York Public Library. He notified Christer Böke about his finding, and the process of obtaining a digitised copy began. Ironically, history has taught us that it is often easier for foreign researchers to obtain digitisation of texts in the USA, since the institutions in question usually encourage Americans to travel to the library in question to make copies on site. However, despite this, the endeavor turned out to be a rather long and tedious process which took several months, and required us to pass through several different obstacles at the library. The request was finally approved, and after having paid a moderate sum of around USD$400, we received our copy of the manuscript in the spring of 2014. The costs were shared by Juan, Christer, and John Koopmans, who had also been looking for this text for many years and had been notified as a result. A few months later, the digital manuscript was suddenly made available to the public on the website of the New York Library.

We may add that, besides the obvious reasons for trying to locate a copy of *La Clef du cabinet hermétique*, another incentive for Juan was that this text was possibly the source of a certain recipe allegedly affording 'proof' for the transmutation of silver into gold, found in the eighteenth-century grimoire, *Le Petit Albert*, and stated there as having been drawn from a text called '*Le Cabinet hermétique*'. Unfortunately, this was not the case, but what it proves is that there were other texts in existence whose title bears resemblance to that of our manuscript. The appendix to this volume explores these texts (and their relation to our manuscript) in more detail.

THE TRANSCRIPTION AND TRANSLATION

The translation has been carried out by all three editors, long-time friends and correspondents within the alchemical community, in a joint effort, with some additonal refinements from the publisher. The translation was prepared in as literal

and true a sense to the original as possible, with the result that some parts may read in a somewhat awkward manner. Christer and John already cooperated previously in a mutual project, the transcription and translation of *The Hermetic Recreations*, published through Rubedo Press in 2017. John has diligently gone through the hand-written transcript and proofed it down to the very details, and it bears his signum of rigor. The transcription not only includes a modernised version of the original Middle French text, but also the equivalent Middle French terminology in the footnotes. Based on the orthographical context alone, it appears that the text was likely written no later than the late-seventeenth century, after which point Middle French was seldom used. As already noted, the modern French version that was made available in 2017 is incomplete and contains inaccuracies and misinterpretations; we therefore hope that this publication will also be of interest to a French audience as well as to an English one.

Bonne lecture,

CHRISTER BÖKE, JOHN KOOPMANS,
& JUAN DUC PEREZ

La clef Du cabinet
hermétique.
auant propos.

Bien des gens m'acuseront de teme
rité et de presomption, Lors qu'ils ver-
rons que j'ose entreprendre d'jnstruire
jcy de tres scauans hommes dans l'-
art chimique, en leur enseignant
des choses qu'ils ont jgnorés jusqu'a
present, en leur faisant remarquer
ce qu'ils ont mal entendus: mays djs-
je qui suis eloigné de la parfaite
connoissance de cet art, cependant
pourriie que je sois utile au publique
et si les scauans trouvent quelques
choses qui ne soit pas de leur goust,
La sincerité auec laquel j'escris, doit
bien moins m'attirer leur jndigna-
tion que de me servir d'excuse auprés
d'eux, et soit que l'erreur m'aye
aueuglé, comme beaucoup d'autres

LA CLEF DU CABINET HERMÉTIQUE

*New York Public Library Manuscripts and
Archives Division, MSS Col 36.*

**TEXTE ET
TRADUCTION**

TEXT AND
TRANSLATION

La Clef du
Cabinet Hermétique

The Key to the
Hermetic Sanctum

PREMIÈRE PARTIE

FIRST PART

AVANT-PROPOS

BIEN DES GENS M'ACCUSERONT DE TÉMÉRITÉ ET DE présomption, lorsqu'ils verront[1] que j'ose entreprendre d'instruire ici[2] de très savants[3] hommes dans l'art chimique, en leur enseignant des choses qu'ils ont ignoré[4] jusqu'à présent, en leur faisant remarquer ce qu'ils ont mal entendu[5] : moi[6] dis-je qui suis éloigné de la parfaite connaissance[7] de cet art. Cependant pourvu[8] que je sois utile au public[9] et si les savants[10] trouvent quelques choses qui ne soit pas de leur goût, La sincérité avec laquelle j'écris, doit bien moins m'attirer leur indignation que de me servir d'excuse auprès d'eux, et soit que l'erreur m'a[11] aveuglé, comme beaucoup d'autres ou qu'un travail[12] certain m'ait[13] conduit à la vérité ; il est toujours très assuré[14] que bien des gens auront cet avantage qu'à l'avenir ils se retireront des dépenses[15] inutiles[16] qu'ils font par des travaux infructueux et de la perte du temps qui leur doit être[17] si précieux[18] et si cher par rapport à leur salut et qui doit être[19] la principale[20] occupation des Chrétiens. cherchez[21] premièrement le royaume de Dieu et tout vous réussira.[22] Dit le Seigneur dans l'Evangile.

1.	verrons.	9.	publique.	16.	inutilles.
2.	icy.	10.	sçavons.	17.	estre.
3.	sçavons.	11.	m'aye.	18.	pretieux.
4.	ignores.	12.	Likely 'travaille'	19.	estre.
5.	entendus.	13.	Likely 'm'ait'.	20.	principalle.
6.	moy.	14.	asseures.	21.	cherches.
7.	connoissance.	15.	depences.	22.	reussirat.
8.	pourvue.				

FOREWORD

MANY PEOPLE WILL ACCUSE ME OF TEMERITY AND presumption when they see that I dare undertake here the instruction of very learned men in the chymical arts, teaching them things they have so far ignored, by pointing out to them what they have misunderstood. I say that I am far removed from the perfect knowledge of this art, however, to see that I am useful to the public, and if the scholars find some things which are not to their liking, the sincerity with which I write must much less induce their indignation as to serve as an excuse for them, and either that error has blinded me, like many others, or that a certain work led me to the truth. It is always very certain that many people will have this advantage, that in the future they will withdraw from the unnecessary expenses which they make by unsuccessful work and of the loss of time which must be so precious to them, and so dear in relation to their salvation, and which must be the principal occupation of the Christians, to first seek the kingdom of God, and all will succeed you. Thus said the Lord, in the Gospel.

La méthode que je me suis proposé pour faire un ouvrage si excellent est toute différente de celle que les autres ont suivi[23] dans ce chemin si glissant et qui conduit tant de personnes au précipice.

J'ai[24] pour garant[25] les grands hommes qui ont écrit[26] sur cette science et surtout le fameux Hermès quoi[27] qu'il[28] nous en ait écrit[29] peu de choses ayant très peu de ses écrits;[30] mais dans ce peu de parole,[31] il nous enseigne néanmoins[32] tout le secret de ce grand ouvrage, et on peut dire que ce traité[33] n'est qu'une explication ou un commentaire de sa table d'émeraude[34] dans laquelle sont renfermes tous les mystères[35] de cet art admirable: C'est pourquoi[36] je l'intitulé la clef du cabinet Hermétique.

Ce traité[37] vous enseigne aussi[38] un moyen d'entendre les philosophes qui ont caché[39] ce divin art sous des paraboles[40] et des signes et sous des noms si différents pour le cacher aux ignorants[41] et aux indignes.

23. suivis.	30. escrits	37. traitté.
24. J'ay.	31. parolle.	38. aussy.
25. garand.	32. neantmoins.	39. cacher.
26. escrit.	33. traitté.	40. parabolles.
27. quoy.	34. d'hemeraude.	41. ignorans.
28. Likely 'qu'il'.	35. misteres.	
29. escrit.	36. pourquoy.	

The method that I have proposed in order to do such an excellent work is quite different from what others have followed in this path, which is so slippery and leads so many people to the precipice.

I have as guarantor[1] the great men who have written on this science, and above all the famous Hermes, however, he has written us few things, having [left] very few of his writings. But in this little speech he nevertheless teaches us the whole secret of this great work, and it may be said that this [i.e., the present] treatise is only an explanation or commentary on his *Emerald Tablet*, in which is contained all the mysteries of this admirable art. This is why I entitled it *The Key to the Hermetic Sanctum*.[2]

This treatise also teaches you a way of understanding the philosophers who have hidden this divine art under parables and signs, and under such different names as to hide it from the ignorant and the unworthy.

1   French *garand* (guarantor, proof).
2   French *Cabinet*, with the meanings that have been outlined in the Preface.

De la matière en général

QU'IL Y A PEU DE GENS QUI AIENT[1] COMPRIS COMME se[2] faite[3] la pierre des philosophes, et ne[4] le comprendrons jamais, si Dieu, par une grâce singulière, ne leur révèle ou quelques philosophes; car qui pourrait[5] s'imaginer que ce que les hommes cherchent avec tant d'empressement depuis si longtemps est néanmoins[6] renfermé[7] dans une matière qu'ils foulent aux pieds et qu'ils jettent par les rues, qu'ils ont toujours devant les yeux, qui se trouve dans les ordures et dans les fumier.[8]

C'est ce qui doit confondre l'orgueil[9] des hommes qui méprisent des choses qu'ils devraient[10] estimer et qui honorent et respectent ce qui n'est rien dans son origine. L'or qui brille à leur yeux les éblouit,[11] ils en font leur idole qui leur coûte[12] souvent[13] de grand soin et de grandes inquiétudes pour l'acquérir au dépend même[14] de leur salut éternel; s'ils savaient[15] la matière dont il est fait, ils n'en auraient[16] peut-être[17] pas une si haute idée et seraient[18] obligés d'avouer que la figure et tout l'éclat de ce monde passe et qu'il n'est rien au sentiment du prophète Roi,[19] toute chair[20] n'est que fumier.

1.	ayent.	8.	fumiers.	15.	sçavoient.
2.	ce.	9.	l'orgueuil.	16.	auroient.
3.	fait.	10.	devroient.	17.	estre.
4.	Likely 'ne'.	11.	eblouys.	18.	seroient.
5.	pourroit.	12.	couste.	19.	Roy.
6.	neantmoins.	13.	sçouvent.	20.	chaire.
7.	remfermé.	14.	mesme.		

FIRST CHAPTER

Of matter in general

THAT THERE ARE FEW PEOPLE WHO HAVE UNDER-
stood how the stone of the philosophers is made, and will
never understand it, if God, by a singular grace does not reveal it to them or some philosophers. For who could imagine
that what men seek so eagerly for so long is nevertheless enclosed in a matter which they trample underfoot, and which
they throw through the streets, which they always have before
their eyes, which is found in the garbage and in the manure.

This is what must confound the pride of men who de-
spise things which they should esteem, and who honor and
respect what is nothing in its origin. The gold which shines
in their eyes dazzles them, they make of it their idol, which
often costs them great concern and great anxiety to acquire it,
even at the very cost of their eternal salvation; if they knew
the matter of which it is made, they might not have such a
high opinion, and would be obliged to admit that the figure
and all the brilliance of this world passes away, and that it is
nothing compared to the sentiment of the prophet King, all
flesh is only manure.

L'Écriture met le verre[21] en comparaison avec l'or, quoi[22] qu'il ne soit fait que de cendre. Souviens-toi[23] homme que tu n'es[24] que cendre.

Les philosophes ont donc eu[25] raison de cacher ce mystère[26] aux yeux de ceux qui n'estiment les choses que par les usages qu'ils leur ont donnes, car si ils connaissaient[27] ou si on leur[28] découvrait ouvertement la matière que Dieu a pris[29] plaisir à[30] cacher dans les choses qui leur paraissent[31] utiles, ils n'en auraient[32] plus d'estime.

La matière est unique dans son principe, la nature n'agissant que par les mêmes[33] principes, elle est seulement différente qu'en l'espèce et la forme, par exemple l'aliment que prend l'homme se[34] change et se[35] convertit en la substance de l'homme. Le même[36] aliment qui sert de nourriture à l'homme peut se changer en la substance de l'animal et en une substance bien plus noble que la matière dont il se nourrit; il en est de même[37] de la pierre des philosophes, quoique[38] la matière soit vile, elle est changée par l'art en une perfection beaucoup plus noble que le sujet dont elle tire la matière.

Les philosophes se sont servis de deux voies[39] pour parvenir à ce si grand secret. La 1ère[40] regarde l'art, et la nature y a peu de part. La 2ème[41] C'est la nature qui le fait et l'art ne fait que l'aider, l'un[42] est difficile[43] et est de dépense,[44] et celle-ci[45] est facile[46] et est de peu de dépense.[47] C'est de celle-ci[48] dont je traite[49] et celle que presque tous les anciens[50] ont suivi.[51]

21. vert, likely 'verre'.	30. 'de' in the MS.	42. l'une.
22. quoy.	31. parroissent.	43. dificille.
23. sçouvient toy.	32. auroient.	44. depence.
24. n'est.	33. mesmes.	45. celle cy.
25. eûs.	34. ce.	46. facille.
26. misteres or mistere	35. ce.	47. depence.
	36. mesme.	48. celle cy.
27. connoissoient.	37. mesme.	49. traitte.
28. word seems to be superfluous.	38. quoyque.	50. antiens.
	39. voyes.	51. suivis.
29. prit.	40. 1re.	
	41. 2me.	

The Scripture puts glass[3] in comparison with gold, even though it is only made of ash. Remember man, you are only ashes.

The philosophers have therefore been right to hide this mystery from the eyes of those who value things only by the usages which they have given them, for if they knew or were openly discovering the matter which God took pleasure in hiding in things that seem useful to them, they would have no more esteem.

The matter is unique in its principle, nature acting only by the same principles, it is only different in species and form; for example, the food that man takes, changes itself, and converts it into the substance of man. The same food which serves as nourishment for man can be changed into the substance of the animal and into a substance much more noble than the matter from which he nourishes himself. It is the same in the stone of the philosophers, though the matter is vile, it is changed by art into a perfection much more noble than the subject from which it draws the matter.

The philosophers have used two ways to achieve this great secret. The first regards art, and nature has little part in it. In the second, it is nature that makes it, and art only helps. The former is difficult and expensive, and the latter is easy and of little expense. It is the latter of which I treat and which almost all the ancients have followed.

3   *Vert* in the manuscript, literally 'green', but reading as *verre*, 'glass'. The scripture alluded to appears to be Revelation 21:21: 'The great street of the city was of gold, as pure as transparent glass' (NIV). See our further comment to the *Table of what is in the manuscript* (n. 71).

La plupart[52] de ceux[53] qui ont écrit,[54] ont suivi[55] cette voie,[56] entre autre Artéphius, Zacaire, Trévisan, Flamel et plusieurs autres, la 1ère,[57] leur a été[58] inconnue, ou du moins s'ils l'ont connu,[59] ils ont publié[60] la dernière sous le nom de la première. Ce qui est très difficile à développer dans la lecture des philosophes; mettant souvent[61] ces deux voies[62] ensemble[63] pour embarrasser les lecteurs. Philalète qui a écrit[64] des derniers nous avertit de ne pas prendre le change. Ces voies,[65] quoique[66] différentes dans leur opération, eu égard au sujet dont ils se sont servi,[67] la matière est toujours unique et la même.[68]

La science de l'alchimie a fait trouver d'autres voies[69] encore différentes. Car les philosophes ont inventé[70] d'autres moyens plus abrégés que la nature n'a pu[71] pour la perfection et la transmutation des métaux.

Le Cosmopolite nous en marque quelques-uns, il dit qu'il y en a qui savent[72] changer le fer en cuivre, que de Jupiter, ils[73] en font du mercure, que de Saturne ils en ont fait de l'argent, et il dit que s'ils savaient[74] joindre à ces transmutations la nature du soleil, ils feraient[75] une chose plus précieuse[76] que l'or même.

Ce sont des arbres fait quoique[77] sauvage, sur lesquels on peut enter[78] des greffes d'arbres solaires et lunaires et par ce moyen on peut faire des améliorations[79] et des transmutations, lesquels arbres portent des fruits conformes à l'espèce solaire et lunaire. C'est à dire que des métaux imparfaits

52. plus part.	62. voyes.	72. sçavent.
53. ceuse.	63. ensembles.	73. il.
54. escrit.	64. escrit.	74. sçavoient.
55. suivis.	65. voyes.	75. feroient.
56. voye.	66. quoyque.	76. pretieuse.
57. 1re.	67. servis.	77. quoyque.
58. esté.	68. mesme.	78. hanter.
59. connus.	69. voyes.	79. meliorations.
60. publies.	70. inventes.	
61. sçouvent.	71. pust.	

Most of those who have written have followed this [latter] path, among them Artephius, Zacaire, Trevisan, Flamel, and many others. The first was unknown to them, or at least if they knew it, they published the last under the name of the first, which is very difficult to develop in the reading of the philosophers, [who are] often putting these two ways together to confuse the readers. Philalethes, who has written of the last, warns us not to accept the exchange. These ways, though different in their operation, considering the subject which they used, the matter is always unique and the same.

The science of alchemy has found other ways even more different. For the philosophers have invented other means more abridged than nature was able to for the perfection and transmutation of metals.

The Cosmopolitan points some out to us. He says that there are some who know how to change iron into copper, that from Jupiter they make mercury, that from Saturn they have made silver, and he says that if they knew how to join to these transmutations the nature of the sun, they would make something more precious than gold itself.

There are trees, though wild, upon which one can attach[4] grafts of solar and lunar trees, and by this means improvements and transmutations can be made, which trees bear fruits conforming to the solar and lunar species. That is to say, imperfect metals, after having reduced them to their first

---

4   The manuscript reads *hanter*, an old form of the French verb, *enter*, which means 'to join, graft'.

après les avoir réduits[80] en leurs premiers[81] principes et les avoir purifiés on y peut joindre l'âme végétative par une seule voie[82] connue des seuls philosophes et non pas par celle que les philosophes vulgaires imaginent[83] et dont ils abusent souvent[84] bien des gens qui ne connaissent[85] pas leur ignorance.

Notre[86] matière est renfermée dans des corps impurs, il faut corrompre ces corps, non pas d'une corruption ladreuse[87] qui détruit tout, mais d'une corruption qui aille à la génération de la mort à la vie, et qui par une résurrection[88] glorieuse, enfante ce fils du soleil qu'il faut donner à son père et le faire rentrer dans le ventre de sa mère; c'est-à-dire lui[89] joindre ce corps fixe et permanent, le vif ressuscitera[90] le mort, et ces 2 corps animes d'un même[91] esprit, produirons des enfants[92] semblables[93] à leur père et à leur mère. Voilà tout ce que[94] ce peut dire de la matière en général.

80. reduit.
81. premier.
82. voye.
83. s'imaginent.
84. sçouvent.
85. connoissent.
86. Nostre.
87. Possibly means 'leprous'. Likely From *ladre*, 'leprous'. Same as *lépreuse*.
88. resurection.
89. luy.
90. resussitera.
91. mesme.
92. enfans.
93. sembable.
94. qui.

principles, and having purified them, the vegetative soul may be joined to it by a single path known only to [true] philosophers, and not by that [path] which the vulgar philosophers imagine, and which is often abused by many people who do not know their ignorance.

Our matter is enclosed in impure bodies. We must corrupt these bodies, not by a leprous corruption which destroys everything, but by a corruption which proceeds to generation from death to life, and which by a glorious resurrection gives birth to this son of the sun, which must be given to his father, and made to return to his mother's womb; that is to say, to join him to this fixed and permanent body, [so that] the living will resurrect the dead, and these two bodies, animated by the same spirit, will produce children similar to their father and mother. That is all that can be said of matter in general.

De la matière en particulier

C'EST UNE HUMIDITÉ ONCTUEUSE QUI EST RENFER-
mée dans tous les êtres[2] de la nature, une matière visqueuse
et gluante, elle se cache profondément dans le centre des Eléments qui les unit si étroitement[3] qu'il est impossible de les
séparer sans un moyen seul, connu des philosophes. Elle se
couvre du manteau des éléments et n'ont point de puissance
sur elle; non pas mémé le feu, quelque violent qu'il puisse
être,[4] étant[5] fixe et inaltérable de sa nature. C'est pourquoi[6]
les philosophes disent qu'elle est permanente au feu, elle est
la matière prochaine de leur pierre, c'est ce qui a fait dire à
Basile[7] Valentin ces admirables[8] paroles.[9] Cherchez[10] dit-il
dans les entrailles de la terre, vous y trouverez[11] notre[12] pierre
cachée et la vraie[13] médicine. Elle est la 1ère[14] matière des
métaux qui sont plus ou moins parfaits, selon qu'elle est jointe
à des matières plus ou moins parfaites si elle est jointe à une
matière pure elle forme l'or, si elle est moins pure, elle forme
l'argent, si elle est encore plus impure, elle forme le plomb.
Ainsi[15] des autres; C'est l'humidité sèche[16] de Geber, qui ne
mouille pas les mains.

1.	2me.	7.	Bazile.	13.	vrais.
2.	estres.	8.	admiribles.	14.	1re.
3.	estroitement.	9.	parolles.	15.	Ainsy.
4.	estre.	10.	Cherches.	16.	seiche.
5.	estant.	11.	trouveres.		
6.	pourquoy.	12.	nostre.		

SECOND CHAPTER

Of matter in particular

IT IS A HUMIDITY, CALLED UNCTUOUS, WHICH IS CON-tained in all the beings of nature, a viscous and gummy matter, it hides deeply in the center of the Elements which unites them so closely that it is impossible to separate them without a single means, known to the philosophers. It covers itself with the mantle of the elements and they have no power over it; not even fire, however violent it may be, [the matter] being fixed and unalterable in its nature. This is why the philosophers say that it is permanent in the fire, it is the proximate matter of their stone, which is what made Basil Valentine say these admirable words: 'Search', he said, 'in the bowels of the earth, you will find there our hidden stone and true medicine'. It is the first matter of metals, which are more or less perfect according to whether it is joined to matters more or less perfect. If it is joined to a pure matter, it forms gold, if it is less pure, it forms silver, if it is even more impure, it forms lead. Similarly, the others. It is the dry humidity of Geber, which does not wet the hands.

Or cette matière quoique[17] très fixe en sa nature, se volatilise facilement par le moyen des éléments qui lui[18] servent de véhicule, se développe et se joint à eux sans néanmoins[19] altérer sa nature de la manière du feu qui est mêlé[20] dans tous les êtres[21] et qui est toujours feu, lorsqu'il est réduit de la puissance en acte; ainsi[22] que le soleil qui répand[23] ses influences sur toute la terre et qui est toujours[24] soleil. C'est pourquoi[25] elle est susceptible des impressions des éléments et des influences des astres qu'elle attire et retient. C'est l'aimant et l'acier des sages.

Elle monte de la terre au Ciel et descend[26] du Ciel en terre et se remplit des influences du Ciel et principalement[27] du grand luminaire, elle sert à la multiplication et à la génération de tous les Astres.[28] C'est par son moyen qu'ils reçoivent leurs[29] actions et leur mouvement. Les Animaux reçoivent la vie par elle et tout ce qui est animé dans la nature, L'homme même[30] ne s'en peut passer, elle entretient sa vie et son mouvement, elle fait dans la nature la fonction de femelle en recevant du Ciel et des Astres et principalement[31] du soleil qui est le mâle,[32] l'action et le mouvement; elle est comme les sperme, la matrice qui reçoit la semence masculine; elle fait le mariage entre le Ciel et la Terre. C'est elle qui renferme le feu caché des sages, sans lequel l'Artiste ne peut parvenir à la fin dont nous traiterons[33] un chapitre en particulier.

De ces deux spermes, est formée la matière du mercure des philosophes. C'est pourquoi[34] le grand Hermès nous dit ces admirables paroles,[35] le soleil en est le père et la lune la mère, l'air le porte dans son ventre qui en est la matrice et le réceptacle. Le Cosmpolite[36] dit qu'il se trouve dans le ven-

17. quoyque.	24. toutjours.	31. principallement.
18. luy.	25. pourquoy.	32. masle.
19. neantmoins.	26. dessend.	33. traittons.
20. mesle.	27. principallement.	34. pourquoy.
21. estres.	28. Estres.	35. parolles.
22. ainsy.	29. leur.	36. Cosmopolitte.
23. repend.	30. mesme.	

Now this matter, although very fixed in its nature, easily volatalises by means of the elements which serve it as a vehicle, develops and joins itself to them without nevertheless altering its nature in the manner of fire which is mingled in all beings and which is always fire, when it is reduced from potency into action; as well as the sun which spreads its influences all over the earth, and which is always sun. This is why it is susceptible to the impressions of the elements and the influences of the stars which it attracts and retains. It is the magnet and the steel of the sages.

It ascends from earth to heaven and descends from heaven to earth and fills itself with the influences of heaven, primarily of the great luminary, and it serves the multiplication and generation of all the Stars. It is by its means that they receive their actions and their movement. Animals receive life by it, and all that which is animated in nature; man himself cannot do without it, it maintains his life and his movement, it performs the function of a female in nature by receiving the action and the movement from heaven and from the stars, and principally from the sun, which is the male. It is like sperm; the womb[5] that receives the male seed; it performs the marriage between heaven and earth. It is that which contains the hidden fire of the sages, without which the artist cannot reach the end, which we will deal with in a specific chapter.

From these two sperms is formed the matter of the mercury of the philosophers. That is why the great Hermes said these admirable words to us: 'the sun is the father, and the moon the mother, the air carries it in its belly which is the womb and the receptacle'. The Cosmopolitan says that it is

5 *Matrice*, 'womb' also means 'matrix'.

tre du Bélier,[37] signifiant par le Bélier[38] le commencement du printemps, lorsque le soleil entre dans ce signe céleste qui est le renouvellement de cet esprit qui anime pour lors toute la nature. C'est cette semence jetée dans la mer des Sages qui est notre[39] air qui donne toute la fécondité[40] à notre[41] pierre, c'est cette semence qu'ils savent[42] extraire par des moyens inconnus aux Chymistes vulgaires et savent[43] joindre à un soufre pur; ils appellent cette semence argent vif. C'est pourquoi[44] ils disent que leur pierre est composée d'argent vif et d'un soufre pur, ils donnent à la première le nom de lune et au second, celui[45] du soleil, ce sont les 2 grands luminaires que vous devez[46] extraire de la pierre.

Le commerce du ciel et de la terre est parfaitement bien décrit[47] dans le Cosmopolite,[48] et par une comparaison. Il vous marque du doigt ce que doit faire le philosophe qui doit être[49] l'imitateur de la nature que Dieu a ainsi[50] formé, ayant joint le Ciel avec la terre qui a ses astres qui sont soleil et lune et notre[51] Maître[52] nous dit que tout ce qui est en haut, est comme tout ce qui est en bas; de même[53] le philosophe[54] doit joindre le ciel avec la terre, il doit tirer du chaos, c'est-à-dire de son sujet les luminaires, séparer la lumière des ténèbres et par l'union de l'esprit en faire un tout parfait, imitant en cela Dieu en la création du monde, c'est sous ce dernier regard que notre[55] art est appelé[56] un art Divin.

Ayant tiré ces luminaires et ces éléments; après les avoir dépouillés de leurs[57] grossièretés et de leur terrestréités, ils en font un tout homogène et un composé qu'ils appellent Elixir qui contient la force du Ciel et de la terre qu'Hermès appelle

37.	Bellier.	45.	celuy.	53.	mesme.
38.	Bellier.	46.	deves.	54.	philosophes.
39.	nostre.	47.	d'escrit.	55.	nostre.
40.	faecundité.	48.	Cosmopolitte.	56.	appellé.
41.	nostre.	49.	estre.	57.	leur.
42.	sçavent.	50.	ainsy.		
43.	sçavent.	51.	Nostre.		
44.	pourquoy.	52.	Maistre.		

found in the belly of Aries, signifying by Aries the beginning of spring, when the sun enters into that celestial sign which is the renewal of that spirit which animates all nature at that time. It is this seed, thrown into the sea of the sages, which is our air which gives all the fertility to our stone. It is this seed which they know how to extract by means unknown to the vulgar chymists, and [which they] know how to join with a pure sulphur. They call this seed *argent vive* [quicksilver].⁶ That is why they say that their stone is composed of *argent vive* and pure sulphur, they give to the first the name of the moon, and to the second that of the sun. These are the two great luminaries that you must extract from the stone.

The commerce of heaven and earth is perfectly well de-scribed in the Cosmopolitan by a comparison. He points out to you what the philosopher must do, who is to be the imita-tor of nature that God so formed, having joined heaven with earth, which has its stars, which are the sun and the moon, and our Master tells us that all that which is above, is like all that which is below. Similarly, the philosopher must join heaven with the earth, he must draw from the chaos, that is to say from his subject, the luminaries, to separate the light from the darkness, and by the union of the spirit to make a perfect whole, imitating by this [act] God in the Creation of the world. It is according to this last perspective that our art is called a Divine art.

Having drawn [out] these luminaries and these elements, after having stripped them of their filth and their earthliness,⁷ they make of it a homogeneous whole, a compound which they call Elixir, which contains the power of Heaven and

---

6   French, *l'argent vif,* from Latin *argentum vivum,* literally 'living silver'; compare English 'quicksilver', in which 'quick' has the archaic sense of 'living, alive'.

7   *Les terrestréités,* literally 'terrestrialities', chemical term for the grossest parts of the substance.

la force des forces, qui réduit tout de puissance en acte, et toute cette puissance est réduite dans un peu de poudre. C'est pourquoi[58] il ne faut pas s'étonner[59] si elle fait de si grands effets, tant pour la santé que pour la perfection des métaux imparfaits.

Car cette divine poudre a la vertu de purifier les éléments de l'homme et les met dans leur égalités naturelles dont le dérangement est la cause prochaine de la destruction.

Nous traiterons dans un chapitre exprès de ses vertus qui sont innombrables, elle ne fait pas de moindres effet[60] sur les métaux; d'imparfaits, elle les rend parfaits. Le Dessein de la Nature étant[61] de les faire parfaits et de les faire or, mais ayant été[62] empêchée[63] dans son opération, et ne pouvant arriver à sa fin, elle en fait des métaux imparfaits, non pas l'or et ce que la nature fait en un grand nombre d'années, le philosophe le fait en peu d'heures.

Ainsi[64] il n'y rien qui soit plus digne de l'occupation de l'homme qu'à travailler[65] à cette divine œuvre ou rechercher,[66] puisqu'il peut acquérir par cette science la santé et les richesses, qui doit être[67] préférée à toutes autres sciences, excepte celle du salut de son âme qui doit être[68] sa principale[69] occupation. Cherchez[70] premièrement, dit le Seigneur dans son Évangile,[71] le Royaume des cieux et tout vous sera donné, par surcroît.[72] On peut dire encore que cette science est Divine, parce qu'il n'y a que Dieu qui la donne, il la enseigné à Moïse, à sa sœur Aaron, aux patriarches, et à leur descendants,[73] à Salomon qui en avait[74] une parfaite connaissance et qui a été[75] conservée jusqu'au temps d'Esdras qui en

58. pourquoy.
59. s'estonner.
60. effets.
61. estoit.
62. esté.
63. empeschée.

64. Ainsy.
65. trauvailler.
66. recherche.
67. estre.
68. estre.
69. principalle.

70. Cherches.
71. Evangille.
72. surcrois.
73. dessendants.
74. avoit.
75. esté.

earth, which Hermes calls the power of powers, which reduces everything from potency into action, and all this potency is reduced into a small amount of powder. That is why it is not surprising if it has such great effects, both for health and for the perfection of imperfect metals.

For this divine powder has the virtue of purifying the elements of man and brings them to their natural equilibrium, whose disturbance is the proximate cause of destruction.

We shall deal with its virtues, which are innumerable, in a special chapter. It has no less effect on metals. Of the imperfect, it makes them perfect. The Purpose of Nature is to make them perfect and to turn them [into] gold. But having been prevented in its operation, and being unable to reach its end, it makes imperfect metals, not gold, and that which nature achieves in a great number of years, the philosopher does in a few hours.

Thus there is nothing more worthy of the occupation of man than to work on this divine work or to search, since he can acquire health and wealth by this science, which must be preferred to all other sciences except for that of the salvation of his soul, which must be his principal occupation. Seek first, says the Lord in his Gospel, the Kingdom of Heaven, and all things will be given to you as well.[8] It may also be said that this science is Divine, because it is only God who gives it, and who taught it to Moses, to his sibling Aaron, to the patriarchs, and to their descendants, to Solomon who had a perfect knowledge [of it] and which was preserved until the time of Ezra, who rebuilt the temple after the captivity of

8   Matthew 6:33.

Réédifia[76] le temple après la captivité de Babylone;[77] Sem l'un des fils de Noé l'avait[78] fait dépeindre sur des colonnes[79] qui se trouvèrent après le déluge. Sem l'avait[80] apprise d'Adam, c'est par son moyen qu'ils vivaient[81] si longtemps, elle s'est conservée et communiquée cabalistiquement à quelques juifs. Il n'y a donc que Dieu et un ami[82] à qui Dieu l'avait[83] inspirée, qui peut vous la communiquer; si vous avez[84] ce bonheure, conservez[85] le comme un trésor[86] précieux,[87] mais surtout ne le communiquez[88] pas aux indignes; car vous attirerez[89] sur vous la malédiction de Dieu qui vous punirait[90] non moins que d'une mort subite, ou vous mettrait[91] entre les mains des puissances qui vous feraient[92] périr dans une prison.

Quant à la possession de la pierre des philosophes, elle n'est pas si difficile[93] que la plupart[94] se l'imaginent.[95] C'est la Nature qui agit, et elle agit toujours certainement par des principes certains: à moins qu'elle ne trouve en son chemin des obstacles certains. Mais si vous savez[96] ôter[97] ces obstacles; elle arrivera infailliblement à sa fin et au terme que Dieu lui[98] a prescrit.

Il est vrais que, quant à la matière particulière, il est impossible à l'homme de la déterminer, Dieu par sa puissance a déterminé tous les Êtres[99] de la nature pour faire une telle forme. Ainsi[100] l'homme ne peut rien créer, et Salomon dit qu'il n'y a rien de nouveau sous le Ciel. Dieu a imposé cette loi[101] à toute la nature, de faire et de se multiplier chacun selon son espèce par son grand mot de Fiat. Cette loi[102] est enfer-

76.	Redifia. Likely réédifié, 'rebuilt'.	85.	conserves.	95.	l'jmagine.
77.	Babylonne.	86.	thresor.	96.	sçaves.
78.	l'avoit.	87.	pretieuse.	97.	oster.
79.	Colomnes.	88.	communiques.	98.	luy.
80.	l'avoit.	89.	attireries.	99.	Estres.
81.	vivoient.	90.	puniroit.	100.	Ainsy.
82.	amy.	91.	mettroit.	101.	loy.
83.	l'avoit.	92.	feroit.	102.	loy.
84.	aves.	93.	difficille.		
		94.	plus part.		

Babylon. Shem, one of the sons of Noah had it depicted on the pillars that were found after the deluge. Shem had learned it from Adam. It was by its means that they lived so long. It was preserved and communicated cabalistically to some of the Jews. Therefore only God or a friend God has inspired can communicate it to you. If you have this privilege, preserve it as a precious treasure, but above all, do not communicate it to the unworthy. For you will draw upon yourself the curse of God, who will punish you with no less than a sudden death, or put you in the hands of powers that would make you perish in a prison.

As for the possession of the stone of the philosophers, it is not as difficult as most imagine it. It is Nature which acts, and it certainly always acts by certain principles, unless it finds certain obstacles in its way. But if you know how to remove these obstacles, it will infallibly come to its end, and to the conclusion that God has commanded.

It is true that, as to the particular matter, it is impossible for man to determine it. God by his power has determined all the beings of nature to make such a form. Thus man cannot create anything, and Solomon says that there is nothing new under Heaven. God has imposed this law on all nature, to make and multiply each according to his species by his grand word, *Fiat*. This law is enclosed in every seed that inviolably

mée en chaque semence qui la suit inviolablement, et chaque
être[103] obéit à cette loi,[104] comme nous disons tous les jours
dans notre[105] *pater Fiat voluntas tua sicut in caelo et in terra.*[106]

Le philosophe ne prétend donc rien faire de lui-même,[107]
et ne peut déterminer aucun être[108] pour faire une telle espèce, car ce serait[109] une espèce de création qui est réservée au
souverain Créateur de l'univers; mais il se sert de la matière
générale[110] qu'il met de la puissance en acte, qu'il sait[111] extraire des choses imparfaites[112] en la séparant des matières imparfaites et des grossièretés, et impuretés qui la mettent[113] hors
d'état d'agir pour d'imparfaite qu'elle était,[114] la rendre plus
que parfaite[115] et d'une perfection à perfectionner chaque
chose selon son espèce: Dans les végétaux par exemple, elle
les fait crôitre[116] à moins de temps, ils donnent leur fruits en
plus grande abondance. Dans les minéraux, elle transmue les
métaux en or plus fort en couleur que l'or vulgaire.[117] Dans
l'homme, elle purifié ses humeurs, les met dans une égalité
parfaite, elle entretient et conserve ce feu Céleste qui fait sa
vie, son mouvement et son action, elle communique cette[118]
huile incombustible et cette[119] humeur radicale au cœur où
réside la vie et le mouvement. Ainsi[120] il n'est pas difficile de
comprendre qu'elle procure une longue vie.

Quant au sujet, je vous dirai[121] comme les philosophes,
qu'il est partout, puisque la nature en est le sujet et la matière
générale; mais ils en ont cependant une particulière qui renferme tout ce qui est nécessaire pour faire ce grand ouvrage;
car qui voudrait travailler indifféremment[122] sur tous les su-
jets de la Nature, la vie ne serait[123] pas assez[124] longue pour en

---

103. estre.
104. loy.
105. nostre.
106. (Latin).
107. luy mesme.
108. estre.
109. seroit.
110. generalle.

111. sçait.
112. imparfaite.
113. mettoient.
114. estoit.
115. parfaitte.
116. croistre.
117. vulguair.
118. cet.

119. cet.
120. Ainsy.
121. diray.
122. indifferament.
123. seroit.
124. assée.

follows it, and every being obeys this law, as we say every day in our *pater Fiat voluntas tua sicut in caelo et in terra.*[9]

The philosopher does not pretend to do anything by himself, and cannot determine any being to make such a species, for it would be a kind of creation that is reserved for the sovereign Creator of the universe. But he makes use of the general matter which he moves from potency to actuality, which he knows how to extract from imperfect things by separating it from imperfect matters, from the filth and impurities which render it incapable of acting, in order that, from its former imperfection it is rendered more than perfect, and of a perfection capable of perfecting everything according to its species. In plants, for example, it makes them grow in less time; they give their fruits in greater abundance. In minerals it transmutes metals into gold stronger in colour than common gold. In man, it purifies his humours, puts them in a perfect equilibrium, it maintains and preserves that celestial fire which makes his life, his movement and his action. It communicates this incombustible oil and this radical humour to the heart where life and movement reside. So it is not difficult to understand that it provides a long life.

As for the subject, I will tell you as philosophers, that it is everywhere, since nature [itself] is the subject and the general matter. But they have, however, one [subject] in particular which contains all that is necessary to achieve this great work. For whoever would work indiscriminately on all the subjects of nature, life would not be long enough to achieve it. Every mixture demands

9   'Thy will be done on earth as it is in heaven' (The Lord's Prayer, or *Pater Noster*).

venir à bout. chaque mixte demande[125] des travaux[126] différents, les uns sont trop éloignés de la matière dont ils composent leur pierre, et de la matière particulière qui est la matière prochaine, et leur feu sans lequel ils ne peuvent rien faire, serait[127] encore plus difficile[128] à trouver les mélanges,[129] et les poids de nature lui[130] sont inconnus, et par les longs travaux[131] qu'ils seraient[132] obligés de faire et les dépenses;[133] il serait[134] contraint d'abandonner l'ouvrage.

Pour l'affaire de notre[134] sujet, la dépense[136] est modique, et le Triomphe hermétique dit, qu'elle ne dépasse[137] pas la somme de dix sols pour avoir le sujet de la matière pour faire l'œuvre. Ce sujet paraît[138] sous une forme très vile, ce qui le rend méprisable aux yeux des hommes, quoiqu'il[139] renferme un trésor[140] précieux,[141] il est couvert de quelques haillons; mais sous ces haillons, vous y verrez[142] bientôt[143] de vos propres yeux l'or brillant, la couleur céleste de l'arc en ciel, signes qui vous feront connaitre[144] ce qu'il renferme et de quoi[145] il est capable; vous y verrez[146] dans la 2ème[147] opération la lumière sortir des ténèbres et de son chaos,[148] vous y verrez[149] les deux luminaires qui vous feront apparaître[150] le sec, et le Saturne orné de robe[151] noire, le noir Dragon en peu de jours vous verrez[152] l'esprit se faire corps, vous y verrez[153] la Diane, vous verrez[154] les deux montagnes d'où découle le ruisseau précieux[155] qui sort de la pierre plus claire que le cristal, enfin les 1ers[156] éléments dont les philosophes forment leur

125. demende.
126. traveaux.
127. seroit.
128. difficille.
129. meslanges.
130. luy.
131. trauvaux.
132. seroit.
133. depences.
134. seroit.
135. nostre.
136. depence.
137. passe.
138. parroist.
139. quoyqu'il.
140. thresor.
141. pretieux.
142. verres.
143. bientost.
144. connoistre.
145. quoy.
146. verres.
147. 2me.
148. cahos.
149. verres.
150. apparoistre.
151. robbe.
152. verres.
153. verres.
154. verres.
155. pretieux.
156. 1rs.

different works. Some are too far removed from the matter of which they compose their stone, and from the particular matter which is the proximate matter. And their fire, without which they can do nothing, would be even more difficult to find. The mixtures and the weights of nature are unknown to them; and due to the long labors which they would be obliged to perform, and the expenses, he [the alchemist] would be forced to abandon the work.

For what concerns our subject, the expense is moderate, and the *Hermetic Triumph*[10] says that it does not exceed the sum of ten *sols*[11] to have the subject matter to do the work. This subject appears in a very vile form, which renders it despicable to the eyes of men, though it contains a precious treasure, it is covered with some rags. But under these rags, you will soon see with your own eyes the shining gold, the celestial colour of the rainbow, signs that will make you know what it contains and what it is capable of. You will see there in the second operation, the light come out of the darkness and its chaos. You will see there the two luminaries that will appear dry to you, and Saturn adorned with a black robe, the black Dragon. In a few days you will see the spirit become a body, you will see Diana, you will see the two mountains, from which flows the precious stream which emerges from the stone brighter than crystal, and finally the first elements from which the philosophers form their mercury and their

10   Alexandre-Toussaint de Limojon de St Didier, *Le Triomphe Hermétique ou la pierre philosophale victorieuse*. Amsterdam: Henry Wetstein, 1699.

11   Currency originating in antiquity (from Latin *solidus*, originally made from gold); in France it became a subdivision of the livre, comparable to shillings in relation to the British pound.

mercure[157] et leur argent vif, vous verrez[158] toutes ces opérations, sans que vous y mettiez[159] les mains. C'est ce sujet que le
père cache à son fils et le fils à son père; il n'y a que Dieu et un
ami[160] qui peut le révéler.

157. mercures.
158. verres.
159. meties.
160. amy.

argent vive. You will see all these operations without putting your hands on them. It is this subject that the father hides from his son, and the son from his father. It is only God and a friend who can reveal it.

De la préparation des Eléments et de leur séparation en géneral

JE VOUS DIRAIS[2] D'ABORD EN GÉNÉRAL QUE LA préparation de nos éléments n'est pas proprement une séparation mais plutôt[3] une dépuration des principes spirituels qui composent[4] notre[5] pierre; que la nature y a plus de part que l'Artiste; les philosophes ne vous disent-ils pas que leur pierre se sublime, se dissout, s'engrossit, se coagule et se fixe d'elle-même:[6] Ne voyons-nous pas dans les animaux, et dans les hommes que les aliments qui descendent dans l'estomac;[7] il ne se fait aucune séparation de substance et que tout est réduit en une substance homogène, et sous une forme que nous appelons[8] chyle,[9] à l'exception de quelques excréments qui s'en séparent.

Il arrive la même[10] chose dans notre[11] pierre, nous ne séparons rien des substances et des principes de la pierre; et ce qui paraît[12] imparfait, grossier et immonde, nous le changeons en une matière plus subtile, plus parfaite et plus capable de pouvoir recevoir les principes spirituels, ce qui se[13] fait par le moyen de notre[14] feu que nous savons[15] introduire dans notre[16] matière; C'est ce feu qui n'est pas tiré de la matière

1.	3me.	7.	l'estomach.	13.	ce.
2.	diray.	8.	appellons.	14.	nostre.
3.	plustost.	9.	chile.	15.	sçavons.
4.	compose.	10.	mesme.	16.	nostre.
5.	nostre.	11.	nostre.		
6.	d'elle mesme.	12.	parroist.		

THIRD CHAPTER

Of the preparation of the elements and their separation in general

I WILL TELL YOU FIRST IN GENERAL, THAT THE preparation of our elements is not properly a separation, but rather a depuration of the spiritual principles which compose our stone; which nature has more of a part of than the Artist. Do the philosophers not tell you that their stone sublimes, dissolves, grows, coagulates, and fixes itself: do we not see in animals and in men that [in regards to] the food which descends into the stomach, there is no separation of substance, and everything is reduced into a homogeneous substance, and into a form which we call chyle [hyle], with the exception of a few excrements which separate from it.

The same thing happens in our stone, we do not separate anything from the substances and principles of the stone; and what appears imperfect, gross, and unclean, we change it into a more subtle matter, more perfect, and more capable of being able to receive the spiritual principles, which is done by means of our fire, which we know to introduce into our matter; it is this fire which is not drawn from the matter, as

comme dit Pontanus, qui change tout ce qui est grossier, imparfaite et immonde, en être[17] et en une substance plus épurée, plus subtile[18] et plus parfaite.

Il est vrai[19] que dans cette dépuration il se sépare quelques fèces[20] qui sont des excréments qui sont accidentels à la matière et qui ne font point partie de sa nature. Ainsi[21] cela ne s'appelle pas une véritable séparation, les principes demeurant[22] toujours unis et conjoints. La lie qui se sépare du vin,[23] ne fait pas partie du vin, quoiqu'elle[24] sorte de la matière qui compose le vin, dans l'accroissement des métaux; nous ne voyons pas de séparation sensible, la nature donc se subtilise, se transforme en d'autres formes plus parfaites[25] se dégageant par degré, s'épure d'elle-même[26] de plus en plus par l'action de son feu interne jusqu'à ce qu'elle soit arrivée à son terme de perfection.

Nous faisons la même[27] chose dans notre[28] œuvre, il est vrai[29] néanmoins[30] que nous séparons quelques substances principalement[31] dans le premier et second œuvre, mais cette séparation de substance n'est pas une véritable séparation de principes comme s'imaginent les chymistes vulgaires qui ne comprennent pas le sens des philosophes; car chaque substance qu'ils séparent contient les autres, l'eau, qu'on distille d'une plante, contient toute la vertu de la plante, et quoique[32] ce qui reste au fond du vaisseau[33] soit séparé de l'eau distillée et paraît[34] sous une autre forme, elle contient les mêmes[35] vertus et les mêmes[36] principes de l'eau distillée: quand donc les philosophes parlent de la séparation des éléments, ce n'est pas une séparation essentielle de principes,

17. estre.	24. quoy qu'elle.	31. principallement.
18. subtille.	25. parfaites.	32. quoyque.
19. vrais.	26. d'elle mesme.	33. vesseau.
20. faeces.	27. mesme.	34. parroisse.
21. Ainsy.	28. nostre.	35. mesmes.
22. demeurants.	29. vrais.	36. mesmes.
23. vine.	30. neantmoins.	

Pontanus says, which changes all that is gross, imperfect, and unclean, into being and into a purer, more subtle, and more perfect substance.

It is true that in this depuration a few feces are separated, which are excrements accidental to the matter, and which are not part of its nature. Thus it is not called a true separation, the principles remaining always united and conjoined. The dregs which separate from the wine, are not part of the wine, although it comes out of the matter that makes up the wine. During the growth of metals, we see no perceptible separation, so nature becomes subtilised, transforms itself into other, more perfect forms, clears by degrees, purifies itself more and more by the action of its internal fire, until it has come to its end of perfection.

We do the same thing in our work; it is nevertheless true that we separate a few substances principally in the first and second works, but this separation of substance is not a true separation of principles, as the vulgar chymists imagine, who do not understand the meaning of philosophers; for every substance which they separate contains the others, the water which is distilled from a plant contains all the virtue of the plant, and although what remains at the bottom of the vessel is separated from the distilled water and appears under another form, it contains the same virtues and principles of distilled water: when the philosophers speak of the separation of the elements, it is not an essential separation of principles, but a separation of the substances that they call by a name of an

mais une séparation de substances qu'ils nomment d'un nom d'élément ou premières substances les plus subtiles[37] et les plus dégagées de la matière et qu'ils appellent air et feu; et les plus grossières, terres et eau; par rapport à la nature des éléments qui veut dire proprement séparer le subtil de l'épais, comme dit Hermès.

C'est donc faussement que plusieurs s'imaginent que par les termes d'éléments nous entendons les éléments communs, car ce serait[38] une espèce de création, si l'homme par le mélange qu'il ferait,[39] pouvait[40] former quelques choses. Dieu a tout crée en nombre, en poids et en mesure. Ainsi[41] le philosophe n'ajoute rien à la perfection de ce que Dieu a fait, ni[42] ne forme rien et ne crée rien.

Dans le 1er[43] œuvre, il est vrai[44] qu'on sépare quelques substances pour les réunir après son dégagement; mais à[45] l'égard des principes et des luminaires, ils se séparent d'eux même.[46] C'est la nature qui le fait sans que l'Artiste y mette la main pour en faire un composé qui est une mixtion,[47] un assemblage, ou plutôt[48] une union de ces mêmes[49] principes sous une même[50] forme, sous laquelle forme, sont renfermées deux substances spirituelles qu'ils appellent du nom d'air et de feu qui sont invisibles; et deux corporelles qui sont l'eau et la terre qui sont visibles, et ils appellent ce composé, pierre.

Dans le second œuvre, ou dans la seconde dépuration, c'est l'Artiste qui fait cette séparation, et c'est dans cette œuvre où il faut appliquer tout qu'ils disent des opérations, et tous les termes de distillation, sublimation, coagulation et semblables termes dont ils se servent, qui ne marquent autre chose qu'une sublimation plus parfaite et plus dégagée de la matière; ce qui ne se fait pas autrement que ce que l'on fait

37. subtilles.	42. ny.	47. mixion.
38. seroit.	43. 1r.	48. plustost.
39. feroit.	44. vrais.	49. mesmes.
40. pouvoit.	45. a.	50. mesme.
41. Ainsy.	46. mesme.	

element, or the most subtle and free first substances of matter, and which they call air and fire; and the coarsest, earth and water, compared to the nature of the elements, which means properly separating the subtle from the dense, as Hermes says.

It is therefore falsely that many imagine that by the terms of elements we mean the common elements, for it would be a kind of creation, if man by the mixture that he would make could form some things. God created everything in number, in weight, and in measure. Thus the philosopher adds nothing to the perfection of what God has done, there is nothing to form and nothing to create.

In the first work, it is true that some substances are separated to reunite them after its disengagement; but with regard to the principles and the luminaries, they separate from themselves. It is nature that does this without the Artist applying his hand to it to make of it a compound that is a mixture, an assemblage, or rather a union of these same principles under one form, under which form, are contained two spiritual substances which they call [by] the name of air and fire which are invisible; and two corporeal ones that are water and earth that are visible, and they call this compound, stone.

In the second work, or in the second depuration, it is the artist who makes this separation, and it is in this work, where everything they say of the operations must be applied, and all the terms of distillation, sublimation, coagulation, and the like terms which they use, which mark nothing but a more perfect sublimation more free from matter; which is not done differently than what is done in ordinary chymistry, which teaches us that in order to purify a matter, salt, sulphur, and mercury must be extracted from it, and the feces separat-

dans la chymie ordinaire qui nous enseigne que pour dépurer une matière, il en faut tirer le sel, le soufre et le mercure et en séparer les fèces,[51] et joindre ensemble les trois principes pour en faire une liqueur et une substance plus parfaite. Nous faisons la même[52] chose dans le second œuvre qui sont toujours les mêmes principes et les mêmes[53] substances.

Ces substances réunies, paraissent[54] sous la forme d'une eau qu'ils appellent argent vif; et la terre, ils l'appellent soufre. Ainsi[55] ils disent que leur pierre est composée de soufre et d'argent vif. D'autres donnent à l'eau le nom de lune et la terre le nom de soufre et sous plusieurs autres termes que nous expliquerons en un chapitre particulier, mais on ne doit pas s'attacher à la diversité des noms.

La Cosmopolite dit que la composition de cette eau est très cachée,[56] les philosophes n'en parlent presque point, et s'ils en parlent, ce n'est que pour en décrire[57] la puissance et les vertus. C'est pourquoi[58] il dit encore qu'elle est rare, puisqu'elle fait tout le composé de l'œuvre; nous en parlerons plus particulièrement en son lieu.

Ils disent que cette eau prend son origine de l'air, conformément à ce que dit le grand Hermès, que l'air la porte dans son ventre et l'auteur[59] de l'Escalier[60] des sages; notre[61]

---

51. fæces.
52. mesme.
53. mesmes.
54. parroissent.
55. Ainsy.
56. cachées.

57. d'escrire.
58. pourquoy.
59. l'autheur.
60. L'Escallier.
61. nostre.

ed, and the three principles joined together to make it into a liquor and a more perfect substance. We do the same thing in the second work, which are always the same principles and the same substances.

These united substances appear in the form of a water which they call *argent vive*; and the earth, they call it sulphur. Thus they say that their stone is composed of sulphur and *argent vive*. Others give to the water the name of the moon, and to the earth the name of sulphur, and under several other terms, which we shall explain in a particular chapter, but we must not attach ourselves to the diversity of names.

The Cosmopolitan says that the composition of this water is very hidden, the philosophers scarcely ever speak of it, and if they [do] speak of it, it is only to describe the power and the virtues. That is why he says again that it is rare, since it makes the entire compound of the work; we will speak more particularly about it in its place.

They say that this water takes its origin from the air, according to what the great Hermes says, that the air carries it in its belly, and [also] the author of the *Ladder of the Sages*;[12]

12   There appear to be only two texts that this might refer to. One is the medieval Latin text called *Scala Philosophorum* (The Ladder of the Philosophers), the other is the seventeenth century text entitled *Escalier des Sages* (Groningen, 1686). From the closer-matching title, one would think that this second text is the one our anonymous author is referring to, but there does not seem to be any such statement about 'our Philosophical Child' being 'born in the air' in this text. But in the *Scala Philosophorum* there is the following statement which might be what he had in mind: 'Therefore, it should be noted, that water conserves the fetus in the mother's womb for three months. Air, also, nurtures it for three months, and fire guards it for the same amount of time, which, on completion, the blood that nourishes in the womb, is cut off and goes to the breasts, and there takes the whiteness of snow. Yet the child would never leave until it takes up a breath of air. Then goes out and opens its mouth and is suckled'. (*Igitur sciendum, quod tribus mensibus aqua foetum in matrice conservat. Aer quoque tribus mensibus fovet, ignis vero totidem custodit, quibus completis, sanguis eius qui fovetur*

enfant philosophique, dit-il, prend naissance dans l'air. C'est pourquoi[62] notre[63] eau a la force de donner la vie à la terre, c'est remettre l'âme dans son corps, ce qui se[64] fait sur la fin du 1er[65] œuvre. (mais cela se[66] fait dans la 2ème[67] qu'ils confondent avec la première).

D'autres philosophes disent qu'il faut le prendre à l'heure de sa naissance. C'est-à-dire dans le lieu de sa naissance. Cet air est celui[68] que nous cherchons dont nous composons notre[69] eau et notre[70] feu. Ce ne sont point l'air et le feu que nous sentons et que nous respirons.

C'est dans cette eau que nous introduisons ce feu: nous faisons la paix entre les ennemis,[71] nous faisons que l'eau et le feu soient amis. C'est ce que dit le même[72] auteur[73] cité au 3ème[74] degré. (C'est, dit-il, que notre[75] eau est la clef de l'œuvre, elle contient l'Esprit et l'âme de la pierre. La terre ou le corps ou le soufre est nôtre[76] airain et nôtre[77] airain c'est nôtre[78] or. Mais tout soufre n'est pas notre[79] airain ni[80] l'or vulgaire n'est pas notre[81] or, quoiqu'ils[82] soient frères utérins, venant de la même[83] mère et du même[84] père.

62. pourquoy.
63. nostre.
64. ce.
65. 1r.
66. ce.
67. 2me.
68. celuy.
69. nostre.
70. nostre.
71. ennemys.
72. mesme.
73. autheur.
74. 3e.
75. nostre.
76. nostre.
77. nostre.
78. nostre.
79. nostre.
80. ny.
81. nostre.
82. quoyqu'ils.
83. mesme.
84. mesme.

our Philosophical Child, he says, is born in the air. That is why our water has the strength to give life to the earth, it is to put the soul back into its body, which is done at the end of the first work (but this is done in the second, which they confuse with the first).

Other philosophers say that it must be taken at the time of its birth. That is to say, in the place of its birth. This air is that which we seek, of which we compose our water and our fire. It is not the air and fire that we feel and breathe.

It is in this water that we introduce this fire: we make peace between the enemies, we make water and fire become friends. This is what the same author quoted to the third degree. (It is, he says, that our water is the key to the work, it contains the Spirit and soul of the stone). The earth, or the body, or the sulphur, is our bronze,[13] and our bronze is our gold. But all sulphur is not our bronze, nor is the vulgar gold our gold, although they are uterine brothers, coming from the same mother and the same father.

---

in umbilico, eo praeciso egreditur ad mammas, ibique candorem nivis assumit. Igitur infanti nunquam patebit egressus quousque aeris flatus exhauriat. Tunc autem egressus aperitur & os eius, & lactatur). 'Liber Scala Philosophorum Dictus', in *De Alchimia Opuscula Complura Veterum Philosophorum* (1550), vol. 1, page 103v.

13   The French word *airain* is derived from the Latin word *aes* 'copper'. The word *airain* was generally used to signify bronze (an alloy of copper and tin), but it sometimes also applied to copper alone.

Des Eléments en particuliers
et de leur préparation

QUANT À LA MATIÈRE DONT NOUS TIRONS NOS
éléments; je vous ai[2] déjà dit[3] qu'elle se trouvait[4] partout,
mais que les philosophes avaient[5] un sujet particulier d'où ils
les tiraient;[6] vous les trouverez[7] infailliblement et plus pro-
chainement dans le métaux et plusieurs philosophes les y ont
trouvés et en ont fait l'œuvre; mais la méthode en est plus
difficile[8] parce qu'il en faut ouvrir les barrières par un moyen
qui est connu de peu de personnes, nous d'écrirons cette œuvre dans un autre traité[9] dans les demis[10] minéraux et dans les
végétaux; elle est presque impossible, la matière étant[11] trop
éloignée[12] et il faudrait[13] toujours réduire et le joindre à la nature métallique, ce qui serait[14] un travail[15] trop long.

Ayant trouvé le sujet dégagé de la matière qui les envi-
ronne et qui le cache à la vue des hommes, prennez les[16] au
moment de leur naissances, c'est-à-dire dans le lieu de leur
naissance; et si, comme dit Virgile, les Dieux vous sont favor-
ables en ayant découvert[17] un, l'autre l'apparaîtra[18] bientôt.[19]

1.	4me.	8.	dificille.	15.	travaille.
2.	ais.	9.	traitté.	16.	prenes-les.
3.	dis.	10.	demys.	17.	descouvert.
4.	trouvoit.	11.	estant.	18.	l'apparoistra.
5.	avoient.	12.	esloignée.	19.	bientost.
6.	tiroient.	13.	faudroit.		
7.	trouvesres.	14.	seroit.		

FOURTH CHAPTER

Of the elements in particular and their preparation

AS FOR THE MATTER FROM WHICH WE EXTRACT our elements; I have already told you that it was found everywhere, but that the philosophers had a particular subject from which they drew them; you will find them unfailingly and more proximally in the metals, and many philosophers have found them there, and have done the work; but the method is more difficult because we must open the barriers by a means known to few people, we shall write this work in another treatise: on the semi-minerals and plants; it is almost impossible, the matter being too remote and it would always be necessary to reduce it and join it to the metallic nature, which would be too long a work.

Having found the subject freed from the matter which surrounds them and which hides it from the sight of men, take them at the time of their birth, that is to say, at the place of their birth; and if, as Virgil says, the gods are favorable to you when you have discovered one, the other will soon

Cherchez-les[20] les dans le soleil et dans la lune où ils sont vifs, cherchez-les[21] dans l'air qui les renferme et quand vous les aurez[22] trouvé;[23] c'est à dire par la méditation, comme dit le grand Hermès, faites[24] en sorte qu'ils paraissent[25] aux yeux; donnez-leur[26] des habillements conformes à leur nature. Mettez-les[27] dans la matrice, car si vous les remettez[28] dans des matières impures, vous les corromprez[29] et ne vous produiront que des avortons inutiles[30] et pernicieux.[31]

Il faut donc les dépouiller des corps impurs dont ils sont environnés et c'est pour vous aider en cette pratique, que nous voulons bien vous en donner les moyens; réservant néanmoins[32] ce qui n'est pas permis de dire, ni[33] moins encore d'écrire.[34] Cependant je vous parlerai[35] plus clairement qu'aucun philosophe n'ait[36] fait, pour peu que vous ayez[37] connaissance[38] de cet œuvre et que vous en connaissiez[39] le sujet. Vous trouverez[40] le reste et pour en faire part à quelques amis qui se connaitront[41] capables de travailler à cet œuvre. C'est pourquoi[42] je m'y explique plus clairement; ce que je pourrais[43] faire plus obscurément, si j'écrivais[44] pour le public, principalement lorsqu'il s'agit d'entrer dans la pratique.

Je pourrais[45] me servir de métaphores de hiéroglyphes, de figures énigmatiques, de paraboles, de similitudes, de comparaisons, de supposition et d'autres que j'aurais[46] pu[47] inventer, comme ont faits les philosophes mes Confrères, sous lesquels voiles ils ont caché[48] les mystères[49] de ce grand

20.	cherches les.	30.	inutils.	40.	trouverres.
21.	cherches les.	31.	pernitieux.	41.	connoistront.
22.	aures.	32.	neantmoins.	42.	pourquoy.
23.	trouves.	33.	ny.	43.	pourrois.
24.	faite.	34.	d'escrire.	44.	j'éscrivois.
25.	parroissent.	35.	parleray.	45.	pourrois.
26.	donnes leurs.	36.	n'aye.	46.	J'aurois.
27.	mettes les.	37.	ayes.	47.	pus.
28.	remettes.	38.	connoissance.	48.	caches.
29.	corromperes.	39.	connoissies.	49.	misteres.

appear. Seek them in the sun and in the moon, where they are alive, look for them in the air which contains them, and when you find them; that is to say, by meditation, as the great Hermes says, make them appear to the eyes; give them clothes according to their nature. Put them in the womb, for if you put them back into the impure matters, you will corrupt them and will only produce useless and pernicious abortions.

We must therefore strip them of the impure bodies with which they are surrounded, and it is to help you in this practice that we are willing to give you the means [to do so]; reserving nevertheless, what is not permitted to be said, let alone write. However, I will speak to you more clearly than any philosopher has done, provided you have knowledge of this work and that you know the subject of it. You will find the rest and share it with some friends who know themselves capable of working on this opus. That is why I explain more clearly what I could [say] more obscurely if I were to write for the public, especially when it comes to getting into the practice.

I could use metaphors, hieroglyphics, enigmatic figures, parables, similitudes, comparisons, supposition, and others that I could have invented, as my brothers the philosophers did, under which veils they have hidden the mysteries of this

ouvrage de la nature aux yeux des indignes et que ceux[50] des véritables philosophes aperçoivent très bien au travers de ces voiles.

C'est pourquoi[51] ils disent qu'il faut avoir des yeux de Lynx[52] pour voir au travers, qu'il faut tirer le rideau, qu'il ne faut pas s'arrêter[53] à la lettre,[54] mais au sens de la chose, non pas au son des paroles, mais à ce qu'elles signifient.

Il en est de même[55] de la connaissance[56] des principes, il ne faut pas s'attacher à leur extérieur, il faut pénétrer dans l'intérieur, il faut les dépouiller de leurs[57] haillons, il en faut séparer l'écorce, pour leur donner des habits Royaux, c'est-à-dire les rendre blanc comme la lune et resplendissants comme le soleil; leur ôter[58] toutes obscurités, faire sortir la lumière des ténèbres, afin de concilier ce qui est te plus opposé, joindre l'humide avec le sec, le feu avec l'eau, le chaud au froid, tirer l'air de l'eau, et l'eau de l'air; la terre, la faire eau; et derechef d'eau, en faire la terre; la terre la faire air; et d'air la faire terre; le fixe le rendre volatil et le volatil, le rendre fixe; dissoudre et coaguler, tout cela paraît[59] des paradoxes et des antithèses à ceux qui n'en ont pas connaissance:[60] ce qui néanmoins[61] sont paroles[62] très véritables, comme vous en serez[63] persuadés après la lecture de ce traité,[64] ce que j'explique en particulier en ce chapitre.

J'éviterais[65] tous ces termes sous lesquels les philosophes ont caché[66] cet admirable ouvrage; l'ayant écrit[67] pour me ser-

50.	ceuse.	57.	leur.	64.	traitté.
51.	pourquoy.	58.	oster.	65.	J'éviteray.
52.	Linx.	59.	parroist.	66.	caches.
53.	s'arrester.	60.	connoissance.	67.	escrit.
54.	lestre.	61.	neantmoins.		
55.	mesme.	62.	parolles.		
56.	connoissance.	63.	seres.		

great work of nature from the eyes of the unworthy, and that those of the true philosophers perceive very well through these veils.

That is why they say that it is necessary to have the eyes of the Lynx to see through, that we must draw the curtain [back], that we must not stop at the letter, but in the meaning of the thing, not at the sound of words, but what they signify.

It is the same with the knowledge of the principles, we must not attach ourselves to their exterior, we must penetrate into the interior, we must strip them of their rags, we must separate the bark, to give them royal garments, that is to say, to make them as white as the moon and as resplendent as the sun; to remove all darkness from them, to bring the light out from the darkness in order to reconcile what is more opposed, to join the humid with the dry, the fire with the water, the hot with the cold, to draw the air from the water, and water from the air; to make the earth water, and water earth again; to make earth air, and air earth; the fixed volatile and the volatile fixed; to dissolve and to coagulate; all these things appear as paradoxes and antitheses to those who have no knowledge of them: words which are nonetheless very true, as you will be persuaded after reading this treatise, which I explain in particular in this chapter.

I would avoid all those terms under which the philosophers have hidden this admirable work; having written it to

vir de mémorial et d'agenda pour m'y appliquer, quand Dieu
par sa miséricorde m'en aura procuré l'occasion pour instruire celui[68] à qui je laisserai[69] cet écrit[70] par testament. C'est
le seul bien que je possède; n'ayant pas eu[71] jusqu'à présent
les moyens d'y travailler et de m'y appliquer entièrement. Car
ce travail[72] demande[73] une application entière: les procès,[74] les
affaires domestiques m'en[75] ont toujours empêche;[76] car pour
la dépense,[77] elle est très modique, et cela ne doit point arrêter l'application qu'on peut avoir, est un travail[78] naturel de
l'homme qui ne passe point ses forces, elle n'est point contraire au salut, parce que son but principal est de soulager les
pauvres, les délivrer de leur misères, de leur maladie et glori-
fier Dieu en fondant des maisons Religieuses,[79] des hôpitaux,
et bâtissant[80] des temples à l'honneur de Dieu, à fonder des
sacrifices et des prières pour le soulagement de son amé: elle
est utile[81] à l'état,[82] à la patrie en donnant des moyens aux puissances pour lever des Armées pour la défense de l'État.

On fait donc un grand mal de persécuter[83] ceux qui s'ap-
pliquent à cet art et ceux qui n'ont point de charge dans la ré-
publique, qui ne sont pas marchands,[84] ni[85] artisans,[86] qui ont
du bien raisonnablement, devraient[87] s'y appliquer, plutôt[88]
que de mener une vie molle et fainéante et s'amuser à la bag-
atelle et à des choses indignes de l'application d'un homme
de bien.

68.	celuy.	76.	empeches.	84.	marchand.
69.	laisseray.	77.	depence.	85.	ny.
70.	escrit.	78.	travaille.	86.	artisants.
71.	eus.	79.	Relligieuses.	87.	devroient.
72.	travaille.	80.	battissant.	88.	plustot.
73.	demande.	81.	utille.		
74.	procez.	82.	L'éstat.		
75.	m'ent.	83.	persecutter.		

serve as a memorial and an agenda for my application, when God by his mercy has given me the opportunity to instruct he to whom I will leave this writing by testament. It is the only good I possess; having not hitherto had the means to work on it, and to apply myself entirely to it. For this work requires an entire application: the lawsuits, the domestic affairs, have always prevented me; because with regards to the expenditure it is very modest, and this must not stop the application that one may have, [it] is a natural labour of man, which does not expend his strength; it is not contrary to salvation, because its main purpose is to relieve the poor, to deliver them from their miseries, of their sickness, and to glorify God by founding religious houses and hospitals, by building temples to the honor of God, to establish sacrifices and prayers for the relief of his soul: it is useful to the state, to the country by giving means to the Powers to raise Armies for the defense of the State.

It is therefore a great evil to persecute those who apply themselves to this art, and those who have no office in the republic, who are neither merchants nor artisans, who are reasonably well off, should apply themselves to it rather than lead a soft and idle life amusing themselves with trivialities and things unworthy of a good man's attention.

Des opérations en général

IL Y EN A 12 QUI SONT AUTANT DE CLEFS POUR ouvrir les portes de notre[2] Cabinet Hermétique et de notre[3] sujet philosophique. Ces opérations sont la calcination, la trituration, la dissolution, la sublimation, l'inhumation, la lotion, la conjonction, la fixation et la nutrition.

La Calcination pour notre[4] œuvre n'est pas une opération violente qui se fait par la violence du feu, comme le croient[5] les chymistes vulgaires. C'est proprement un dessèchement[6] de la matière dont nous voulons la dépouiller de son humidité flegmatique,[7] ce qui se[8] fait par un feu médiocre, il y a une calcination physique[9] de la nature, où l'Artiste ne met pas les mains; la matière se calcine d'elle-même,[10] ce qui arrive au milieu[11] et à la fin de l'œuvre; au milieu[12] lorsque le noir commence à paraitre,[13] que le soleil s'éclipse et le corps du soleil se met sous la lune; les philosophes m'entendent bien ou[14] dans sa vie, lorsque de la coagulation et de la fixation.

1.	5me.	7.	phlegmatique.	13.	parroistre.
2.	nostre.	8.	ce.	14.	Could also be *où*,
3.	nostre.	9.	phisique.		'where'. Neither
4.	nostre.	10.	elle mesme.		make sense.
5.	croyent.	11.	mileux.		
6.	deseichement.	12.	mileux.		

FIFTH CHAPTER

Of operations in general

THERE ARE TWELVE [OPERATIONS] WHICH ARE AS many [as the] keys to open the gates of our Hermetic Sanctum[14] and of our philosophical subject. These operations are calcination, trituration, dissolution, sublimation, inhumation, ablution,[15] conjunction, fixation, and nutrition.

Calcination, for our work, is not a violent operation that is done by the violence of fire, as the vulgar chymists believe. It is properly a drying out[16] of the matter, which we wish to strip of its phlegmatic humidity, which is done by a mediocre fire. There is a physical calcination of nature, where the Artist does not use his hands; the matter calcines itself, which occurs in the middle and at the end of the work. In the middle, when the blackness begins to appear, the sun disappears and the body of the sun goes behind the moon. Philosophers hear me well, or in its life, when coagulation and fixation [begins to occur].

14   *Cabinet* (see Preface).
15   *La lotion*, 'washing, ablution'.
16   *Dessèchement*, 'dessication'.

Sous la Calcination, est compris[15] la rubification qui est une espèce de sublimation du corps blanc de la lune, qui par cette opération, en augmentation le feu d'un degré, devient rouge.

La Trituration est une opération qui précède presque toujours la calcination il faut broyer notre[16] matière: quand je parle ici[17] de notre[18] matière dans les opérations [il faut toujours entendre le corps de la pierre, ou le sujet dont est formé le corps, cela se[19] dit, pour les opérations.] Broyer notre[20] matière n'est pas de la broyer dans un mortier, c'est-à-dire réduire la matière en menues parties, la nature le fait dans l'œuvre, sans les mains de l'artiste. C'est, lorsque la terre commence à se sublimer et qu'elle se mêle[21] avec les autres éléments; cela se[22] fait encore dans la dissolution du sujet philosophique, lorsqu'on le fond dans l'eau et se divise en manière de glace qui fond dans l'eau chaude, ou plutôt[23] comme un morceau de chaux vive qui jetée dans l'eau se broie[24] d'elle-même[25] et se divise quasi en atomes.[26] C'est la 3ème[27] préparation que nous donnons à notre[28] sujet.

La Dissolution est la même[29] que l'on entend ordinairement qui est la réduction d'un corps en eau, excepté qu'elle se fait un peu autrement dans notre[30] magistère et dans notre[31] œuvre elle ne se fait pas tout d'un coup; mais par réitérée lotion. Toute la matière se réduit une eau à l'exception de quelques fèces[32] et résidences, lorsque le dit solvant est rempli[33] suffisamment[34] de[35] parties terrestres. C'est dans cette

15.	comprit.	24.	broye.	33.	remplit.
16.	nostre.	25.	d'elle mesme.	34.	suffisament.
17.	icy.	26.	athome.	35.	des.
18.	nostre.	27.	3me.		
19.	ce.	28.	nostre.		
20.	nostre.	29.	mesme.		
21.	mesle.	30.	nostre.		
22.	ce.	31.	nostre.		
23.	plustot.	32.	fæces.		

Under Calcination is understood the rubification, which is a kind of sublimation of the white body of the moon, which by this operation, by increasing the fire by one degree, becomes red.

Trituration is an operation that almost always precedes calcination, we must crush our matter. When I speak here of our matter in the operations (we must always understand the body of the stone, or the subject of which the body is formed, it can be said, for the operations). To grind our matter is not to crush it in a mortar, that is to say, to reduce the matter into small parts, nature does it in the work without the hands of the Artist. It is when the earth begins to sublime and mingle with the other elements; this is still done in the dissolution of the philosophical matter, when it is melted in water and divided in the manner of ice melting in hot water, or rather like a piece of quicklime thrown into water which grinds itself and divides itself almost into atoms. This is the third preparation that we are giving to our subject.

Dissolution is the same as is commonly understood, which is the reduction of a body into water, except that it is done somewhat differently in our magisterium and in our work it is not done all at once; but by repeated lotion. All the matter is reduced into water with the exception of a few feces and residues,[17] when the said solvent is sufficiently filled with the terrestrial parts. It is in this operation that the

---

17   Old French *résidence*, which can mean 'that which falls to the bottom of liquors; sediment, residuum'.

opération que les parties ignées se mêlant[36] avec l'eau, que le
feu se fait eau et se joint à l'air, que l'air devient eau; qu'ils
appellent proprement une conversion[37] d'Eléments qui est un
mélange[38] des parties ignées, aqueuses, aériennes[39] et terrestres, qui gardent toujours leurs natures d'air, de feu, d'eau, et
de terre, qui occupent un des plus grands espaces entre elles
par l'interposition de l'eau et de l'air qui font qu'elles s'éten-
dent et font un plus grand volume. C'est cette conversion[40]
qui fait le commerce du ciel avec la terre dans le grand monde
comme dans notre[41] divin œuvre.

La main de l'Artiste est nécessaire dans cette opération, la
nature fait cette dissolution, lorsque la terre se change en eau,
c'est dans cette opération, disent les philosophes que la pierre
se dissout elle-même.[42] C'est proprement cette opération qui
est la clef qui ouvre les sept[43] portes de notre[44] Cabinet Hermétique, car à chaque dissolution il s'ouvre une porte; cette
porte ouverte donne entrée dans la 2ème[45] de la 2ème[46] dans
la 3ème[47] ainsi[48] jusqu'à la 7ème[49] porte qui vous donne les 2
luminaires qui sont le commencement comme nous disons
ci-après,[50] et cela se[51] fait par réitérées dissolutions.

Mais cette dissolution ne se fait pas sans qu'elle n'ait[52]
précédé la calcination; cette opération est la plus essentielle de l'œuvre, car comme dit Bernard, tout dépend de tout
dissoudre et coaguler, car la Calcination des philosophes
est proprement une coagulation; c'est ce que dit Philalète,[53]
pour faire l'union de nos natures, il faut une eau homogène
à laquelle on prépare la voie[54] par la calcination qui a
précédé et qu'il se fait auparavant un dessèchement.[55] Cette

36.	meslant.	43.	cept.	50.	cy.
37.	convertion.	44.	nostre.	51.	ce.
38.	meslange.	45.	2me.	52.	n'aye.
39.	aerienes.	46.	2me.	53.	Philalette.
40.	convertion.	47.	3me.	54.	voye.
41.	notre.	48.	ainsy.	55.	deseichement.
42.	elle mesme.	49.	7me.		

igneous parts mingle with the water, that the fire becomes
water and joins with the air, that the air becomes water; that
they properly call a conversion of the Elements, which is a
mixture of the igneous, aqueous, aerial, and terrestrial parts,
which always retain their natures of air, fire, water, and earth
which occupy one of the largest spaces between them, by the
interposition of water and air, which make them extend and
form a larger volume. It is this conversion which makes the
commerce between heaven and earth in the macrocosm as in
our divine work.

The hand of the Artist is necessary in this operation. Nature makes this dissolution when the earth changes into water; it is in this operation, say the philosophers, that the stone
dissolves itself. It is this operation, properly, which is the key
that opens the seven gates of our Hermetic Sanctum,[18] for at
each dissolution a gate opens; this open gate gives entry into
the second, from the second into the third, and so on up to
the seventh gate which gives you the two luminaries which
are the beginning, as we say below, and this is done through
repeated dissolutions.

But this dissolution does not take place without having
[been] preceded [by] the calcination; this operation is the most
essential [part] of the work, for, as Bernard says, everything
depends on dissolving and coagulating, for the calcination of
the philosophers is properly a coagulation; this is what Philalethes says, in order to unite our natures, we need a homogeneous water to which we prepare the way through the calcination which has preceded, and which has previously become a

18 *Cabinet* (see Preface).

dissolution n'est proprement, dit-il, qu'une réduction en atomes[56] de l'eau avec la terre par le crible de la nature qui est l'air et les atomes[57] sont plus déliés et plus subtiles.

La sublimation est une opération par laquelle, nous purifions de plus en plus notre[58] sujet en dégageant les éléments de leurs terrestres[59] et de leurs impuretés maternelles,[60] en faisant monter les parties terrestres en la partie supérieure du vaisseau[61] par l'action de notre[62] feu aidé du feu de nature, et par ce moyen la terre reçoit la vertu des éléments supérieurs.

Voilà ce que nous appelons[63] sublimation, parce que la terre acquiert une vertu plus puissante et plus sublime. Cela s'appelle aussi[64] donner des ailes[65] à la terre et rendre le fixe volatil.

Philalèthe[66] nous décrit[67] admirablement bien cette sublimation, parce que, dit-il, dans la sublimation qui ce fait, le corps communique alors sa fixité a l'eau et l'eau fait part de sa volatilité au corps. Mais toute l'eau ne monte pas, il en reste une partie avec le corps dans le fond du vaisseau:[68] si vous considérez[69] souvent et attentivement cette opération, vous remarquerez[70] que le corps bout et se crible dans l'eau qui demeure en bas et que par le moyen de cette même[71] eau qui perce et ouvre le reste du corps, et par cette circulation, l'eau devenant plus subtile,[72] elle tire à la fin l'âme[73] du soleil doucement et sans violence.

Or cette sublimation est bien opposée à celle des chymistes qui par la violence du feu, rendent une matière subtile[74] en la faisant monter dans des aludels; nos aludels et nos vaisseaux[75] sont les éléments. C'est pourquoi[76] nous n'avons

56.	atosmes.	63.	appellons.	70.	remarqueres.
57.	atosmes.	64.	aussy.	71.	mesme.
58.	nostre.	65.	ailles.	72.	subtille.
59.	terrestreites.	66.	Philalette.	73.	l'ame.
60.	maternelle.	67.	d'escrit.	74.	subtille.
61.	vesseau.	68.	vesseau.	75.	vesseaux.
62.	nostre.	69.	consideres.	76.	pourquoy.

dessication. This dissolution, he says, is properly only a reduction into atoms of the water with the earth by the sieve of nature, which is the air, and the atoms are more penetrating and more subtle.

Sublimation is an operation by which we purify our subject more and more by disengaging the elements from their terrestrial bodies and their maternal impurities, by making the terrestrial parts rise to the upper part of the vessel by the action of our fire, aided by the fire of nature, and by this means the earth receives the virtue of the superior elements.

This is what we call sublimation, because the earth acquires a more powerful and sublime virtue. This is also called giving wings to the earth and making the fixed volatile.

Philalethes admirably describes this sublimation to us, because, he says, in the sublimation that results, the body then communicates its fixity to the water, and the water shares its volatility to the body. But not all the water rises, and a part of it remains with the body in the bottom of the vessel: if you consider this operation often and carefully, you will notice that the body boils and is sieved in the water which remains below, and that by means of this same water which pierces and opens the rest of the body, and by this circulation, the water, becoming more subtle, finally draws the soul of the sun gently and without violence.

Now this sublimation is quite contrary to that of the chymists, who, by the violence of fire, render a matter subtle by making it rise in aludels; our aludels and vessels are the elements. That is why we do not need so many vessels and

pas besoin de tant de vaisseaux[77] et tant d'alambics, nous en parlons en un chapitre particulier. Voilà ce que nous entendons par sublimation, la distillation est souvent confondue avec le terme de sublimation, parce que le corps ou la terre, en se sublimant, se distille en passant par le filtre de la nature qui est l'air et l'air se coagulant, forme des gouttes, et ces gouttes se réduisent en eau qui arrive dans notre[78] distillation. l'air est le chapiteau de l'alambic de la nature. Le récipient est l'eau et la cucurbite[79] c'est la terre. Ainsi[80] vous voyez[81] que nous n'avons pas besoin de tant d'alambics[82] et de tant de[83] vaisseaux;[84] nous avons besoin pourtant d'une espèce d'alambic pour séparer l'esprit de l'eau et pour le déflegmer, qui est l'esprit blanc, et pour tirer l'esprit solaire de notre[85] corps qui sont nos 2 premiers luminaires et le mercure blanc et le mercure citrin que nous mettons à part dont nous parlons dans la pratique et dans les opérations en particulier.

L'inhumation est une opération très essentielle dans l'œuvre. C'est de rendre à la terre son humidité; de spirituelle la faire corporelle; le volatil se rend fixe et d'une fixité d'autant plus parfaite qu'on réitère souvent cette opération. Ce qui se[86] fait par réitérée imbibition, en humectant la terre, jusqu'à ce qu'elle ait[87] bu[88] toute son eau, C'est encore par cette opération qu'on blanchit le noire et qu'on coupe[89] la tête[90] au Corbeau; C'est aussi[91] par elle qu'on sublime la terre et qu'on lui[92] donne des ailes, aidée par la sublimation et la distillation; car les opérations se font les unes par les autres; elles ont une très grande[93] connexité. C'est pourquoi[94] les philosophes ont raison de dire que toutes ces opérations se succèdent les unes aux autres, et se font néanmoins par une même[95] opération

77. vesseaux.
78. nostre.
79. cucurbitte.
80. Ainsy.
81. voyes.
82. d'alembic.
83. des.
84. vesseux.
85. nostre.
86. ce.
87. aye.
88. buë.
89. couppe.
90. teste.
91. aussy.
92. luy.
93. grandes.
94. pourquoy.
95. mesme.

so many alembics. We talk about them [further] in a specific chapter. This is what we mean by sublimation. Distillation is often confused with the term sublimation, because the body or the earth, in its sublimation, is distilled by passing through the filter of nature which is air, and air coagulates, forms drops, and these drops are reduced to water which arrive in our distillation. The air is the head[19] of the alembic of nature. The receiver is the water and the cucurbit is the earth. So, you see that we do not need so many alembics and so many vessels; we still need a kind of alembic to separate the spirit from the water and to dephlegm it, which is the white spirit, and to draw the solar spirit from our bodies, which are our first two luminaries and the white mercury, and the citrine mercury, that we set apart [and] of which we talk about in the practice and in the particular operations.

Inhumation is a very essential operation in the work. It is to restore to the earth its humidity; to make the spiritual corporeal; to render the volatile fixed and of a fixity all the more perfect when this operation is frequently repeated. It is that which is done by repeated imbibition, by moistening the earth until it has drunk all its water. It is again by this operation that the black is whitened and that the head of the raven is cut off; it is also through [this operation] that the earth is sublimed and wings are given, aided by sublimation and distillation. Because the operations are performed by each other, they have a very great connection. This is why the philosophers are right in saying that all these operations succeed one another, and are nevertheless performed by the same operation and in the same vessel. This

19 *Le chapiteau*, or 'capital'.

et dans le même[96] vaisseau.[97] Cette opération se[98] fait principalement[99] dans la fin de l'œuvre et Philalèthe[100] en parle en ces termes. Cuisez[101] donc la matière continuellement avec un feu qui lui[102] soit propre; de sorte que dans votre[103] vaisseau,[104] vous voyez[105] monter une rosée, et un espèce de brouillard[106] qui retomberont incessamment[107] en goutte, jour et nuit; par cette circulation le mercure monte tout sel ainsi qu'il est en sa 1ère[108] nature et que le corps demeure en bas au fond du vaisseau[109] tout de même[110] en sa 1ère[111] nature, jusqu'à ce que par un assez[112] long temps, le corps commence à retenir quelque peu d'eau; ainsi[113] le corps et l'eau se[114] sont fait l'un et l'autre participant des degrés de qualité[115] qu'ils ont chacun séparément. C'est à dire que le corps communique sa fixité à l'eau, et l'eau fait part de sa volatilité au corps. Puis il ajoute, ainsi[116] par l'entremise de l'âme, l'esprit est réconcilié avec le corps, ils s'unissent tous deux dans la couleur noire.

La lotion est une opération par laquelle nous blanchissons le corps noire de l'or, par réitérée imbibition de son eau dont il a été[117] tiré, Comme nous blanchissons ce noir, nous l'appelons[118] lavement ou lotion. C'est pourquoi[119] quelques philosophes ont dit que leur ouvrage était[120] un ouvrage de femme, parce qu'ils blanchissent: elle n'est en usage que lorsque la pierre est au noire dans la 1ère[121] et 2ème[122] œuvre, car dans la 3ème[123] [le blanchiment[124] se fait autrement][125] il

96. mesme.	107. incessament.	118. l'appellons.
97. vesseau.	108. 1re.	119. pourquoy.
98. ce.	109. vesseau.	120. estoit.
99. principallement.	110. mesme.	121. 1re.
100. Philalette.	111. 1re.	122. 1me.
101. Cuises.	112. asses.	123. 3me.
102. luy.	113. ainsy.	124. blanchissament.
103. vostre.	114. se.	125. Marginal note.
104. vesseau.	115. qualites.	
105. voyes.	116. ainsy.	
106. brouillart.	117. esté.	

operation is done mainly in the end of the work and Philalethes speaks of it in these terms. Cook the matter continually
with a fire of its own, so that in your vessel you will see a dew
rise, and a kind of fog which will incessantly fall drop by drop,
day and night; by this circulation the mercury raises every
salt, as it is in its first nature, and the body remains below at
the bottom of the vessel, still completely in its first nature,
until [after] quite a long time the body begins to retain some
of the water; thus the body and the water are each made of
each other participating in the degrees of quality which they
each have separately. That is to say, the body communicates
its fixity to the water, and the water imparts its volatility to
the body. Then he adds, through the medium of the soul, the
spirit is thus reconciled with the body, and they both unite in
the colour black.

Ablution [washing] is an operation by which we whit-
en the black body of gold by repeated imbibition of its water
from which it was drawn. As we whiten this black, we call it
washing or lotion. This is why some philosophers have said
that their work was a woman's work, because they whiten:[20]
it is used only when the stone is black in the first and second
works, for in the third (the whitening is done differently)[21]

20   That is, through washing.
21   Marginal note in manuscript.

ne faut pas confondre ce que disent les auteurs[126] qui divisent seulement la pierre en 2 œuvres. Nous en faisons un plus grand éclaircissement. Consultez[127] le chapitre où nous en traitons.[128]

La Conjonction est une union de deux substances que nous mêlons[129] ensemble, les substances sont le mercure blanc et le mercure rouge que nous joignons ensemble pour faire le mercure animé et le mercure citrin de la 1ère[130] préparation dont nous tirons nos deux luminaires, soleil et lune qui en se réunissant d'eux même[131] sans la main de l'Artiste, paraissent[132] sous un corps blanc qui est l'or blanc de Philalèthe[133] et la lunaire des philosophes que quelques-uns d'eux d'écrivent, lorsqu'ils disent que pour lors la femelle monte sur le mâle;[134] ces deux corps mis en putréfaction se changent en un corps noir; pour lors l'éclipse[135] du soleil se fait des philosophes, semblable à celle du soleil du grand monde qui arrive par l'interposition de la lune au soleil, il arrive la même[136] chose dans notre[137] petit monde philosophique. Nous faisons encore cette opération, lorsque nous joignons la lune au corps du soleil, lorsqu'il faut couper la tête[138] au corbeau et blanchir le corps noir de l'or. C'est le 1er[139] mariage et la 1ère[140] conjonction du mâle[141] et de la femelle dans le dernier œuvre de la 1ère[142] partie. Cette conjonction se fait encore plus parfaitement; mais la nature le fait sans l'aide de l'Artiste.

La putréfaction, nous n'entendons pas dans cette opération une putréfaction ladreuse qui détruit tout, mais seulement une putréfaction qui va à la génération, et c'est plutôt[143] une mortification des substances lunaires et solaires, de laquelle mortification nous formons nos luminaires, après

---

126. autheurs.	132. parroissent.	138. teste.
127. Consultes.	133. Philalette.	139. 1r.
128. traittons.	134. masle.	140. 1r.
129. meslons.	135. Esclipse.	141. masle.
130. 1re.	136. mesme.	142. 1re.
131. mesme.	137. nostre.	143. plus tost.

one must not confuse what the authors say who only divide the stone into two works. We make it much more clear. Consult the chapter where we deal with this.

Conjunction is a union of two substances, which we mix together. The substances are the white mercury and the red mercury which we join together to make the animated mercury and the citrine mercury of the first preparation from which we draw our two luminaries, the sun and the moon, which by uniting by themselves without the artist's hand, appear under a white body which is the white gold of Philalethes, and the moon of the philosophers that some of them write about when they say that when the female mounts the male. These two putrefying bodies change into a black body; for when the eclipse of the sun is made by philosophers, similar to that of the sun of the macrocosm which happens by the interposition of the moon upon the sun, the same happens in our philosophical microcosm.[22] We perform this operation again when we join the moon to the body of the sun, when it is necessary to cut the head off the raven and whiten the black body of gold. It is the first marriage and the first conjunction of the male and the female in the last work of the first part. This conjunction is made even more perfectly; but nature does it without the help of the Artist.

[Concerning] putrefaction, we do not mean in this operation a leprous[23] putrefaction which destroys everything, but only a putrefaction which proceeds to generation, and it is rather a mortification of the lunar and solar substances, from which mortification we form our luminaries, after a due digestion,

22   Literally *grand mond* and *petit mond*, 'great world' and 'small world', the latter referring to the recapitulation of the cosmogonic process on the alchemical level.

23   *Ladreuse*, possibly means 'leprous'.

une due digestion par un feu convenable; les luminaires commencent à sortir de leurs chaos[144] et de leur éclipse,[145] le corps du soleil commence à se coaguler en atomes[146] noirs sur la superficie de l'eau. C'est ce que Philalèthe[147] entend des petits corbeaux qui sortent de leurs nids, et qu'il faut bien prendre garde qu'ils n'y entrent; ayant soin de les prendre subtilement. C'est en ce sens que les philosophes disent de prendre nos luminaires lors de leurs naissances. Et c'est alors, dit Philalèthe,[148] qu'il faut bien gouverner le feu, et ne le point pousser d'une manière que vous épuisiez[149] l'eau et que la terre qui est affaissé[150] n'en ai[151] point du tout, et empêcher que les petits des Corbeux ne retournent dans leurs nids, quand ils en seront une fois sortis qui sont ces petits atomes[152] noirs qui paraissent[153] sur la surface[154] de l'eau, aussi[155] afin que, par faute de chaleur, la terre soit suffoquée et noyée par trop d'eau.

La Coagulation, la Fixation et la Nutrition regardent particulièrement la deuxième partie de l'œuvre qui est la multiplication dont nous traitons[156] un chapitre.

144. cahos.
145. Esclipse.
146. atosmes.
147. Philalette.
148. Philalette.
149. epuissies.
150. affaicée.
151. ay.
152. atosmes.
153. parroissent.
154. surfasse.
155. aussy.
156. traittons.

by a suitable fire. The luminaries begin to emerge from their chaos and their eclipse, the body of the sun begins to coagulate into black atoms on the surface of the water. This is what Philalethes understands by the little ravens coming out of their nests, and it is necessary to be very careful that they do not re-enter, taking care to gather them subtly. It is in this sense that the philosophers say to take our luminaries during their births. And it is then, says Philalethes, that it is necessary to govern the fire well, and not push it in such a way that you exhaust the water, and that the earth that has collapsed has none at all. And [it is necessary] to prevent the young ravens from returning to their nests once they have departed; for they are the tiny black atoms which appear on the surface of the water; [it is] also [necessary to do this] so that, due to lack of heat, the earth will be suffocated and drowned by excess water.

Coagulation, Fixation, and Nutrition are particularly relevant to the second part of the work, which is the multiplication that we deal with in another chapter.

SECOND PART

Des opérations en particulier[1] qui sont absolument nécessaires pour la pratique

AVANT-PROPOS

NOUS AVONS DIT DANS LES CHAPITRES PRÉCÉDENTS tout ce qui était[2] nécessaire pour la connaissance des principes de la pierre et de la théorie, maintenant nous allons entrer dans la pratique.

C'est cette forêt[3] noire dont parlent Philalèthe[4] et Poliphile, qu'il faut pénétrer, et ou tant de gens s'égarent, sans un bon guide qui leur montre un chemin droit et leur donne les moyens d'en sortir, C'est ce dédale et ce labyrinthe[5] a 7 portes décrites[6] par les portes d'où l'on ne peut sortir sans le filet[7] d'Ariadne;[8] C'est cette mer orageuse, où il y a tant d'écueils[9] où tant de personnes font naufrage,[10] à moins d'avoir un pilote expert; enfin cette pratique que les philosophes ont plus caché[11] dans leurs écrits[12] et qu'ils ont mêlés[13] de tant de figures, d'énigmes, de métaphores, de similitudes, de suppositions, de contrariétés, et même[14] d'expressions qu'il est impossible de les comprendre sans l'aide d'un bon Artiste, ou d'un bon Maître.[15] Car lorsqu'ils semblent en parler plus clairement, c'est alors qu'ils sont moins sincères,[16] et lorsqu'ils parlent plus obscurément, c'est alors qu'ils vous disent la vérité. Ils en

1.	particulieurs.	7.	fillet.	13.	mesles.
2.	estoit.	8.	D'Ariane.	14.	mesme.
3.	forest.	9.	d'ecüeuilles.	15.	Maistre.
4.	Philalette.	10.	nauffrage.	16.	sincers.
5.	labyrinte.	11.	caches.		
6.	d'escrittes.	12.	escrits.		

Of the operations in particular which are absolutely necessary for the practice

FOREWORD

WE HAVE SAID IN THE PRECEDING CHAPTERS ALL that was necessary for the knowledge of the principles of the stone and the theory; now we shall enter into the practice.

It is this black forest of which Philalethes and Poliphilus speak, which must be penetrated, and where so many people go astray without a good guide who shows them a straight path and gives them the means to find their way out; this maze and labyrinth has seven gates, defined by the gates from which one cannot leave without the thread of Ariadne. In this stormy sea, there are so many reefs where so many people are shipwrecked unless they have an expert steersman. Finally, the philosophers have hidden this practice further in their writings, which they have mingled with so many figures, enigmas, metaphors, similitudes, suppositions, contrarieties, and even expressions that are impossible to understand without the help of a good Artist or a good Master.[24] Because when they seem to speak most clearly, it is when they are less sincere, and when they speak most obscurely, then they are telling you the truth. They have used

24 That is, an adept.

ont usés ainsi,[17] comme je vous ai[18] déjà dit et fait remarquer
pour cacher notre[19] science aux ignorants[20] et aux gens incapa-
bles de la posséder; Laissant à l'ordre de la Divine providence
de l'inspirer à celui[21] qu'il lui[22] plaira.

Quelques-uns ont suivi[23] une autre méthode, ils n'ont
rien supposé[24] ni[25] figuré;[26] mais ils ont mêlé[27] les opérations
d'une manière qu'on peut facilement[28] confondre une opération avec une autre, en sorte que ce qui convient à l'une, ne
convient pas à l'autre, ils décrivent[29] le commencement, ce
qui doit être[30] la fin; et souvent[31] la fin, ils la mettent au commencement. Ce qui cause une confusion à l'esprit dans la
lecture de leurs écrits[32] qui n'est pas peu considérables. C'est
Philalèthe[33] qui, de tous les philosophes a le plus suivi[34] ce
genre d'écriture,[35] où il mêlé[36] si adroitement ces opérations
distinctes, et il les coud[37] si bien ensemble, qu'il semble qu'il
parle de la même[38] opération, quand on en sait[39] rompre le
tissu.[40] C'est cependant ce philosophe qui parle le plus sin-
cèrement. Il est assez[41] de bonne foi[42] pour avertir le lecteur,
de ne pas prendre le change. C'est ce philosophes qui a le plus
entré dans la pratique qu'aucun autre et qui a écrit[43] le dernier.
C'est pourquoi[44] je le cite souvent et plus que les autres, mais
il s'est particulièrement attaché à d'écrire[45] la pierre minérale
qu'il appelle la difficile[46] dont la matière est l'or et le mercure
vulgaire; pour celle-ci[47] qui est celle des anciens[48] et qui est
la plus facile,[49] qui se fait sans le mercure ni[50] l'or vulgaire et

17.	ainsy.	29.	descrivent.	40.	tissue.
18.	ais.	30.	estre.	41.	asses.
19.	nostre.	31.	sçouvent.	42.	foy.
20.	ignorans.	32.	escrits.	43.	escrit.
21.	celuy.	33.	Philalette.	44.	pourquoy.
22.	luy.	34.	suivit.	45.	d'escrire.
23.	suivis.	35.	d'escrire.	46.	dificille.
24.	supposes.	36.	mesle.	47.	celle cy.
25.	ny.	37.	cout: likely 'coud'	48.	antiens.
26.	figures.		(sews).	49.	facille.
27.	mesles.	38.	mesme.	50.	ny.
28.	facillement.	39.	sçait.		

them in this way, as I have already told you and pointed out, to hide our knowledge from the ignorant and from the people incapable of possessing it, leaving it to the order of Divine Providence to inspire who he pleases.

Some have followed a different method. They have not assumed or imagined anything, but they have mingled the operations in such a way that one can easily confuse one operation with another, such that what is appropriate to one is not appropriate to the other. They describe [at] the beginning what must be [at] the end, and often put the end at the beginning. This causes confusion in the mind when reading their writings, which is not insignificant. It is Philalethes who, of all the philosophers, has followed this style of writing the most, where he so adroitly mingled these distinct operations, and sews them so well together that it seems that he speaks of the same operation; [but] we know how to 'rupture the fabric'.[25] However, it is this philosopher who speaks most sincerely. He has the good faith to warn the reader not to accept the exchange. It is this philosopher who has entered into the practice more than any other, and who was last to have written. That is why I quote him often, and more than the others. But he is particularly attached to writing about the mineral stone, which he calls difficult, whose material is gold and vulgar mercury. For that which is [the way] of the ancients and which is the easiest, is made without mercury or vulgar gold, and

---

25   Literal translation of *rompre le tissu*, to 'break, rupture, or unravel' (*rompre*) the 'fabric' (*tissu*), similar in meaning to 'see behind the curtain', or to 'pierce the veil', i.e., to see what is actually being said.

qui est celle des anciens.[51] Il en parle peu, il mêle[52] néanmoins quelques opérations de la minérale[53] à la pierre des modernes, ce qui appartient avec celle des anciens.[54]

Quand je parle des philosophes, j'entends[55] parler des véritables, il y en a plusieurs qui passent pour philosophes qui ne l'ont jamais été[56] et qui n'ont jamais su[57] la pierre, quoiqu'ils[58] en aient[59] écrit[60] pour paraître[61] savent[62] en cet art dont il se faut donner de garde, car ils sont capables de vous faire quitter le droit chemin, il faut encore plus éviter la lecture de certains manuscrits qu'ils appellent procédés où ils d'écrivent toutes choses de point en point. C'est ce que vous ne verrez[63] jamais dans un véritable philosophe, mais ces sortes d'auteurs[64] ne risquent rien; il n'y a que celui[65] qui travaille avec eux ou selon leur méthode[66] qui perd son temps et son argent, C'est pour vous tirer particulièrement de ce mauvais pas que j'ai[67] fait[68] ce traité,[69] afin que vous puissiez[70] distinguer les faux frères d'avec les véritables, afin que trouvant et connaissant[71] un véritable adepte, il puisse vous conduire[72] et vous enseigner ce qui vous peut faire de peine dans la pratique et vous devez[73] faire société avec lui.[74]

C'est donc pour vous aider en ce chemin épineux et pour résoudre toutes les difficultés qui pourraient[75] vous empêcher de parvenir à la fin désirée que j'ai[76] fait cet écrit;[77] je ne vous dirai[78] pas les choses de point en point, en sorte que vous n'ayez[79] plus rien à découvrir,[80] cela ne m'étant[81] pas permis, il

51. Antiens.	62. sçavent.	73. deves.
52. mesle.	63. verres.	74. luy.
53. mineralle.	64. autheurs.	75. pourroient.
54. Antiens.	65. celuy.	76. jay.
55. entend.	66. metode.	77. escrit.
56. estes.	67. jay.	78. diray.
57. scües.	68. fais.	79. n'ayes.
58. quoyqu'ils.	69. traitte.	80. descouvrir.
59. ayent.	70. puissies.	81. m'estant.
60. escrit.	71. connoissant.	
61. parroistre.	72. conduir.	

is that of the ancients. He does not speak much about it, [but] he nevertheless mixes up several mineral operations with the stone of the moderns, which belongs to that of the ancients.

When I speak about the philosophers, I mean to speak about the genuine ones. There are many who pass for philosophers, but who never were, and who have never known the stone, even though they have written to appear knowledgeable in this art; one must guard against [them], because they can make you abandon the right path. It is even more necessary to avoid reading certain manuscripts, which they call procedures,[26] where they write everything point by point. This is what you will never see in a genuine philosopher. But these kinds of authors risk nothing. Only those who work with them or according to their method lose their time and money. It is specifically to draw you away from this faulty step that I prepared this treatise, so that you can distinguish the false brethren from the genuine, so that [upon] finding and knowing a genuine adept, he can lead you and teach you what you can scarcely do [on your own] in the practice, and [so for this reason] you must associate with him.

It is therefore to assist you on this thorny path and to resolve all the difficulties which might prevent you from reaching the desired end, that I have prepared this writing. I will not tell you things point by point, so that you have nothing left to discover. That was not allowed me. I must leave you

26   Also often known in alchemy as 'particulars' (i.e., the *particularia*, as contrasted with the *universalia*).

faut vous laisser quelques choses à faire; il n'est pas juste que ce qui couté tant de peine et même[82] de dépense[83] pour parvenir à ce grand secret de la nature, vous l'avez[84] sans quelques peines et quelques travaux:[85] je ne me sert d'aucune supposition ni[86] de similitude, mais seulement de quelques expressions figurées. Enfin je vous dis[87] la pure vérité que je caché seulement de quelque petit voile qui est assez[88] clair pour en traverser l'épaisseur.[89]

Pour donc donner quelque ordre à une matière dont les philosophes ont affecté[90] d'écrire[91] sans ordre; je divise la pierre ou notre[92] ouvrage que l'on appelle aussi communément magister en deux parties que les auteurs[93] appellent le 1er[94] et 2ème[95] œuvre.

Le premier regarde toute la composition de la pierre et sa perfection jusqu'à la fermentation.

La deuxième comprend toutes les opérations qu'il est nécessaire de faire pour la 2ème[96] et dernière perfection de la pierre. Je la divise autrement pour plus grand éclaircissement[97] de la première partie.

Cette 1ère[98] partie, je la diviserai[99] en 3 ordres différents, suivant la division de Geber ce grand Roi[100] des Arabes qui en a écrit très doctement. Le 1er je l'appelle comme lui,[101] la médecine ou l'œuvre du 1er ordre. Je dis tout ce qui appartient à cet ordre et à cet œuvre, pour ne pas confondre ce qui appartient au 1er, et ne le pas donner au 2ème[103] et au 3ème[104] et au contraire que je divise en autant de chapitre, ce qui n'est pas d'une petite[105] conséquence pour l'intelligence des écrits[106] des philosophes et pour la pratique de notre[107] divin œuvre.

82. mesme.	91. d'escrire.	100. Roy.
83. depence.	92. nostre.	101. escrit.
84. l'ayes.	93. autheurs.	102. luy.
85. trauveaux.	94. 1r.	103. 2me.
86. ny.	95. 2me.	104. 3me.
87. dit.	96. 2me.	105. petitte.
88. asses.	97. esclaircissement.	106. escrits.
89. l'espaisseur.	98. 1re.	107. nostre.
90. affectes.	99. diviseray.	

some things to do. It is not right that you should obtain this great secret of nature, which requires so much effort and even expense, without some trouble and labour. I do not use any supposition nor similitude, but only a few figurative expressions. Finally, I tell you the pure truth, which I only hide behind a light veil, which is clear enough to penetrate through.

Therefore, to give some order to a matter which the philosophers have affected to write without order, I divide the stone, or our work, which is also commonly called the magisterium, into two parts, which the authors call the first and second works.

The first looks at the whole composition of the stone, and its perfection, until the fermentation.

The second includes all of the operations that are necessary for the second and final perfection of the stone. I divide it differently for greater clarification of the first part.

This first part, I will divide into three different orders, following the division of Geber, that great King of the Arabs who wrote very learnedly. I call the first, like him, the medicine, or the work of the first order. I say everything that belongs to this order and to this work, so as not to confuse what belongs to the first, and not to give it to the second and the third, which on the contrary, I divide into as many chapters, which is not of a small consequence for the intelligence of the writings of the philosophers and for the practice of our divine work.

De l'extraction des teintures

APRÈS AVOIR TIRÉ NOTRE[1] MATIÈRE DE SA MINIÈRE, vous là laverez[2] bien pour lui[3] ôter[4] ses impuretés, et après l'avoir lavé,[5] vous la laissez[6] tomber par résidence et rassoir[7] au fond de l'eau, vous la dessècherez,[8] et la calcinerez,[9] et quand elle sera bien calcinée et pulvérisée et broyée en menue partie, vous la mettrez[10] à part.

Il est nécessaire que vous en ayez[11] une bonne grande quantité, parce qu'elle contient beaucoup de matière mais peu d'esprit. Car c'est de cette seule et unique matière dont nous tirons tout ce qui est nécessaire à l'œuvre par une voie[12] linéaire.

Un certain philosophe décrit[13] parfaitement bien cette opération par ces termes, il dit qu'après l'écoulement des eaux du déluge universel, l'Arche se[14] trouva[15] sur la montagne d'Arménie. Montez,[16] dit-il, *sur cette montagne vous y trouverez*[17] *une terre limoneuse* d'où sortira un ruisseau d'une admirable vertu; et il ajoute, si vous ne m'entendez[18] pas, vous n'êtes[19] pas philosophes et vous ne le serez[20] jamais. Ce philosophe

1.	nostre.	9.	calcineres.	17.	trouveres.
2.	laveres.	10.	mettres.	18.	m'entendes.
3.	luy.	11.	ayes.	19.	n'este.
4.	oster.	12.	voye.	20.	seres.
5.	lavée.	13.	d'escrit.		
6.	laisseres.	14.	ce.		
7.	rassoire.	15.	trouvat.		
8.	deseicheres.	16.	Montés.		

FIRST CHAPTER

Of the extraction of the tinctures

AFTER HAVING DRAWN OUR MATTER FROM ITS MINE, you must cleanse it well in order to remove its impurities, and after having cleansed it, you let the sediment[27] fall and settle at the bottom of the water. Desiccate and calcine it, and when it is well-calcined, pulverised, and crushed into small pieces, set it aside.

It is necessary that you have a good quantity, because it contains a lot of matter but little spirit. For it is from this one and only matter that we draw out all that is necessary for the work in a linear way.

A certain philosopher describes this operation perfectly by these terms: he says that 'after the flow of waters from the universal deluge, the ark found itself on the mountain of Armenia'. 'Climb', he said, '*on this mountain you will find a loamy soil*,[28] from which flows a stream of admirable virtue'. And he adds, 'if you do not understand me, you are not philosophers, and you will never be one'. This philosopher

27   Old French *résidence*, 'residuum'.
28   Underlined in the manuscript to stress its importance.

a raison de parler ainsi,[21] car dans cette opération ici,[22] il faut
qu'il précède un déluge d'eau, après lequel l'Arche repose sur
la montagne qui est notre[23] matière et notre[24] sujet, il faut
pénétrer et traverser cette montagne pour en faire sortir ce
ruisseau et une eau d'une vertu incomparable. C'est de cette
eau que sortent nos luminaires comme vous verrez[25] ci-après.[26]

C'est après le déluge de l'eau que l'Arche reposa sur cette
montagne d'Arménie; de même[27] C'est après les fréquentes
et réitérées ablutions de notre[28] terre que nous en tirons l'axonge et toute l'onctuosité qui est la matière prochaine de la
pierre de laquelle nous frappons la pierre, et le Rocher par la
verge d'Aaron pour en faire sortir cette eau vive propre pour
la santé des esprits et des corps; et toute impure qu'elle est encore, son simple usage guérit[29] plusieurs maladies comme on
en a fait l'expérience; et si vous laissez[30] écouler[31] doucement
l'eau qui couvrit[32] cette montagne; vous verrez[33] de vos yeux[34]
l'Arche du Seigneur [C'est à dire que le soleil et l'or, dans son
1er[35] être,[36] brillera visiblement à vos yeux][37] et le signe de paix,
c'est à dire l'arc en ciel reluira avec toutes ces[38] couleurs.

Mais pour faire ces lotions et ablutions; ne pensez[39] pas
que ce soit avec l'eau commune des fontaines et des Rivières.
L'eau dont nous nous servons a bien d'autres vertus. C'est une
eau qui renferme toutes les vertus du ciel et de la terre; C'est
pourquoi[40] elle est le Dissolvant général de toute la Nature,
elle ouvre les barrières, et c'est elle qui ouvre toutes les portes
de Notre[41] Cabinet Hermétique et Royal où sont renfermés
notre[42] Roi[43] et notre Reine, aussi elle est leur bain, ils s'y
lavent. C'est la Fontaine de Trévisan où le Roi[44] se dépouille

21.	ainsy.	29.	guery.	37.	yeuse.
22.	icy.	30.	laisses.	38.	ses.
23.	nostre.	31.	escouler.	39.	pences.
24.	nostre.	32.	couvroit.	40.	pourquoy.
25.	verres.	33.	verres.	41.	nostre.
26.	Cy apres.	34.	yeuse.	42.	nostre.
27.	mesme.	35.	1r.	43.	Roy.
28.	nostre.	36.	estre.	44.	Roy.

has reason to speak thus, because in this operation here, it must be preceded by a deluge of water, after which the ark rests upon the mountain, which is our matter and our subject. It is necessary to penetrate and pass through this mountain in order to bring out this stream and a water of incomparable virtue. It is from this water that our luminaries come out as you will see below.

It was after the deluge of water that the ark rested on this mountain of Armenia. Likewise, it is after the frequent and repeated ablutions of our earth that we extract from it the lard[29] and all the unctuosity which is the proximate matter of the stone, from which we strike the stone, and the rock by Aaron's rod, to bring out this living water proper for the health of spirits and bodies: and even though it is still impure, its simple use cured several diseases, as has been experienced. And if you let the water that covered this mountain flow gently, you will see with your own eyes the ark of the Lord (i.e., the sun and gold, in its first being, will shine visibly before your eyes) and the sign of peace, i.e., the rainbow, will shine with all its colours.[30]

But to make these lotions and ablutions, do not think that it is with the common water of the fountains and rivers. The water we use has many other virtues. It is a water that contains all the virtues of heaven and earth. That is why it is the general solvent of all Nature. She opens the barriers, and it is she who opens all the gates of our Hermetic and Royal Sanctum[31] where our King and Queen are enclosed, so she is their bath, where they wash themselves. It is the fountain of Trevisan where the King divests himself of his purple cloak

29 *L'axonge*, 'fatty substance', i.e., the 'fatness' of the loamy earth.

30 This is the intriguing passage which Fulcanelli partly quoted in *Les Demeures* and which he believed to refer to the alchemical solvent in its liquid state (he normally thought of it as being a solid 'mineral or metallic salt'). See the *Introduction*.

31 *Cabinet* (see Preface).

de son manteau de pourpre pour se revêtir[45] d'un habit noir qu'il donne à ♄ [Saturne]. L'expression de ce philosophe est admirable, il nous décrit[46] par la naissance du corbeau cette couleur si nécessaire dans l'œuvre et si à souhaiter.[47]

Il est vrai[48] que cette eau est difficile à avoir; C'est ce qui a fait dire au Cosmopolite[49] dans son énigme, qu'elle était[50] rare dans l'île;[51] mais il vous indique le temps de la cueillir[52] par cette figure; il dit que les prés[53] de cette île[54] étaient[55] émaillés[56] de mille fleurs et que dans ces prés,[57] paissent[58] des moutons et des bœufs gardés par deux jeunes Bergers; il nous veut faire remarquer par cette énigme qu'il faut recueillir[59] cette eau au printemps, lorsque le soleil parcoure les 3 signes ♈. ♉ . ♊. [Bélier, Taureau, Gémeaux] célestes, les moutons marquent le signe du Bélier[60] les Bœufs le signé du Taureau;[61] et les deux Bergers le signe des jumeaux qu'on dépeint comme 2 jeunes Enfants, ces prés[62] émaillent[63] de mille fleurs, marquent la qualité de cette eau qui contient des vertus innombrables.

Cet auteur,[64] nous la marque plus particulièrement par ces paroles:[65] elle n'est pas semblable à l'eau qui sort de la nuée,[66] mais elle en a toute l'apparence; en un autre endroit, il nous la décrit[67] sous le nom d'Acier et d'Aimant,[68] car c'est véritablement un aimant[69] qui attire à elle toutes les influences du Ciel, du Soleil, de la lune et des Astres, pour les communiquer à la terre; il dit que cet Acier se trouve dans Ariès qui marque encore le commencement du printemps, lorsque le soleil parcourt le signe du ♈ [Bélier].

45. revestir.	55. estoient.	65. parolles.
46. d'escrit.	56. esmailles.	66. nuë.
47. souhaitter.	57. preds.	67. d'escrit.
48. vrais.	58. paissoient.	68. d'Aymant.
49. Cosmopolitte.	59. recuillir.	69. aymant.
50. estoit.	60. Bellier.	
51. l'isle.	61. Toreau.	
52. cuillir.	62. preds.	
53. preds.	63. esmailles.	
54. isle.	64. Autheur.	

to put on a black garment that he gives to ♄ [Saturn]. The expression of this philosopher is admirable; he describes it to us via the birth of the raven, whose colour is so necessary in the work, and so desirable.

It is true that this water is difficult to obtain. This is what made the Cosmopolitan say in his enigma, that 'it was rare on the island'; but by this figure, he tells you the time to gather it; he says that the meadows of this island were dotted with a thousand flowers, and that in these meadows graze sheep and oxen, guarded by two young shepherds. He wants to point out to us by this enigma that it is necessary to collect this water in the spring, when the sun traverses the three celestial signs: ♈ ♉ ♊ [Aries, Taurus, Gemini]; the sheep marks the sign of Aries; the oxen the sign of Taurus; and the two shepherds the sign of the twins,[32] who are depicted as two young children. These dotted meadows of a thousand flowers mark the quality of this water, which contains innumerable virtues.

This author signifies it for us even more particularly by these words: 'it is not like the water that comes out of the clouds, but it has all the appearance of it'. In another place, he describes it to us under the name of steel and magnet, for it is truly a magnet which attracts to itself all the influences of the sky, the sun, the moon, and the stars, in order to communicate them to the earth. He says that this steel is found in Aries, which still marks the beginning of spring when the sun traverses the sign of ♈ [Aries].

32   That is, Gemini.

Vous ne pouvez[70] avoir cette eau que par le moyen de notre[71] terre qui l'attire à elle de la même[72] manière que l'eau de l'arbre, de la plante, est attiré[73] par ses racines; C'est pourquoi[74] ils ont besoin de fréquents arrosements;[75] de même[76] nous ne pourrons avoir cette eau que par de fréquents arrosements[77] réitérées par lesquels arrosements[78] la terre étant[79] toute remplie d'eau, elle l'a comme par lotion, nous la lavons donc plusieurs fois et dans cette lotion, elle donne toute la vertu à l'eau, non pas à la 1ère[80] fois mais à la 7ème[81] car nous avons dit que notre[82] Cabinet avait[83] sept[84] portes figurées, et par ces 7 lotions. Car le Roi[85] et la Reine n'en sortent que par ce moyen.

70. pouves.	76. mesme.	82. nostre.
71. nostre.	77. arrousements.	83. avoit.
72. mesme.	78. arrousements.	84. cept.
73. attirée.	79. estant.	85. Roy.
74. pourquoy.	80. 1re.	
75. arrousements.	81. 7me.	

You can only have this water by means of our earth, which attracts it in the same way that the water of the tree, or of the plant, is attracted by its roots. That is why they need frequent watering. In the same way, we can only have this water by frequent and repeated watering, through which the earth is completely filled with water, which it obtains via lotion. We wash it several times, and in this lotion it gives every virtue to the water, not the first time, but on the seventh. Because, we said that our Sanctum[33] had seven figurative gates, and via these, seven lotions. For the King and the Queen come out only by this means.

33   *Cabinet* (see Preface).

De la séparation des éléments

IL EST IMPOSSIBLE DE FAIRE UNE VÉRITABLE séparation des éléments dans notre[2] œuvre sans qu'il y ait[3] précédé la putréfaction; C'est par le moyen de cette opération que la nature se dépouille de toutes ses impuretés, parce qu'il y a dans nos principes, dit Philalèthe[4] beaucoup de superfluité de différente nature qui ne peut jamais se rendre assez[5] pure.

Arnaud dit, Chap. 6 que notre[6] pierre se divise en 4 éléments, afin qu'elle se subtilisé d'avantage, et qu'elle se purifie mieux en se[7] séparant de ses fèces,[8] et qu'après on la joigne plus fortement. Car quelque chose que ce soit qui soit née ou qui n'ait, il faut qu'il ait été[9] pourri[10] auparavant, comme le grain de froment qu'il faut qu'il soit jeté[11] en terre, qu'il pourrisse avant qu'il prenne aucune autre forme. C'est l'ordre établi[12] dans la nature. C'est ce feu de fumier si nécessaire à la production des fruits de la terre. C'est ces[13] essieux d'Espagnette qui fait tourner la roue de la nature, ce feu qu'il faut introduire[14] dans la matrice et qui fait toutes les merveilles qu'on remarque dans notre[15] œuvre dont j'ai[16] parlé, et ce premier agent de Flamel et que Pontanus décrit[17] admirablement bien en disant qu'il est aqueux, aérien, igné[18] et terrestre et

1.	2me.	7.	ce.	13.	cette.
2.	nostre.	8.	fæces.	14.	introduir.
3.	aye.	9.	esté.	15.	nostre.
4.	Philalette.	10.	pourry.	16.	jay.
5.	asses.	11.	jetté.	17.	déscrivent.
6.	nostre.	12.	establit.	18.	ignée.

SECOND CHAPTER

Of the separation of the elements

IT IS IMPOSSIBLE TO MAKE A TRUE SEPARATION OF the elements in our work without it first being preceded by putrefaction. It is by means of this operation that nature is stripped of all its impurities. Because there is in our principles, says Philalethes, much superfluity of a different nature, which can never be rendered pure enough.

Arnaldus[34] says, Chapter 6, that our stone is divided into four elements so that it may be further subtilised, and that it may be better purified by separating itself from its feces, and that afterwards it is united more strongly. For whatever has been born or not, it must have been decayed before, like the grain of wheat that must be thrown into the earth so that it rots before it takes any other form. It is the established order in nature. It is this fire of manure that is so necessary for the production of the fruits of the earth. It is these axles of Espagnet[35] that turn the wheel of nature, this fire that must be introduced into the womb, and that makes all the wonders that we notice in our work, of which I have spoken. [It is] this first agent of Flamel, that which Pontanus describes admirably by saying that it is aqueous, aerial, igneous, and terrestrial, and which he compares to the three humors of our body

34   Arnaldus de Villa Nova (c. 1240–1311).
35   Jean d'Espagnet (1564–c. 1637).

qu'il le compare aux 3 humeurs[19] de notre[20] corps en disant qu'il est flegmatique, colérique et mélancolique. Trévisan dit à peu près la même[21] chose, en disant qu'il est vaporeux, circondant, digérant, non brulant. Tout cela nous marque ce feu de putréfaction, participant des quatre[22] qualités; de froid, de chaud, de sec et d'humide; il dit aussi[23] qu'il participe du soufre et qu'il est argent vif. C'est par le moyen de ce feu qui ne vient pas de la matière, mais qui est prit d'ailleurs[24] et qui achèvera tout l'ouvrage sans l'apposition des mains de l'artiste car il putréfie, corrompt, et engendre et perfectionne ce qui est impur et imparfait, il fait apparaître[25] les principales[26] les couleurs de l'œuvre qui sont le noir, le blanc et le rouge, il change, cuit et digère la matière crue par le moyen de quoi[27] on multiplie la pierre. C'est la clef des philosophes qu'ils n'ont jamais enseigné.[28] [cette œuvre s'accomplit donc en peu de temps par le moyen de ce feu et sans l'aide de l'artiste, parce qu'il se putréfie, se corrompt se régénère et se perfectionne de lui-même,[29] comme il est déjà expliqué ci-devant;[30] et de plus il fait apparaître[31] les 3 couleurs qui sont le noir, le blanc et le rouge, et par le moyen de notre[32] feu; la médecine se cuit, se digère et se change et se multiplie, en y ajoutant la matière crue en quantité et qualité. Il est le 1er[33] et le propre agent.

Ce feu se[34] trouve dans le fumier. C'est pourquoi[35] il donne la fécondité à la terre en corrompant et putréfiant[36] les semences. C'est pour cela qu'il est appelé[37] feu de fumier.

Flamel nous en fait une peinture assez[38] juste dans les figures d'Abraham le juif dépeinte dans la bibliothèque[39] chymique: il nous dépeint un vieux chêne[40] creux d'où sort une

19. humeures.	27. quoy.	35. pourquoy.
20. nostre.	28. enseignes.	36. putrifiant.
21. mesme.	29. luy-mesme.	37. appelle.
22. quatres.	30. cy devant.	38. addes.
23. aussy.	31. apparoistre.	39. biblioteque.
24. d'ailleur.	32. nostre.	40. chesne.
25. apparoistre.	33. 1r.	
26. principal.	34. cé.	

by saying that it is phlegmatic, choleric, and melancholic. Trevisan says much the same thing by saying that it is vaporous, circulating, digesting, non-burning. All of this marks the fire of putrefaction, participating in the four qualities: cold, hot, dry, and humid. He also says that it participates in sulphur and that it is *argent vive*. It is by means of this fire, which does not come from the matter, but which is taken from elsewhere, and which will complete the whole work without the apposition of the artist's hands, because it putrefies, corrupts, engenders, and perfects that which is impure and imperfect. It brings out the principal colours of the work, which are black, white, and red. It changes, cooks, and digests the crude matter by the means of which one multiplies the stone. It is the key of the philosophers which they have never taught. This work is thus accomplished in a short time by means of this fire and without the help of the artist, because it putrefies, corrupts, regenerates, and perfects itself, as already explained above. Moreover, it makes the three colours appear, which are black, white, and red. And by means of our fire, the medicine is cooked, digested, changed, and multiplied by adding the crude matter, both in quantity and quality. It is the first and the proper agent.

This fire is found in manure. This is why it gives fecundity to the earth by corrupting and putrefying the seeds. That is why it is called fire of manure.

Flamel makes us a fairly accurate picture of it in *The Figures of Abraham the Jew*, as depicted in the *Chymical Library*.[36] He depicts for us an old hollow oak from which a fountain

---

36   W. Salmon, M. Richebourg, et al., *Bibliotheque des philosophes chymiques, Nouvelle édition, revûë, corrigée & augmentée de plusieurs philosophes, avec des figures & des notes pour faciliter l'intelligence de leur doctrine, par M.J.M.D.R.* Cailleau: Paris, 1740–1754 (tome 2). The edition most likely used by the author would have been that published in Paris by Charles Angot in 1672.

fontaine, et de la même[41] eau un jardinier arrose les plantes et les fleurs d'un parterre; le vieux chêne[42] marque, et qui est creux, le tonneau qui est fait de bois de chêne[43] dans lequel, il faut corrompre l'eau qu'il réserve, pour arroser les plantes, qui est bien meilleur que l'eau cru.[44]

Les philosophes ont bien d'autres feux que j'expliquerai[45] en son lieu et en leur place. Le secret de cette opération, est de savoir le temps préfixé[46] de cette putréfaction; car il faut que vous preniez[47] bien garde qu'elle ne passe en putréfaction ladreuse[48] et vermiculaire, car tout votre œuvre serait[49] détruit.

Si la matière n'est pas aussi[50] corrompue et mortifiée, vous ne pourrez[51] pas extraire nos éléments et nos principes, et pour vous aider en cette difficulté, je vous donnerai[52] des signes pour la connaître.[53]

Quelques philosophes l'ont aussi[54] marquée.[55] Morien[56] dit, il faut qu'on y remarque quelque acidité, et qu'elle ait quelque odeur de sépulcre. Philalèthe[57] dit, qu'il faut qu'elle paraisse[58] comme des yeux de poissons. C'est à dire des petites[59] bouteilles[60] sur la superficie et qu'il paraisse[61] qu'elle écume; car c'est une marque que la matière se fermente et qu'elle bout. Cette fermentation est fort longue, et il faut avoir une grande patience, parce-qu'elle se fait par notre[62] feu secret qui est le seul agent, comme dit l'auteur[63] de la guerre des Chevaliers,[64] qui peut ouvrir,[65] sublimer, putréfier; et ce feu, ajoute-t-il,[66] est une eau céleste qui opère la solution, l'animation et la purification de la pierre.

41. mesme.	49. seroit.	58. parroisse.
42. chesne.	50. aussy.	59. petittes.
43. chesne.	51. pourres.	60. Probably 'bulles'.
44. crië.	52. donneres.	61. parroisse.
45. J'expliqueray.	53. connoistre.	62. nostre.
46. prefix.	54. aussy.	63. l'autheur.
47. prenies.	55. marques.	64. Chevalliers.
48. Possibly means	56. Moriens.	65. ouvrire.
'leprous'.	57. Philalette.	66. ajout il.

emerges, and from the same water a gardener waters the plants and flowers of a garden. The old oak, which is hollow, signifies the barrel which is made of oak; the water stored within it must be corrupted [in this barrel] in order to water the plants, for this water is much better than the crude[37] water.

Philosophers have many other fires, which I will explain in their context and in their place. The secret of this operation is to know the time of this putrefaction in advance. For care must be taken that it does not pass into leprous and vermicular putrefaction, for all your work would be destroyed.

If the matter is not sufficiently putrefied and mortified, you will not be able to extract our elements and principles. And to help you in this difficulty, I will give you signs by which to recognise it.

Some philosophers have also pointed this out. Morienus said: 'it is necessary to notice some acidity, and that it has some odor of the sepulcher'. Philalethes says that it must appear like the eyes of fish, that is to say, like small bubbles[38] on the surface; and it appears to foam, because it is a sign that the matter ferments and boils. This fermentation is very long, and it is necessary to have great patience because it is done by our secret fire, 'which is the only agent', as the author of the *War of the Knights* says, 'which can open, sublimate, and putrefy'.[39] 'And this fire', he adds, 'is a heavenly water that operates the solution, the animation, and the purification of the stone'.

37 That is, common water.

38 Literally *bouteilles* (bottles) in the manuscript. Based on context, the author most likely meant *bulles*, 'bubbles'.

39 Ostensibly from Johann Sternhals, *Ritter Krieg* (Erffordt: Martin Wittel, 1595), the passage is actually from *Lettre aux vrais disciples d'Hermès*, usually attributed to Limojon de Saint-Didier, published in the *Triomphe Hermétique*, which also includes an anonymous text called *L'Ancienne guerre des Chevaliers* that is different from Sternhals' text. Our anonymous author seems to have assumed that the author of the *Lettre* is also the author of the *L'Ancienne guerre des Chevaliers* published in the *Triomphe Hermétique* (cf. Ferguson's arguments and summary, *Bibliotheca Chemica*, pp. 486–487).

Or, c'est ici[67] le lieu de découvrir un des grands mystères[68] de cet art que les philosophes ont caché,[69] sans lequel vaisseau,[70] vous ne pouvez[71] pas faire cette putréfaction et purification de nos éléments: de même[72] qu'on ne saurait[73] faire le vin sans qu'il ait[74] bouilli[75] dans le tonneau. Or comme le tonneau est fait de bois de chêne,[76] de même[77] le vaisseau[78] doit être[79] de bois d'un vieux chêne[80] tourné en rond en dedans comme un demi-Globe[81] dont les bords sont[82] fort épais[83] en carré;[84] à faute de ce, un baril, un autre pareil,[85] pour le couvrir. Presque tous les philosophes ont parlé[86] de ce vaisseau[87] absolument nécessaire pour cette opération. Trévisan dit que proche la fontaine qui doit être[88] le bain du Roi,[89] elle était[90] au pied d'un chêne.[91] Philalèthe[92] le décrit[93] par la fable du serpent python[94] que Cadmus perça d'outre en outre contre un Chêne[95] creux. Flamel rapporte la même[96] fable à ce sujet, et dit qu'il faut prendre garde à ce mot de chêne.[97] Notre[98] chêne,[99] dit Abraham le juif et qui montre la chose plus précisément par la figure rapportée par Flamel dans la Bibliothèque Chymique. Vous y voyez[100] un vieux chêne[101] d'où coule une eau dont le jardinier arrose les plantes d'un parterre qui sort du tronc d'un vieux chêne;[102] il y a deux fleurs[103] et des Roses au-dessus, l'une blanche et l'autre rouge qui marquent que c'est notre[104] eau qui contient le blanc et le rouge, le soleil

67.	icy.	80.	chesne.	93.	d'escrit.
68.	misteres.	81.	Demy Globe.	94.	Pithon.
69.	caches.	82.	soient.	95.	Chesne.
70.	vesseau.	83.	espais.	96.	mesme.
71.	pouves.	84.	quarré.	97.	chesne.
72.	mesme.	85.	pareille.	98.	nostre.
73.	sçavroit.	86.	parles.	99.	chesne.
74.	aye.	87.	vesseau.	100.	voyes.
75.	bouilly.	88.	estre.	101.	Chesne.
76.	chesne.	89.	Roy.	102.	Chesne.
77.	mesme.	90.	estoit.	103.	fleures.
78.	vesseau.	91.	chesne.	104.	nostre.
79.	estre.	92.	Philalette.		

But, this is the place to reveal one of the great mysteries of this art, which philosophers have hidden: without this vessel you cannot make this putrefaction and purification of our elements, just as wine cannot be made without fermenting it in the barrel.[40] Now, as the barrel is made of oak, so the vessel must be of old oak wood, rounded inside like a half-globe whose edges are very stout and square; failing which, a keg, and another to cover it. Almost all philosophers have spoken of this vessel, which is absolutely necessary for this operation. Trevisan says that near the fountain which must be the King's bath, it was at the foot of an oak tree. Philalethes describes it by the fable of the serpent Python, which Cadmus pierced also against a hollow oak. Flamel relates the same fable on this subject, and says that we must be aware of this word, oak. Our oak, says Abraham the Jew, and who shows the thing more precisely by the figure reported by Flamel in the *Chymical Library*. You see there an old oak from which flows a water, which the gardener uses to water the plants of a flower bed, which emerges from the trunk of an old oak tree. There are two flowers and roses above, one white and the other red, which signify that it is our water that contains the white and the red, the sun and the moon. This also indicates that it is

40   Literally 'without having boiled (*bouilli*) it in the barrel', however the context suggests fermenting, which was often likened to boiling insofar as fermenting liquids appear to seethe and 'boil'.

et la lune, cela marque encore que c'est de ces deux substances que nous faisons notre[105] vin marqué par le tonneau.

Il y a une figure, dans le livre des 12 Clefs, qui représente cette même[106] opération, et le vaisseau[107] où elle se fait, C'est un tonneau d'où il sort un grande fumée qui marque la fermentation et l'ébullition de cette eau, et cette fumée ce termine à une fenêtre,[108] où on voit le ciel où sont dépeints[109] le soleil et la lune qui marquent l'origine de cette eau et les vertus qu'elle contient. C'est notre[110] vinaigre mercuriel[111] qui descend[112] du ciel en terre et monte de la terre au ciel.

DE L'EXTRACTION DES DEUX LUMINAIRES, OR ET MERCURE

Il faut premièrement distiller ce vinaigre, il n'est pas d'un grand usage pour ainsi[113] dire. Vous le mettez[114] dans un alambic de verre, adapté avec son chapiteau et son récipient; vous distillerez[115] d'abord à feu lent, et lorsqu'il ne distillera plus rien, vous remettrez[116] sur les fèces,[117] l'eau qui aura distillé dans le récipient, puis vous recommencerez[118] la distillation, si au même[119] feu il ne distille plus rien, vous augmenterez[120] un peu le feu, et vous continuerez[121] ce même[122] degré, jusqu'à ce

105. nostre.
106. mesme.
107. vesseau.
108. fenestre.
109. depeint.
110. nostre.
111. mercuriale.
112. dessend.
113. ainsy.
114. mettres.
115. distilleres.
116. remettres.
117. fæces.
118. recommenceres.
119. mesme.
120. augmenteres.
121. continures.
122. mesme.

of these two substances that we make our wine, indicated by the barrel.

There is a figure in the book of the *Twelve Keys*,[41] which represents this same operation and the vessel in which it is made. It is a barrel from which a great [cloud of] smoke emanates, which marks the fermentation and the boiling of this water, and this smoke ends at a window where we see the sky, in which the sun and the moon are depicted, which mark the origin of this water and the virtues it contains. It is our mercurial vinegar, which descends from heaven to earth and ascends from earth to heaven.[42]

OF THE EXTRACTION OF THE TWO LUMINARIES, GOLD AND MERCURY

This vinegar must first be distilled, [otherwise] it is not of much use, so to speak. Put it in a glass alembic fitted with its capital[43] and its recipient.[44] Distil at first with a slow fire, and when nothing more will distill, put the water which will have distilled in the recipient back on the feces.[45] Then restart the distillation. If the same fire no longer distils anything, in-

41   Basilius Valentinus, *Zwölff Schlüssel*, in *Ein kurtz summarischer Tractat, von dem grossen Stein der Uralten*, Eißleben: Hornigk, 1599.

42   This passage is notably quoted in its entirety by Fulcanelli in *Le Mystère des Cathédrales*. Although it is unclear whether the reference to the 'oak barrel' was originally intended in a literal or metaphorical sense, Fulcanelli seems to suggest it may have been metaphorical (see our *Introduction*). Despite Fulcanelli's insistence that 'the spirit gives the light, but the letter kills', the possibility of a literal interpretation cannot be ruled out. The author of the *Cabinet* could very well have meant oak—known for being rich in tannin and gallic acid among other things—or as a hint at oak-related processes such as the formation of tartrates (used in some procedures for making the stone).

43   *Le chapiteau*, 'capital, head'.

44   *Le récipient*, 'container, receptacle, receiver'.

45   That is, the matter that remains in the alembic.

qu'il ne monte plus rien en haut de l'alambic.[123] Alors remettez[124] ce qui est distillé dans l'alambic[125] et recommencerez[126] la distillation et faites[127] de même[128] que ci-dessus,[129] augmentant le feu à proportion que vous voulez[130] faire monter l'eau. Vous ferez[131] le 1er[132] au B.M.[133] Le 2me aux cendres, et le 3 me au feu de sable et lorsqu'il ne montera plus rien par le feu de sable, vous laisserez[134] refroidir le vaisseau[135] et ayant versé l'eau qui se trouvera dans la cucurbite[136] par inclination, vous prendrez[137] les fèces[138] qui sont au fond, calcinez[139] les jusqu'à blancheur; ensuite vous mettrez[140] votre eau à part, et vous la distillerez[141] par une petite[142] cornue. Cette eau est l'esprit blanc et lunaire avec laquelle on tire l'esprit rouge de la terre blanche. Pour lors elle se teindra[143] en rouge étant[144] en digestion ou jaune citrin au B.M.[145] [car cette terre blanche contient l'esprit rouge et le sel]. Quand elle aura cette couleur; versez[146] l'eau par inclination que vous mettrez[147] à part, puis de nouvelle eau distillée; après avoir calciné la terre et réverbéré,[148] vous mettrez[149] du[150] nouveau vinaigre distillé sur la matière qui est dans la cornue jusqu'à ce qu'il ne teinte[151] plus; puis poussé la par la cornue, il passera d'abord un esprit blanc, puis un esprit rouge qui se teindra par réitérée cohobation avec le susdit vinaigre distillé et quand le vinaigre ne prendre plus de teinture [après lui[152] avoir donné le feu de sable]. Cette opération vous donnera le mercure rouge et le mercure citrin]. Vous prendrez[153] ce qui restera au fond de la cornue,

123. l'alembic.
124. remetté.
125. lalembic.
126. recommenceres.
127. faite.
128. mesme.
129. cy dessus.
130. voules.
131. feres.
132. 1r.
133. = bain marie.
134. laisseres.
135. vesseau.
136. cucurbitte.
137. prendres.
138. fæces.
139. calcines.
140. mettres.
141. distilleres.
142. petite.
143. teindrat.
144. estant.
145. = bain marie.
146. verses.
147. mettres.
148. reverberer.
149. mettré.
150. de.
151. teigne.
152. lui.
153. prendres.

crease the fire a little, and continue at the same degree until [the water] no longer rises to the top of the alembic. Then put the distillate[46] back into the alembic, and start the distillation again, and do the same as above, increasing the fire proportionally so that the water rises. Do the first one in the B.M.,[47] the second in the ashes, and the third in the sand bath. And when nothing more rises by the sand bath, let the vessel cool down. And having poured the water which is found in the cucurbit by inclination,[48] take out the feces which are at the bottom, and calcine them to whiteness. Then set your water apart, and distill it with a small retort. This water is the white and lunar spirit, with which one draws the red spirit from the white earth. For then it will be dyed red in digestion, or citrine yellow by B.M. (because this white earth contains the red spirit and the salt). When it has obtained this colour, pour out the water by inclination, which you then set apart. Then add new distilled water. After calcining the earth and reverberating it, put the distilled vinegar back on the matter that is in the retort, until it no longer tinges. Then, pushed through the retort, it will first pass as a white spirit, then as a red spirit, which will be dyed by repeated cohobation with the aforesaid distilled vinegar.[49] And when the vinegar no longer absorbs any more dye (after having been submitted to the sand bath), this operation will give you the red mercury and the citrine mercury. Take what remains at the bottom of the retort, then

---

46   Literally *ce qui est distillé*, 'that which is distilled'.

47   Bain-marie, or water bath.

48   *L'inclination*, laboratory term for decantation (to pour the liquid by gently tilting the vessel).

49   That is, the white spirit.

puis vous le mettrez[154] au fourneau du petit réverbère[155] pendant 24 heures, et quand elle sera bien réverbérée et blanche et parfaitement broyée; vous mettrez[156] cette matière dans un petit vaisseau[157] de verre, et vous verserez[158] dessus quatre doigts[159] de vinaigre distillé, puis ayant bouché le vaisseau,[160] vous le mettrez[161] au B.M.[162] pendant 8 jours, au bout desquels, vous verserez[163] le vinaigre par inclination, prenant bien garde de troubler le fond.

Ensuite vous mettrez[164] de nouveau vinaigre et vous ferez[165] comme à la 1ère[166] fois, et vous verserez[167] par inclination le dit vinaigre; vous jetterez[168] après les fèces[169] comme inutiles.[170]

Ensuite vous évaporerez[171] les dits vinaigres à feu lent et vous trouverez[172] au fond du vaisseau,[173] un sel qui a des vertus admirables: et si vous voulez[174] encore le rendre plus parfait, vous recommencerez[175] la même[176] opération comme ci-devant,[177] et votre sel sera blanc comme cristal. Ce sel est le corps de la lune qui sert pour l'ouvrage au blanc et à la composition du mercure des philosophes comme il est dit au chapitre 2ème.[178] [v.p.10].

Vous verserez[179] dans un petit matras ce sel précieux[180] qui se dissoudra en versant dessus l'esprit blanc distillé par la cornue et le mettrez[181] au B.M. pendant 8 jours. Puis versant le tout par inclinaison[183] et rejetant[184] les fèces;[185] vous aurez[186] le mercure de la lune et l'esprit blanc. C'est la Diane et la femelle

154. mettres.
155. reverbe.
156. mettres.
157. vesseau.
158. verseres.
159. doits.
160. vesseau.
161. mettres.
162. bain marie.
163. verseres.
164. mettres.
165. feres.
166. 1re.
167. verseres.
168. jetteres.
169. fæces.
170. inutils.
171. evapores.
172. trouveres.
173. vesseau.
174. voules.
175. recommenceres.
176. mesme.
177. cy devant.
178. 1me.
179. verseres.
180. pretieux.
181. mettres.
182. = bain marie.
183. inclination.
184. rejettant.
185. fæces.
186. aures.

put it in the little reverberation furnace for 24 hours. And when it is well reverberated, and white, and perfectly crushed, put this matter in a small glass vessel and pour over it four fingers of distilled vinegar. Then, having stopped the vessel, put it to the B.M. for eight days, at the end of which, pour the vinegar by inclination, being careful not to disturb the bottom.

Then put on new vinegar and proceed as the first time, and pour out the vinegar by inclination. Afterwards, discard the feces as useless.

Then evaporate the said vinegars on a slow fire, and you will find at the bottom of the vessel a salt which has admirable virtues: and if you want to make it even more perfect, repeat the same operation as above, and your salt will be as white as crystal. This salt is the body of the moon, which serves for the white work, and the composition of the mercury of the philosophers, as stated in chapter 2.

Pour this precious salt into a small matrass. It will dissolve when you pour the white spirit distilled in the retort on it and put it in the B.M. for 8 days. Then, pouring everything by inclination and rejecting the feces, you will have the mercury of the moon and the white spirit. This is Diana, the

qui est encore vierge, n'ayant pas encore souffert les embrasse-ments du mâle,[187] la lune vive.

Vous joindrez[188] ensemble le mercure blanc et le mercure rouge 2 parties du mercure blanc sur une partie du mercure rouge. Cette liqueur ainsi[189] mélangée[190] s'appelle 1er[191] élixir, dont on tire les luminaires, en la manière qui est ci-après.[192] Ceux-ci[193] ne sont rien que les esprits, et ceux qui suivent les esprits se sont les corps.

Les auteurs[194] qui ont parlé[195] de cette opération, sont premièrement Penot qui en parle sous la préparation de sa marcassite dans une lettre[196] écrite[197] en latin, où il avertit de ne pas prendre à la lettre[198] ce qu'il en dit, car auparavant, dit-il, il faut bien méditer sur ce que disent les philosophes dans leurs livres et qu'il ne faut pas prendre ce qu'ils disent mot à mot, mais il en faut prendre le sens. [C'est pourquoi[199] qu'un chacun s'attache et s'applique à découvrir ce que les philoso-phes veulent dire; et d'interpréter le sens de leurs[200] paroles et non pas leurs[201] paroles mêmes,[202] il faut donc les bien étudier, les bien approfondir[203] et les méditer d'une manière à pouvoir les comprendre, c'est le seul moyen de parvenir à leurs sciences.

187. masle.
188. joindres.
189. ainsy.
190. meslangée.
191. 1r.
192. cy apres.
193. Ceux cy.
194. autheurs.
195. parles.
196. lestre.
197. escrite.
198. lestre.
199. pourquoy.
200. leur.
201. leur.
202. mesmes.
203. aprofondir.

living moon, the female who is still a virgin, having not yet suffered the embraces of the male.

Join together the white mercury and the red mercury: two parts of the white mercury to one part of the red mercury. This liquor, thus mixed, is called the first elixir from which the luminaries are drawn, in the manner that follows. These are nothing but spirits, and those who follow the spirits are the bodies.

The authors who have spoken of this operation are first of all Penotus,[50] who speaks of it under the preparation of his marcasite[51] in a letter written in Latin, where he warns us not to understand what he says according to the letter, because beforehand, he says, it is necessary to meditate on what the philosophers say in their books, and not to take what they say according to the letter, but according to the meaning. (That is why each person must commit and apply himself to discover what the philosophers mean to say).[52] In order to interpret the meaning of their words, and not their words themselves, it is therefore necessary to study them well, to go deeply into them, and to meditate on them in a way that they can be understood. This is the only way of attaining to their sciences.

---

50   Bernardus Georgius Penotus, who possibly died in 1617.

51   The author seems to be referring to *Philippi Aureoli Theophrasti Paracelsi Utriusque Medicinae doctoris celeberrimi, centum quindecim curationes experime[n]taque: e Germanico idiomate in Latinu[m] versa. Accesserunt Quaedam praeclara atque utilissima a B. G. a Portu Aquitano* [i.e. Bernard Georges Penot] *annexa* (1582). Pages 76–80 contain a text by Penotus that deals with operations with a '*marcasita plumbea*' (plumbeous marcasite). An English translation of this text exists in: *A hundred and fouretene experiments and cures of the famous physitian Philippus Aureolus Theophrastus Paracelsus; translated out of the Germane tongue into the Latin. Whereunto is added certaine excellent and profitable workes by B.G. a Portu Aquitano. Also certaine secrets of Isacke Hollandus concerning the vegetall and animall worke. Also the spagericke antidotarie for gunne-shot of Iosephus Quirsitanus. Collected by Iohn Hester—Centum quindecim curationes experimentaque è Germanico idiomate in Latinum versa* (1596), pp. 17–19.

52   Closing bracket implied.

Vous trouverez[204] beaucoup de ces opérations dans Isaac Hollandus,[205] si vous savez[206] en séparer les fausses opérations qu'il y mêle[207] dans son extraction du miel et du sucre et sa petite herbe de rose solaire; si vous en savez[208] prendre, comme l'abeille, le véritable miel et le véritable rosée et que vous connaissiez[209] que ce qu'il entend par ces mots de miel, de herbe solaire et de sucre qui n'est pas une petite[210] difficulté, et que vous puissiez[211] distinguer les vrais opérations des fausses avec tous les vaisseaux[212] inutiles dont les philosophes disent se servir pour cacher leurs opérations aux faux philosophes et aux chymistes vulgaires: car les auteurs[213] qui parlent plus clairement, ce sont ceux dont il faut bien se donner de garde de les suivre à la lettre.[214] C'est pourtant celui[215] de tous les philosophes qui entre le plus, dans la pratique des opérations.

Arnauld de Villeneuve est aussi[216] le philosophe qui écrit[217] dans ce genre, il semble dire les opérations à la lettre.[218] Geber, Raymond[219] Lulle et Ripley[220] ont presque suivis la même[221] méthode;[222] il faut lire les philosophes avec un grain de sel.

Basil Valentin est encore fort prolixe dans ses 12 clefs; ce qui donne bien de la peine au commencement. Il vaut mieux s'attacher à la lecture de ceux qui continuent d'écrire[223] toute l'œuvre en peu de paroles[224] et s'attacher à savoir[225] les principes de ce grand ouvrage avant de mettre la main à l'œuvre, afin d'avoir des règles certaines des principes, pour connaître[226] et distinguer ce que les philosophes disent de vrai[227] et de faux.

204. trouveres.
205. Holandois.
206. sçaves.
207. mesle.
208. sçaves.
209. connoisies.
210. petitte.
211. puissies.
212. vesseaux.
213. autheurs.
214. lestre.
215. celuy.
216. aussy.
217. escrit.
218. lestre.
219. Raimond.
220. Riplée.
221. mesme.
222. metode.
223. d'escrire.
224. parolles.
225. sçavoir.
226. connoistre.
227. vrais.

You will find many of these operations in [the works of] Isaac Hollandus, if you know how to separate the false operations, which he mixes in [with] his extraction of honey and sugar and his little solar rose herb. If you know, like the bee, how to take the true honey and the true dew, then you know what he means by these words: 'honey', 'solar herb', and 'sugar', which is no small difficulty. And you can [therefore] distinguish the true operations from the false, with all the useless vessels that the philosophers say they use, to hide their operations from the false philosophers and the vulgar chymists. For the authors who speak the most clearly are the ones we must be most careful about following to the letter. Nevertheless, of all the philosophers, he is the one who enters most into the practice of the operations.

Arnaldus de Villanova is another philosopher who writes in this genre. He seems to speak of the operations according to the letter. Geber, Raymond Lull, and Ripley have almost followed the same method. We must therefore read the philosophers with a grain of salt.

Basil Valentine is even more verbose in his *Twelve Keys*; which causes much trouble in the beginning. It is preferable to focus on the reading of those who continue to write about the whole work with only a few words, and to endeavor to know the principles of this great work before putting the hand to the work, in order to have distinct rules for the principles, to know and distinguish whether what the philosophers say is true or false. It is in order to help you in this

C'est pour vous aider dans cette pratique que je vous ai[228] donné[229] d'abord les principes qui vous doivent servir de guides
pour vous faire sortir de ce labyrinthe,[230] et vous donner des
lumières pour vous éclairer,[231] afin que vous ne puissiez[232] pas
vous égarer[233] dans cette forêt[234] noire et sortir de ces ténèbres.
C'est de ce dont je veux[235] vous avertir avant que de passer à
la suite des autres opérations. Philalèthe[236] dit que ces opérations ici,[237] sont les travaux[238] d'hercule, qu'il faut essayer les
autres étant[239] beaucoup plus faciles,[240] parce que la nature y a
plus de part que l'art; parce que, dit-il, c'est ce qui a fait dire au
fameux auteur[241] du secret hermétique que ce 1er[242] travail[243]
est un travail[244] d'hercule parce qu'il y a dans nos principes
beaucoup de superfluité hétérogène, c'est à dire de différente
nature qui ne peuvent jamais être[245] rendue assez[246] pures pour
servir à notre ouvrage et qu'il faut absolument ôter[247] avant
qu'on puisse tirer le sang menstruel[248] de notre[249] prostituée;
c'est à dire de notre[250] mercure, Ce n'est pas qu'une femme ne
puisse faire cet ouvrage, pourvu[251] qu'elle en fasse son ouvrage
principal.[252] Mais quand une fois qu'on[253] a le mercure des philosophes tout préparé, alors on a trouvé le repos.

On peut, dit-il, trouver en un autre endroit notre[254]
matière et notre[255] or philosophique en une matière impure et
imparfaite en une semaine; c'est notre[256] voie[257] qui est aisée,
mais rare. Dieu l'ayant réservé pour les pauvres et pour les
gens de bien qui sont dans le mépris.[258] C'est celle-ci[259] que
nous décrivons; l'autre plus difficile est la minérale: l'une et

228. ais.	239. estant.	250. nostre.
229. donnes.	240. facils.	251. pourvue.
230. labirinte.	241. autheur.	252. principale.
231. esclairer.	242. 1r.	253. on.
232. puissies.	243. travaille.	254. nostre.
233. esgarer.	244. travaille.	255. nostre.
234. forest.	245. estre.	256. nostre.
235. veus.	246. asses.	257. voye.
236. Philalette.	247. oster.	258. meprit.
237. cy.	248. menstrual.	259. Celle cy.
238. traveaux.	249. nostre.	

practice, that I first gave you the principles that should guide you out of this labyrinth, and serve as a beacon to enlighten you so that you cannot get lost in this black forest, but rather escape from this darkness. This is what I wanted to warn you about before proceeding to the other operations. Philalethes says that these operations are the work of Hercules, that it is necessary to attempt other ways, being much easier, because nature has a greater role here than art. Because, he says, this is what made the famous author of the *Hermetic Secret*[53] say that this first work is a work of Hercules, because in our principles there is much heterogeneous superfluity, i.e., different natures which can never be made pure enough to serve our work, and which must be absolutely removed before we can draw the menstrual blood from our prostitute, that is to say, from our mercury. It is not that a woman cannot do this work, provided that she makes it her principal work; but once we have the mercury of the philosophers fully prepared, then we have found repose.

One can, he says, find our matter in another place, and our philosophical gold in an impure and imperfect matter in a week. This is our way, which is easy, but rare, god having reserved it for the poor and for the good people who are [held] in contempt. This is what we describe; the other more difficult [path] is the mineral. Each of these two ways are true

53   Jean d'Espagnet, *Arcanum Hermeticae philosophiæ*, 1623.

l'autre de ces 2 voies[260] sont[261] véritables parce que ce n'est qu'une même[262] manière d'agir dans la fin, quoi[263] qu'elles soient différentes au commencement, car notre[264] soleil n'est pas l'or vulgaire et néanmoins il est dans l'or vulgaire: mais cette voie[265] de le chercher est la plus longue et si avec cela, il ne sera pas encore si puissant ni[266] si excellent que celui[267] que la nature nous a laissé et comme mis[268] entre les mains, et cependant tournant la Roue pour une 3ème[269] fois, vous trouverez[270] le même[271] dans tous les deux. Mais celle-ci[272] ce fait en 7 mois et elle est la plus aisée, et l'autre en un an et demi[273] et c'est la pierre minérale.[274]

Sachez[275] donc que l'on ne trouve que cette seule difficulté, en lisant les livres des philosophes les plus sincères; qui est que tous tant qu'ils sont, donnent le change dans le seul régime, et lorsqu'ils parlent d'un ouvrage, ils mêlent[276] le régime et la pratique de l'autre.

260. voyes.
261. Likely 'sont'.
262. mesme.
263. quoy.
264. nostre.
265. voye.
266. ny.
267. celuy.
268. mit.
269. 3me.
270. trouveres.
271. mesme.
272. celle cy.
273. demy.
274. mineralle.
275. Saches.
276. meslent.

because there is only one way of acting in the end, no matter how different they are at the beginning, because our sun is not vulgar gold and nevertheless it is in vulgar gold. But this way of searching for it is the longest, and so with that, it will not be as powerful nor as excellent as that which nature has left us and put in our hands. And yet, turning the wheel for a third time, will you find the same in both. But this [our work] is finished in seven months, and it is the easiest; the other takes a year and a half, and it is [called] the mineral stone.

Know, therefore, that this singlular difficulty can only be found by reading the books of the most sincere philosophers: that all [of them], such as they are, make a substitution[54] in one regimen, and when they speak of a work, they mix the regimen [of one] with the practice of the other.

54   The expression *donner le change*, literally 'give the (ex)change', i.e., 'bring about the change', is also idiomatic for 'throw [someone] off the scent or track', i.e., to exchange something sought with a decoy, to 'make the switch', as it were, in order to hide or deceive.

De l'extraction des corps
des deux luminaires soleil et lune

IL N'Y A RIEN DE SI CACHÉ DANS LES PHILOSOPHES que cette opération qui est suivie de plusieurs autres et dont ils ont très peu parlé;[2] bien que la perfection de notre[3] mercure en dépende. Les plus sincères[4] comme Artephius, le Trevisan et Flamel, ont passé[5] sous silence, ces opérations qu'ils ont supposées[6] et ceux qui en ont parlé; ils l'ont fait si confusément, que sans une inspiration du ciel où sans le secours[7] d'un ami,[8] il est impossible de sortir de ce labyrinthe.[9] Ces opérations consistent dans la séparation et purification de notre[10] mercure qui se fait par une dissolution parfaite et glorification et purification du corps dont il prend naissance et par l'union de l'âme avec le corps du soleil pur, C'est à dire de la lune avec le corps du soleil, dont l'esprit est l'unique lien qui opère cette conjonction, c'est la fin et le but de ces opérations qui se terminent à la génération d'une nouvelle substance plus noble que la première, dont il se[11] fait le mercure des philosophes.

Tout le secret de ces opérations consiste à séparer le corps de la lune, de celui[12] du soleil[13] renfermé dans la teinture rouge que nous avons appelé[14] esprit rouge dans le chapitre précé-

---

1. 3me.	6. supposes.	11. ce.
2. parles.	7. secour.	12. celuy.
3. nostre.	8. amy.	13. soleile.
4. sincers.	9. labirinte.	14. appelles.
5. passes.	10. nostre.	

THIRD CHAPTER

Of the extraction of the bodies of the two luminaries, sun and moon

THERE IS NOTHING SO HIDDEN BY THE PHILOSOPHERS as this operation, which is followed by several others, and of which they have given very few words, although the perfection of our mercury depends on it. The most sincere, such as Artephius, Trevisan, and Flamel, have passed over those operations which they have assumed, and those who have spoken of them, in silence. They have done it with such confusion, that without an inspiration from heaven, or without the help of a friend, it is impossible to get out of this labyrinth. These operations consist of the separation and purification of our mercury, which is done by a perfect dissolution and glorification and purification of the body from which it originates, and by the union of the soul with the body of the pure sun, i.e., of the moon with the body of the sun, whose spirit is the only bond that performs this conjunction. This is the end and goal of these operations, which terminate in the generation of a new substance more noble than the first, which gives rise to the mercury of the philosophers.

The whole secret of these operations consists in separating the body of the moon from that of the sun, enclosed in the red dye, which we have called red spirit in the preceding

dent, et où nous vous avons enseigné[15] le moyen de le tirer.
Vous mettrez[16] cet esprit rouge ou la teinture ☉ [solaire] dans
un vaisseau[17] plat et dont le fond soit assez[18] large que vous
couvrirez[19] d'une espèce de chape[20] de verre qui ferme exactement le vaisseau[21] et ayant lutté les jointures avec un lut convenable dans ce vaisseau,[22] vous y joindrez[23] deux fois autant
d'esprit blanc que vous mettre[24] d'abord au B.M.[25] pendant 8
jours, comme le conseille Arnauld de Villeneuve en son Rosaire, parce que, dit-il, dans cette distillation, il n'y a que les
parties de l'eau qui se pénètrent et se subtilisent, ce qui se fait
presque sans chaleur [et ce sont[26] les plus subtiles parties de la
matière qui se réduisent en nature comme d'eau simple dans
le vaisseau[27] et à l'égard de la terre qui contient le feu et l'air,
comme ils sont attachés à des parties plus grossières; il est besoin d'un feu de cendre. Le Rosaire chapitre sept.[28]

Cette distillation se[29] fait sans alambic et dans le même[30]
vaisseau:[31] la séparation se fait de la terre et de l'eau, sans que
l'Artiste y mette les mains. Les 8 jours passés et lorsque vous
verrez[32] que le rouge commencera à s'obscurcir, vous chang-
erez[33] le feu et vous mettrez[34] un feu de cendre, sans laisser
refroidir votre matière, vous ouvrirez[35] de temps en temps
votre vaisseau[36] lorsque vous verrez[37] surnager sur la superficie
de l'eau, une cendre noire comme une terre subtile;[38] vous la
cueillerez[39] en manière qu'on cueille[40] la crème[41] du lait. C'est
la comparaison qu'en donne Philalèthe,[42] lorsqu'il dit notre[43]

15.	enseignes.	25.	= bain marie.	35.	ouvrires.
16.	mettres.	26.	c'est.	36.	vesseau.
17.	vesseau.	27.	vesseau.	37.	verres or verses?
18.	asses.	28.	cept.	38.	subtille.
19.	couvrires.	29.	ce.	39.	cuilleres.
20.	chappe.	30.	mesme.	40.	cuille.
21.	vesseau.	31.	vesseau.	41.	cresme.
22.	vesseau.	32.	verres.	42.	Philalette.
23.	joindres.	33.	changeres.	43.	nostre.
24.	mettres.	34.	mettres.		

chapter, where we have taught you the means to extract it. Put this red spirit or ☉ [solar] tincture in a flat vessel whose bottom is wide enough that you [can] cover with [it] a kind of glass hood[55] that closes the vessel perfectly. Having sealed the joints with a suitable lute for this vessel, you will add twice as much of the white spirit as you originally put on the B.M. for eight days, as advised by Arnaldus de Villanova in his *Rosary.*[56] For in this distillation, he says, it is only the parts of the water which penetrate and subtilise, and this is achieved almost without [any external] heat (and it is the most subtle parts of the matter that are reduced in nature, like simple water in the vessel). And with regard to the earth which contains fire and air, as they are attached to coarser parts, it is necessary to use an ash bath. [Refer to] *The Rosary*, Chapter Seven.

This distillation is done without an alembic, and in the same vessel: the separation is made of the earth and the water, without the Artist putting his hands on it. [When] eight days [have] passed, you will see that the red will begin to darken. Change the fire and put it on an ash bath without letting your matter cool down. Open your vessel from time to time, and when you see a black ash like a subtle earth floating on the surface of the water, collect it in the same way as cream is collected from milk. This is the comparison given by Philalethes, when he says that our sun coagulates in the manner of flowers or

---

55   French *chappe*, literally 'cape', likely means a type of covering in this
      context.

56   Arnaldus de Villanova, *Omnia, quae exstant, opera chymica : videlicet,
      Thesaurus thesaurorum: seu, Rosarius philosophorum ac omnium secre-
      torum maximum secretum. Lumen novum, Flos florum, & Speculum
      alchimiae. Quibus nimirum artis huius mysteria etiam secretissima lu-
      culenter enodantur, & quam maximalicet, & potest fieri perspicuitate
      explicantur*, Francofurti: Typis Ioachimi Bratheringij, 1603.

soleil en se coagulant en la façon de fleures et crème[44] de lait et ce soufre doit surnager au-dessus des eaux en la façon d'une terre ou cendre subtile.[45] Cette terre subtile[46] est le soufre fixe et le corps mort qu'il faut animer, en lui[47] donnant son âme étant[48] enfermé dans son sépulcre, signifiant par là, sa noirceur.[49]

Aristée[50] très savant[51] philosophe nous décrit[52] admirablement cette opération dans sa 3ème[53] énigme en ces termes. C'est une racine qui se conservé avec son suc vert rempli[54] de force et de sa propre humidité et convenable à la nature solaire; après cela on le met dans le vaisseau[55] où il se[56] purifie, jusqu'à ce que son esprit ou sa racine saline apparaisse[57] par la lotion liquide et teignant[58] qu'il faut tout prendre avec le corps sans les fèces[59] et les parties grossières qui restent par la teinture rouge qu'il tire de cette racine. Il enseigne la 1ère[60] teinture qu'il faut encore rectifier et clarifier, et de cette dernière qui est notre[61] esprit, Il en faut séparer les fèces,[62] et cette séparation se[63] fait en exposant cette teinture au soleil, ou a un feu semblable à celui[64] du soleil; puis il ajoute qu'il est renfermé dans ce corps et terre noire, une substance fusible et pure qui ne se peut tirer qu'avec beaucoup de travail et d'industrie.

Arnauld de Villeneuve, au chap. 4, décrit[65] encore cette opération en ces termes; C'est pour lors que cette terre noire est le corps de la matière étant[66] dissoute, prenez[67] la toute et mettez[68] la en digestion en une chaleur tempérée, afin qu'elle se putréfie et se digère plus facilement[69] pendant un

44. cresme.
45. subtille.
46. subtille.
47. luy.
48. estant.
49. noirceure.
50. Aristeus.
51. sçavent.
52. d'escrit.
53. 3me.
54. remplit.
55. vesseau.
56. ce.
57. apparoisse.
58. teingeante.
59. fæces.
60. 1re.
61. nostre.
62. fæces.
63. ce.
64. celuy.
65. descrit.
66. estant.
67. prenes.
68. mettes.
69. facillement.

cream of milk. And this sulphur must float above the waters in the manner of an earth or subtle ash. This subtle earth is the fixed sulphur and the dead body which must be animated by giving to it its soul [which is] shut up in its sepulcher, meaning, its darkness.

Aristeus, a very learned philosopher, describes this operation admirably, in his third enigma, in these terms: 'It is a root that is conserved with its green juice, filled with strength and its own moisture, and suitable to the solar nature. After that, it is put into the vessel where it is purified, until its spirit or saline root appears via the liquid, tincturing lotion that must be completely taken with the body, leaving the feces and the coarse parts that remain, by the red tincture that it draws from this'. He teaches us about the first tincture that still needs to be rectified and clarified, and the latter which is our spirit. It is necessary to separate the feces, and this separation is done by exposing this tincture to the sun, or to a fire similar to that of the sun. Then he adds that it is enclosed in this body and black earth, a fusible and pure substance that can only be extracted with much labour and industry.

Arnaldus de Villanova, in Chapter 4, also describes this operation in these terms: 'it is for this reason that this black earth is the body of the matter being dissolved. Take it all and put it into digestion in a temperate heat, so that it putrefies and digests more easily during a philosophical month, that is

mois philosophique, c'est à dire 30 jours, et faites[70] la cuire à un feu doux en sorte que le tout s'évapore et se subtilise, et il ajoute parce que la chaleur agissant sur la ıère[71] humidité la noirceur, laquelle noirceur est la tête[72] du corbeau, mais le principe de notre[73] œuvre est de dissoudre notre[74] pierre dans l'eau mercuriale.

Or vous ne pouvez[75] avoir cette eau mercuriale que nous appelons le lunaire, que par la séparation de cette terre noire; c'est pour lors que cette terre noire est le corps du soleil et l'eau est le corps de la lune. Il faut mettre à part cette eau et cette terre noire qu'il faut joindre par après comme nous l'enseignerons au chapitre suivant, dit le triomphe Hermétique page. 110. Vous avez[76] pu[77] remarquer que dans les principales[78] opérations de l'art, ce sont toujours 2 choses qui en produisent une, qui de ces 2 choses, l'une tient lieu de mâle,[79] et l'autre de femelle, l'une est le corps, l'autre est l'esprit ou le mâle[80] et sa femelle; le corps et l'esprit ne sont autres choses que le corps et le sang, et que ces 2 choses sont d'une même[81] nature et d'une espèce; de sorte que la solution du corps dans son propre sang est la solution du mâle[82] par la femelle comme nous dirons ci-après:[83] Ces paroles[84] sont tirées de L'auteur de la guerre des Chevaliers.[85] C'est ce que j'ai[86] voulu vous marquer parce qu'ils conviennent précisément à ces opérations. Vous devez[87] encore connaître,[88] comme le dit le triomphe Hermétique, page 109, que l'intention générale[89] de notre[90] art, est de purifier exactement et de subtiliser une matière d'elle-même[91] immonde et grossière et que pour arriver à cette

70.	faite.	78.	pricipalles.	86.	jay.
71.	ıre.	79.	masle.	87.	deves.
72.	teste.	80.	masle.	88.	connoistre.
73.	nostre.	81.	mesme.	89.	generalle.
74.	nostre.	82.	masle.	90.	nostre.
75.	pouves.	83.	cy apres.	91.	d'elle mesme.
76.	aves.	84.	parolles.		
77.	pus.	85.	Chevalliers.		

to say thirty days. And cook it at a gentle fire so that every-thing evaporates and is subtilised', he adds, 'because the heat is acting on the first humidity of blackness, this blackness be-ing the head of the raven. But the principle of our work is to dissolve our stone in mercurial water'.

Now you cannot have that mercurial water which we call the luminary, other than by the separation of this black earth. It is then that this black earth is the body of the sun, and the water is the body of the moon. It is necessary to set aside this water and this black earth, which must be joined afterwards, as we will teach in the following chapter, says the *Hermetic Triumph*, page 110. You may have noticed that in the main operations of the art, it is always two things that produce one. Of these two things, one takes the place of the male, and the other of the female. One is the body, the other is the spirit, or the male and his female. The body and the spirit are nothing but the body and the blood, and these two things are of the same nature and kind. So the solution of the body in its own blood is [the same as] the solution of the male by the female, as we will say hereafter. These words are taken from the author of the *War of the Knights*. That is what I wanted to remark to you, because they are precisely suited to these operations. You must still know, as the *Hermetic Tri-umph* says, page 109, that the general intention of our art is to purify exactly and to subtilise a matter from its own filth and coarseness, and that in order to attain to this end several

fin, plusieurs opérations sont requises[92] qui ne sont proprement qu'une même[93] opération diversement continuée.[94]

Dans cette opération, ce n'est pas proprement une séparation: mais plutôt[95] une conversion, comme le dit le triomphe Hermétique.

Cette opération est encore précisément marquée dans le petit traité[96] d'Aristotle qui se trouve dans l'art aurifère[97] en ces termes, qu'il dit avoir pris[98] d'Avicenne.

Quand vous verrez[99] paraître[100] la noirceur sur la superficie de l'eau; recueillez[101] là adroitement et soyez persuadé que votre pierre est dissoute en partie; distillez[103] la toute par un linge, et ce qui restera, recuisez la,[104] et réitérez[105] jusqu'à ce que le tout vienne en noirceur au feu du 1er[106] degré chaud et humide; et si vous faites[107] un feu plus fort, la noirceur ce convertira en rougeur, ce qui prouve qu'elle sera brûlée.[108] C'est pourquoi[109] si vous dirigez[110] bien votre feu selon l'art vous trouverez[111] la tête[112] du corbeau qui est la noirceur.

Il faut prendre garde qu'à mesure que se[113] fait et se[114] séparée[115] cette cendre noire; il faut avoir soin de la mettre à part, puis remettre votre[116] vaisseau[117] au B.M.[118] et continuer ainsi[119] jusqu'à[120] ce que le rouge n'en donne plus ce signe que vous en aurez,[121] est que l'eau deviendra blanche. Après avoir desséché[122] cette terre noire mettez[123] à part par un feu lent, vous la mettrez[124] dans une cucurbite[125] ou un matras et

92. requisent.	104. recuisé la.	116. vostre.
93. mesme.	105. reiteré.	117. vesseau.
94. continuées.	106. 1r.	118. = bain marie.
95. plus tost.	107. faite.	119. ainsy.
96. traitte.	108. bruslée.	120. jusques a.
97. aurifaire.	109. pourquoy.	121. aures.
98. prit.	110. diriges.	122. desseiché.
99. verres.	111. trouvesres.	123. mit.
100. parroistre.	112. teste.	124. mettres.
101. recuilles.	113. ce.	125. cucurbitte.
102. soyes.	114. ce.	
103. distilles.	115. separt.	

operations are required which are properly one and the same operation diversely continued.

In this operation, it is not properly a separation, but rather a conversion, as the *Hermetic Triumph* says.

This operation is still precisely marked in the little treatise of Aristotle, which is found in the *Artis Auriferæ* in these terms, which he says he took from Avicenna.

When you see the blackness appear on the surface of the water, collect it adroitly and be persuaded that your stone is partially dissolved, distill[57] the whole through some linen, recook what is left, and repeat until everything becomes black in the fire of the first degree, warm and humid; and if you make a stronger fire, the blackness will turn into redness, which proves that it will be burnt. That is why if you direct your fire according to art you will find the head of the raven, which is the darkness.

It is necessary to take care that as this black ash is made it is separated; it is necessary to take care to set it apart, then put your vessel back to the B.M. and continue thus until the red gives no more. The sign that you will have is that the water will become white. After drying this black earth, set it apart by a slow fire, put it in a cucurbite or a matrass and reserve the

---

57   The word 'distillation' was not limited only to the operation we acknowledge as such today. It also included other methods for separating the 'sediments' or 'dregs' from a liquid or even a molten substance. Many writers distinguished these different methods in order to avoid confusion. Thus 'distillation' through a filter was often accompanied by *per filtrum* in order to clearly distinguish it from proper distillation. See, for example, Geber's *Summa Perfectionis*, where he describes both proper distillation as well as per capillary action, and even through melting (*per descensum*), under the same general label of 'distillation'.

vous réserverez[126] dessus l'eau blanche ou la lunaire ci-dessus[127] décrite[128] et vous mettez[129] ces 2 substances au feu de putréfaction pendant un mois philosophique ainsi,[130] que dit Avicenne ne rapporté dans le petit traité[131] d'Aristotle. Prenez,[132] dit-il, ce qui est dissous,[133] mettez-le[134] dans une cucurbite[135] et versez[136] dessus la poudre noire que vous avez[137] ci-devant[138] ramassée, enfermez-la dans le l'alambic[139] que vous mettrez[140] après sur un feu lent pendant un mois philosophique afin qu'il soit plus corrompu et putrifié.

126. reserveres.
127. cy dessus.
128. d'escritte.
129. mettes.
130. Ainsy.
131. traitte.
132. Prenes.
133. dissout.
134. mettes le.
135. cucurbitte.
136. verses.
137. aves.
138. cy devant.
139. lembic.
140. mettres.

white water or the lunaria as described above, and put these two substances to the fire of putrefaction for a philosophical month. As said, Avicenna reports in the little treatise of Aristotle: 'Take', he says, 'what is dissolved, put it in a cucurbite, and pour over it the black powder which you have gathered before, shut it up in the alembic, which you will put on a slow fire for a philosophical month so that it will be more corrupted and putrefied'.

De la Conversion des éléments et la conjonction des deux luminaires, la lune et le soleil

LE TEMPS DE CETTE PUTRÉFACTION ÉTANT[2] ACHEVÉ,[3] vous ajouterez[4] sa chapiteau[5] et le récipient à la cucurbite,[6] vous distillerez[7] par un feu très lent, de peur de brûler les teintures, ce qui ferait[8] changer le corps noire en un rouge qui serait[9] le signe qu'il serait[10] brûlé. Ce qu'il faut soigneusement éviter comme nous avertit Aristote[11] dans son petit traité[12] de la pierre des philosophes. Fermez,[13] dit-il votre vaisseau[14] de peur que ce que vous y aurez[15] mis[16] dedans ne s'évente,[17] et pendant 8 mois philosophiques,[18] et faites[19] le distiller doucement, et prenez[20] bien garde que vous ne brûliez [pas] la teinture par un trop grand feu. Rhazès[21] dit aussi[22] que le secret de cette opération consiste à préparer subtilement et que si on brûlé la teinture, l'Artiste n'en doit attendre aucun bon effet.

Arnauld de Villeneuve chapitre 8 dit la même[23] chose, et remettre le tout en digestion, au[24] cas que cela arrive[25] et recommence[26] les opérations.

1.	4me.	10.	seroit.	19.	faite.
2.	estant.	11.	Aristotte.	20.	prenes.
3.	achevé.	12.	traitté.	21.	Rasis.
4.	ajouteres.	13.	Fermes.	22.	aussy.
5.	Likely 'chapiteau'.	14.	vesseau.	23.	mesme.
6.	cucurbitte.	15.	aures.	24.	en.
7.	distilleres.	16.	mit.	25.	arriuve.
8.	feroit.	17.	s'evante.	26.	recommencier.
9.	seroit.	18.	philosophique		

Of the conversion of the elements & the conjunction of the two luminaries, the moon and the sun

THE TIME OF THIS PUTREFACTION BEING COMPLETED, you will add its head and the receiver to the cucurbite, you will distill by a very slow fire, for fear of burning the tinctures, which would change the black body into a red that would be the sign that it would be burnt. This must be carefully avoided, as Aristotle warns us in his little treatise on the stone of the philosophers. 'Close', said he, 'your vessel for fear that what you have put into it will not vent out for eight philosophical months, and distill it gently, and take good care that you do not burn the tincture by too great a fire'. Rhazes also says that the secret of this operation is to prepare subtly and that if the tincture is burned, the artist must expect no good effect.

Arnaldus de Villanova, chapter 8, says the same thing, and in the event that this happens, he puts the whole back to digestion and restarts the operations.

Il conseille de se servir pour cela du feu de fumier, c'est à dire d'un feu vaporeux et humide.

Pour faire cette opération comme il faut, qui consiste à blanchir ce corbeau qui s'appelle aussi[27] ablution et inhumation; il faut distiller toute l'eau au dit B.[28] et vous trouverez[29] une terre noire au fond de la cucurbite[30] et après avoir distillé jusqu'à siccité,[31] vous l'arroserez[32] doucement et l'imbiberez[33] de son eau distillée, puis dessécherez;[34] puis vous lui[35] donnerez[36] de nouveau à boire de la même[37] eau peu à chaque fois. Car si vous faite autrement et si vous mettiez[38] trop d'eau, vous éteindriez[39] le feu de la dite[40] terre ou vous la dissoudriez[41] trop promptement; vous lui[42] ferez[43] boire autant d'eau qu'elle en pourra boire. Or par les réitérées arrosements et distillations la terre se blanchira. Avicenne[44] dit qu'à la 7ème[45] distillation, elle sera blanche et claire comme cristal, ce qu'il entend par la 2ème[46] opération qui suit celle-ci.[47] Car dans celle-là, elle est seulement blanche, alors l'on tire le sel armoniac ou le sel nitre du Cosmopolite[48] avec l'esprit lunaire pour extraire le mercure des philosophes, comme nous le dirons ci-après;[49] confondant les 2 opérations ensemble. Continuez[50] donc doucement le feu et mettez[51] un récipient pour recevoir l'eau qui en sort, car ce qui se[52] distille le premier est l'eau flegmatique qui n'est jamais pure, ensuite le feu vient après avec l'air qui est mêlé[53] avec lui,[54] les gardant ensemble jusqu'à ce que vous la divisiez,[55] et ce qui reste au fond, c'est

27. aussy.	37. mesme.	47. celle cy.
28. = bain (marie).	38. metties.	48. Cosmopolitte.
29. trouveres.	39. esteindries.	49. cy apres.
30. cucurbitte.	40. ditte.	50. Continué.
31. ciccité.	41. dissoudries.	51. mettes.
32. l'arrouseres.	42. luy.	52. ce.
33. l'imbiberes.	43. feres.	53. mesle.
34. desseicheres.	44. Avisennes.	54. luy.
35. luy.	45. 7me.	55. divisies.
36. donneres.	46. 2me.	

He advises to use for this the fire of manure, that is to say, of a vaporous and humid fire.

To do this operation properly, which consists in whitening this raven, which is also called ablution and inhumation, all the water must be distilled in the said B.M. and you will find a black earth at the bottom of the cucurbite, and after having distilled to the point of dryness, water it gently and imbibe it with its distilled water, then dry it; then let it drink again from the same water a little each time. For if you did otherwise and put too much water, you would extinguish the fire of the said earth, or you would dissolve it too quickly; make it drink as much water as it can drink. But by the repeated waterings and distillations the earth will be whitened. Avicenna says that in the seventh distillation, it will be white and clear as crystal, by which he means the second operation which follows it. For in this one, it is only white, so one draws the sal armoniac or the niter salt of the Cosmopolitan with the lunar spirit to extract the mercury of the philosophers, as we shall hereafter say; conflating the two operations together. So continue the fire gently and put [on] a receiver to receive the water that comes out, because that which is distilled first is the phlegmatic water that is never pure, then the fire comes next with the air that is mixed with it, keeping them together until you divide it, and what remains at the bottom

la terre brûlée et séchée.[56] Ainsi[57] vous avez les 4 éléments séparés en parties, mais qui ne sont pas encore purifiés; le 1er[59] élément qui sort, est l'eau pure froide et humide de sa nature, qui'il faut distiller 7 fois, et elle sera très belle et claire et blanche comme cristal.

Il y a encore d'autres philosophes qui mêlent[60] ces deux opérations la ensemble.

Arnauld de Villeneuve confond de mêm[61] ces 2 opérations; des deux n'en faisant qu'une, lorsqu'il la décrit[62] en ces termes, que toutes les terres et fèces[63] qui viennent des séparations des éléments et des principes, il les faut joindre à la terre noire. Il ajoute encore de l'eau qui a est été[64] distillée 7 fois, on doit la partager aussi[65] en 7 et les mettre l'une après l'autre sur la terre, parce qu'elle est le mercure des philosophes. Ainsi[66] si on ne connait[67] pas les principes de notre[68] science, il est facile de se tromper par la lecture des livres de ces philosophes, parce qu'ils joignent souvent, différentes opérations ensemble et qu'ils entremêlent[69] souvent[70] de fausses, pour cacher leur[71] sciences aux ignorants.[72]

L'auteur[73] du Combat des Chevaliers,[74] nous marque fort doctement et d'une manière palpable, au livre du Triomphe Hermétique, page 132 par ces mots. Après que le sage ait[75] fait sortir de la pierre une source d'eau vive qu'il a exprimé le suc de la vigne des philosophes et qu'il a fait leur vin. [C'est la liqueur qu'il a mise[76] dans le creux[77] du chêne,[78] dont il a tiré le vin]. Il doit remarquer que dans cette substance homogène qui paraît[79] sous la forme d'eau [C'est à dire, lorsqu'elle est

56.	seiche.	64.	esté.	72.	ignorans.
57.	Ainsy.	65.	aussy.	73.	L'autheur.
58.	aves.	66.	Ainsy.	74.	Chevalliers.
59.	1r.	67.	connoit.	75.	a.
60.	meslent.	68.	nostre.	76.	mit.
61.	mesme.	69.	entremeslent.	77.	creuse.
62.	drescrit.	70.	sçouvent.	78.	chesne.
63.	fæces.	71.	leurs.	79.	parroist.

is the burnt and dried earth. Thus you have the four elements separated into parts, but which are not yet purified; the first element that comes out is the cold, moist, pure water of its nature, which must be distilled seven times, and it will be very beautiful and clear and white as crystal.

There are still other philosophers who mingle these two operations together.

Arnaldus de Villanova similarly confounds these two operations; of the two, making only one, when he describes it in these terms: that all the earths and feces which come from the separations of the elements and principles must be joined to the black earth. He adds more water that has been distilled seven times, it must be divided also into seven and put one after the other on the earth, because it is the mercury of the philosophers. Thus, if we do not know the principles of our science, it is easy to deceive ourselves by reading the books of these philosophers, because they often join different operations together, and often mingle false ones, to hide their sciences from the ignorant.

The author of the *War of the Knights* marks [for] us very learnedly and in a palpable manner, in the book of the *Hermetic Triumph*, page 132, with these words. After the wise man has brought out a spring of living water from the stone, he pressed out the juice from the vine of the philosophers and made their wine. (This is the liquor that he has put in the hollow of the oak, from which he has drawn the wine). He must observe that in this homogeneous substance, which appears in the form of water (that is, when it is separated from

séparée du noir] elle contient [néanmoins en puissance] trois substances différentes et 3 principes naturels de tous les corps, sel, soufre, et mercure qui contient l'esprit, l'âme et le corps.

C'est pourquoi[80] on dit que notre[81] pierre a esprit, corps, et âme; et bien qu'ils paraissent[82] purs et parfaitement unis ensemble; il s'en faut beaucoup qu'ils le soient encore, car lorsque par la distillation, nous tirons l'eau qui est mêlée[83] avec l'âme et l'esprit; le corps demeure au fond du vaisseau[84] comme une terre noire morte et féculente,[85] Mais comme dit Pontanus, tout ce qu'il y a de superflu,[86] d'immonde et de féculent[87] reste au fond. Enfin toute la substance du composé se perfectionne par l'action de notre[88] feu. Puis il ajoute que les Enfants[89] de la science ne doivent pas ignorer que le feu et le soufre sont cachés dans le centre de la terre, ou de cette terre noire qu'il faut laver avec son esprit, c'est à dire plus exactement avec le corps lunaire qui est l'esprit blanc avec son blanchissement pour en extraire, comme le même[90] auteur[91] ajoute, le Baume, le sel fixe qui est le sang de notre[92] pierre; d'où se forme, comme[93] nous enseignons ci-après[94] le mercure des philosophes et le dissolvant des corps parfaits du soleil et de la lune, tant pour le blanc que pour le rouge. Ce qui est confirmé par Arnauld de Villeneuve au chapitre 8. Cette eau qui a été[95] distillée 7 fois, vous en mettrez[96] une des sept parties[97] sur cette terre précieuse[98] ou ce sel fixe, parce qu'elle est le mercure des philosophes et qui fait le mariage, et c'est cette eau qui lave le laton, et l'esprit qui aura dissous[99] le corps du soleil servira seulement pour le rouge, se[100] donnant bien de garde de ne les pas confondre ensemble. Ce qu'Arnauld

80. pourquoy.	87. fæculante.	94. Cy apres.
81. nostre.	88. nostre.	95. este.
82. parroissent.	89. Enfans.	96. mettres.
83. meslée.	90. mesme.	97. partie.
84. vesseau.	91. autheur.	98. pretieuse.
85. fæculante.	92. nostre.	99. dissout.
86. superflus.	93. com.	100. ce.

the black), it contains (albeit in potency) three different substances and three natural principles of all bodies, salt, sulphur, and mercury, which contains spirit, soul and body.

That is why it is said that our stone has spirit, body, and soul; and though they appear pure and perfectly united together, it is far from being so; for when by distillation we draw the water which is mixed with the soul and the spirit, the body remains at the bottom of the vessel like a dead and feculent black earth, but as Pontanus says, everything superfluous, foul, and feculent remains at the bottom. Finally, all the substance of the compound is perfected by the action of our fire. Then he adds that the Children of Science must not ignore that the fire and sulphur are hidden in the center of the earth, or that this black earth must be washed with its spirit, that is to say, more precisely, with the lunar body, which is the white spirit with its whitening, to extract from it, as the same author adds, the Balm, the fixed salt which is the blood of our stone; from which is formed, as we teach below, the mercury of the philosophers, and the dissolvent of the perfect bodies of the sun and the moon, as much for the white as for the red. This is confirmed by Arnaldus de Villanova in chapter 8. [Of] this water which has been distilled seven times, you will put one of the seven parts on this precious earth or fixed salt, because it is the mercury of the philosophers and that which performs the marriage. And it is this water which washes the Laton, and the spirit that will have dissolved the body of the sun will serve only for the red, taking good care not to conflate them together. [This is] what

de Villeneuve nous donne à entendre dans le même[101] endroit cité. Vous agirez[102] de la même[103] manière, de l'eau rouge, comme vous avez[104] fait de l'eau blanche, parce que c'est la même[105] méthode[106] qu'il faut observer et qui fait le même[107] effet, si ce n'est que cette eau blanche sert pour faire le blanc, et la rouge pour faire le rouge. Ne mêlez[108] donc pas ces deux eaux ensemble parce que vous perdriez[109] votre ouvrage et c'est ainsi[110] que vous serez[111] sûr,[112] en observant ce que l'on vient de dire.

Vous avez[113] par ces opérations la lune jointe au corps du soleil qui ne sont qu'un corps; laquelle terre est appelée des philosophes de plusieurs noms, comme arsenic, leur venin, leur terre fouillée,[114] parce qu'elle est comme en feuillé,[115] de laquelle se tire le sel fixe et le sel armoniac et le mercure sublimé, pour faire le mercure des philosophes. Nous vous enseignerons la manière de le faire au chapitre suivant, en quoi[116] consiste le grand secret de cet art.

101. mesme.
102. agires.
103. mesme.
104. aves.
105. mesme.
106. metode.
107. mesme.
108. mesles.
109. perdries.
110. ainsy.
111. seres.
112. sçure.
113. aves.
114. fœuillée.
115. fœuillée.
116. quoy.

Arnaldus de Villanova makes us understand in the same cited place. Act in the same manner with the red water as you did with the white water, because it is the same method that must be observed, and it has the same effect, except that this white water serves to make the white, and the red to make the red. Do not mix these two waters together because you will lose your work. This is how you will be sure: by observing what we have just said.

With these operations you have joined the moon to the body of the sun, which are but one body. The philosophers call this earth by many names, such as arsenic, their poison, or their foliated earth, because it is leafy. From this [earth], the fixed salt, the sal armoniac, and the sublimed mercury are extracted in order to make the mercury of the philosophers. We will teach you how to do this in the next chapter, in which consists the great secret of this art.

Du mercure des philosophes

C'EST ICI[2] LE LIEU DE PARLER DE CETTE EAU admirable dont les philosophes disent tant de vertus, et qu'ils appellent par excellence leur mercure dont ils ont caché[3] la Composition par une infinité[4] de termes seuls connus des véritables philosophes, par des allégories, des similitudes et par mille noms empruntés, et sous des termes non seulement équivoques, mais même[5] opposés. Ce qui paraît[6] une contrariété étonnante[7] à ceux qui ne sont pas initiés dans nos mystères[8] philosophiques. Ce qui les oblige[9] d'en user ainsi,[10] c'est que quand on est une fois parvenu au moyen de faire cette eau, le travail[11] est beaucoup moindre que les précédentes opérations; elle a néanmoins encore quelques impuretés qu'il faut séparer, et doit encore passer par les degrés avant qu'elle vienne à sa perfection pour en faire le parfait Elixir.

Cette eau est la clef et le chef-d'œuvre de la philosophie Hermétique puisque par elle, ce commence, se perfectionne, et s'achève enfin leur grand œuvre qu'ils appellent leur pierre; et le grand hermès n'en dit les propriétés et les vertus qu'avec Exclamation qu'il décrit,[12] sans dire un mot comment[13] elle se

1.	5me.	6.	parroist.	11.	travaille.
2.	icy.	7.	estonnante.	12.	descrit.
3.	caches.	8.	misteres.	13.	comme.
4.	infinites.	9.	obligent.		
5.	mesme.	10.	ainsy.		

FIFTH CHAPTER

Of the mercury of the philosophers

THIS IS THE PLACE TO SPEAK OF THAT ADMIRABLE water, of which the philosophers tell so many virtues, and which they call their mercury *par excellence*, the composition of which they have hidden by an infinity of terms only known to the true philosophers, by allegories, similitudes, and by a thousand borrowed names, and under terms not only equivocal, but even opposed. That appears to be a surprising annoyance to those who are not initiated into our philosophical mysteries. What obliges them to do so is, that when one has once succeeded in making this water, the labor is much less than the preceding operations; it nevertheless still has some impurities which must be separated, and must still pass through the degrees before it comes to its perfection to make it into the perfect Elixir.

This water is the key and the masterpiece of the Hermetic philosophy, since by it, it begins, perfects itself, and finally completes their great work, which they call their stone; and the great Hermes speaks of its properties and virtues only with exclamation which he describes without saying a

fait et de ce dont elle est tirée. [Ô bienheureuse forme aqueuse, par ce qu'elle dissout tous les Éléments] il dit encore, les éléments de la pierre ne peuvent être[14] dissous[15] que par cette eau toute divine par une digestion et putréfaction proportionnée.

Artephius, Flamel, le Trévisan et il ne s'en trouve presque pas un qui n'ait[16] supposé sa préparation, quoique[17] la plus importante. Car c'est elle qui fait la sublimation de la pierre et la conversion des principes et des éléments, ainsi[18] que le marqué l'auteur[19] des combats des Chevaliers,[20] qui fait l'eau de la terre, l'air de l'eau et le feu de l'air, par laquelle voie,[21] notre[22] mercure peut être[23] fait et préparé.

Le triomphe Hermétique page 130 dit que c'est dans elle qu'est contenu le feu sacré des sages qui par conséquent est l'unique instrument qui puisse opérer cette sublimation. Je vous ai[24] décrit[25] ce feu, et je vous ai[26] révélé ce puissant agent qui opère toutes les merveilles de cet art. Si vous ne l'avez[27] pas compris,[28] vous devez[29] prier Dieu qu'il vous éclaire.[30] Car la connaissance de ce secret, dit l'auteur[31] du triomphe Hermétique, est plutôt[32] un dont[33] du Ciel qu'une lumière acquise par le raisonnement; C'est par le moyen de ce feu qui est renfermé dans cette eau et notre[34] mercure qu'elle dissout, dit l'auteur[35] du triomphe Hermétique, la pierre naturellement et sans violence, et la fait résoudre en eau dans la grande mer des sages par la dissolution qui se fait des rayons du soleil et de la lune qui est la vigne des sages, leur eau de vie rectifiée et leur vinaigre très aigre.

14. estre.	22. nostre.	30. esclaire.
15. dissouts.	23. estre.	31. l'autheur.
16. n'aye.	24. ais.	32. plus tost.
17. quoyque.	25. d'escrit.	33. 'dont' in MS.,
18. ainsy.	26. ais.	likely an error.
19. l'autheur.	27. l'aves.	34. nostre.
20. Chevalliers.	28. comprit.	35. l'autheur.
21. voye.	29. deves.	

word about how it is made and of what it is drawn from. (O blessed aqueous form, by which it dissolves all the Elements). He says again: the elements of the stone can only be dissolved by this all-divine water by a proportionate digestion and putrefaction.

Artephius, Flamel, Trevisan, and there is hardly one who has not presumed its preparation, though [it is] the most important one. For it is that which makes the sublimation of the stone and the conversion of the principles and elements, as is noted by the author of the *War of the Knights*, which makes the water from the earth, the air from the water, and the fire from the air, by which way our mercury can be made and prepared.

The *Hermetic Triumph*, page 130, says that it is in [this water] that the sacred fire of the sages is contained, which is consequently the only instrument that can carry out this sublimation. I have described to you this fire, and I have revealed to you that powerful agent that works all the marvels of this art. If you do not understand, pray that God will enlighten you. For the knowledge of this secret, says the author of the *Hermetic Triumph*, is rather a gift from Heaven than a light acquired by reasoning; it is by means of this fire which is contained in this water and in our mercury, says the author of the *Hermetic Triumph*, that it dissolves the stone naturally and without violence and causes it to resolve into water in the great sea of the Sages by the dissolution which is made from the rays of the sun and the moon which is the vine of the sages, their rectified water of life and their sharpest vinegar.

C'est donc la plus importante de toutes les opérations de notre[36] pratique et comme c'est le[37] Dédale où le disciple de notre[38] Art demeure infailliblement sans en pouvoir trouver l'issue heureuse.[39] C'est pourquoi[40] je m'étendrai[41] un peu plus que les philosophes n'ont fait, qui ne parlent si confusément de cette eau, que sans une inspiration du Ciel, il n'est pas possible de le comprendre.

Vous voyez[42] par la, qu'il n'y a rien de si rare et de si précieux[43] que cette liqueur qu'ils ont caché[44] sous mille noms différents, Les uns l'appellent leur eau de vie, les eaux, l'eau de Diane, la grande lunaire, l'eau d'argent vif, notre[45] mercure, notre[46] huile incombustible qui au froid se congèle comme la glace et se liquéfie a la chaleur comme le beurre.[47] Hermès l'appelle la terre feuillée[48] ou la terre des feuilles.[49] Car la matière dont elle est tirée, est toute feuillée:[50] en un mot la fontaine très claire dont le Comte de Trévisan fait mention, et le triomphe Hermétique page 144 qu'elle est enfin le grand Alkaest[51] qui dissout radicalement[52] les métaux parfaits, elle est la véritable eau permanente, qui après les avoir dissout, elle s'unit inséparablement à eux, et en augmente le poids et la teinture.

Je m'assure que vous, qui êtes[53] les véritables Enfants[54] de la science, vous recevrez[55] une très grande satisfaction de l'éclaircissement de ces mystères cachés qui regardent la séparation et la purification des principes de notre[56] mercure, dont je vous ai[57] touché au chapitre précédent la préparation des plus grossières et de la matière dont et d'où il prend ses orig-

---

36.	nostre.	44.	caches.	52.	radicallement.
37.	la.	45.	nostre.	53.	estes.
38.	nostre.	46.	nostre.	54.	Enfans.
39.	heureux.	47.	beure.	55.	recevres.
40.	pourquoy.	48.	fæuillée.	56.	nostre.
41.	m'estendray.	49.	fæuilles.	57.	ais.
42.	voyes.	50.	fæuillée.		
43.	pretieux.	51.	Alkaet.		

It is therefore the most important of all the operations of our practice, and as it is the Maze in which the disciple of our Art inevitably remains if they cannot find the desired exit. That is why I will extend a little more than the philosophers have done, who speak so confusedly of this water that it is not possible to understand it without an inspiration from Heaven.

You see by this that there is nothing so rare and so precious as that liquor which they have hidden under a thousand different names. Some call it their water of life (*eau de vie*), the waters, the water of Diana, the great Lunaria, the water of *argent vive*, our mercury, our incombustible oil which congeals like ice in the cold and melts like butter in the heat. Hermes calls it the foliated earth or the earth of leaves. For the matter from which it is drawn is quite foliated: in a word, the very clear fountain mentioned by Count Trevisan and the *Hermetic Triumph* page 144 is ultimately the great Alkahest which radically dissolves the perfect metals; it is the true permanent water, which, after having dissolved them, is inseparably united to them, increasing the weight and tincture.

I assure you that you who are the true Children of Science will receive a great satisfaction from the clarification of these hidden mysteries which concern the separation and purification of the principles of our mercury, which I touched upon in the previous chapter: the preparation of the coarsest; and of the matter: from what and where it takes its origins. In

ines. Dans ce chapitre ici[58] les éléments sont plus spirituels et dégagés de la matière; je suivrai[59] donc par ordre tout ce qui regarde la purification de cette eau divine, et je suivrai[60] par ordre tout ce qui en dépend jusqu'à son entière perfection, et j'y ajouterai[61] tout ce que les auteurs[62] les plus fameux ont dit plus précisément et très confusément.

Or, comme l'intention des sages est de donner à l'or plus de perfection qu'il n'a reçu[63] par la nature, et lui[64] donner la vertu de se multiplier pour en faire leur médecine universelle. Sur ce principe il est évident que l'or commun n'est point leur or, puisqu'il est fini[65] et qu'il ne peut acquérir une plus grande perfection. C'est ce que dit le triomphe Hermétique dans le Dialogue de la pierre avec l'or vulgaire; l'or, dit-il, est un métal[66] parfait lequel à cause de sa perfection ne saurait[67] être[68] poussé à un degré plus parfait. De sorte que, de quelque manière que l'on puisse travailler avec l'or, soit qu'on sache[69] extraire sa couleur et sa teinture, l'Artiste n'en fera jamais plus d'or et ne teindre[70] jamais une plus grande quantité de métal.[71] Raymond[72] Lulle dit, ce qui doit être[73] rendu meilleur, ne doit pas être[74] parfait; parce que dans ce qui est parfait, il n'y a rien à changer et qu'on détruirait[75] bien plutôt[76] sa nature.

Il y a, dit Geber dans la profondeur de notre[77] mercure, un soufre qui le cuit et qui le digère. C'est ce soufre qui est leur or vif qui donne la vie même[78] à l'or commun, qui fait végéter et multiplier par le moyen de notre[79] eau, et qui forme et accomplit notre[80] grand œuvre, qu'ils appellent communément pierre philosophale.[81]

58. icy.
59. suivres.
60. suivres.
61. ajouteray.
62. autheurs.
63. receu.
64. luy.
65. finit.
66. metail.
67. sçavroit.
68. estre.
69. sçache.
70. tiendra.
71. metail.
72. Raimond.
73. estre.
74. estre.
75. detruiroit.
76. plus tost.
77. nostre.
78. mesme.
79. nostre.
80. nostre.
81. philosophalle.

this chapter the elements are more spiritual and freed from matter; I will therefore follow by order all that pertains to the purification of this divine water, and I follow in order all that depends on it to its full perfection. And I will add to it all that the most famous authors have said more precisely and very confusedly.

Now, as the intention of the sages is to give gold more perfection than it has received by nature, and to give it the virtue of multiplying to make it their universal medicine, on this principle, it is evident that common gold is not their gold, since it is finite, and it cannot acquire greater perfection. This is what the *Hermetic Triumph* says in the *Dialogue of the stone with vulgar gold*. Gold, he says, is a perfect metal which, because of its perfection, cannot be pushed to a more perfect degree. Thus, whatever may be done with gold, whether one knows how to extract its colour and its tincture, the artist will never make more gold and never tinge a greater quantity of metal. Raymond Lull says: what must be made better must not be perfect, because in that which is perfect, there is nothing to change, and that one would instead destroy its nature.

There is, says Geber, in the depths of our mercury, a sulphur which cooks and digests it. It is this sulphur which is their living gold, which even gives life to common gold, which makes [it] vegetate [i.e. grow][58] and multiply by means of our water, and which forms and accomplishes our great work, which they commonly call [the] philosophers' stone.

---

58   French *végéter* is cognate with English 'vegetate' and means 'grow'. (Importantly, the word does not have the negative connotation of the modern English equivalent, i.e., 'to be inactive', used pejoratively). For our author, this 'growth' is notably accomplished 'by means of our water'. This comparison to the growth or cultivation of vegetables is a popular one among the alchemists precisely because it is accomplished by their secret solvent or 'water', just like plants also 'grow' by means of common water.

Il faut remarquer en passant que le terme de pierre, est pris en plusieurs sens différents de l'œuvre; ce qui fait dire à Geber qu'il y a 3 pierres qui sont les 3 médecines répondant[82] aux 3 degrés de perfection de l'œuvre: de sorte que la pierre du 1er[83] ordre, est la matière des philosophes parfaitement purifiée et réduite en pure substance mercuriale La pierre du 2ème[84] ordre, est la même[85] matière cuite,[86] digérée et fixée en soufre incombustible. La pierre du 3ème[87] ordre, est cette même[88] matière fermentée, multipliée et poussée a la dernière perfection de teinture fixe permanente et teignent.[89]

Pour connaitre[90] ce qu'entendent les philosophes par leur or; il faut savoir[91] qu'il y a 3 sortes d'or: Le 1er[92] est un or astral qui est produit par la lumière et les Rayons du soleil, dont son corps est le centre; C'est une substance ignée et une continuelle Émanation des corpuscules[93] solaires qui remplissent tout l'univers et qui se mêlent[94] dans tous les mixtes. Le 2ème[95] est un or élémentaire et la plus pure partie du soufre fixe renfermé dans le profondeur[96] des Éléments et dont chaque mixte renferme un grain de ce précieux[97] or qui est multiplié par cet or Astral dont il en est l'aimant[98] et qui forme l'or des philosophes: lorsque cet or a été[99] parfaitement calciné et exalté, c'est à dire réduit en un sel blanc comme la neige, pour lors il a une grande sympathie avec cet or Astral, d'où il est visiblement l'aimant.[100] Le 3ème[101] est l'or métallique et vulgaire qui est un corps sans âme, qui ne saurait[102] être[103] vivifié que par notre[104] or vivant, ou par le moyen de notre[105] magistère.[106]

82. repondants.	91. sçavoir.	100. l'aymant.
83. 1r.	92. 1r.	101. 3me.
84. 2me.	93. corpusculles.	102. sçavroit.
85. mesme.	94. meslent.	103. estre.
86. cuitte.	95. 2me.	104. nostre.
87. 3me.	96. profond.	105. nostre.
88. mesme.	97. pretieux.	106. magister.
89. teingente.	98. l'aymant.	
90. connoistre.	99. esté.	

It should be noted in passing that the term stone is taken in several different senses in the work; this is what makes Geber say that there are three stones which are the three medicines corresponding to the three degrees of perfection in the work. The stone of the first order is the matter of the philosophers perfectly purified and reduced to pure mercurial substance. The stone of the second order is the same matter cooked, digested, and fixed into incombustible sulphur. The stone of the third order is the same fermented matter multiplied and pushed to the last perfection of the fixed, permanent, and tingeing tincture.

To know what the philosophers mean by their gold, you must know that there are three kinds of gold. The first is an astral gold which is produced by the light and rays of the sun, whose body is the center; it is an igneous substance and a continual emanation of the solar corpuscles which fill the whole universe and blend with all mixts. The second is an elementary gold, and the purest part of the fixed sulphur contained in the depths of the Elements, and of which each mixt contains a grain of that precious gold, which is multiplied by this Astral gold, of which it is the magnet, and which forms the gold of the philosophers: when this gold has been perfectly calcined and exalted, that is to say reduced to a white salt like snow, then it has a great sympathy with this Astral gold, from which it is visibly the magnet. The third is the metallic and vulgar gold, which is a body without soul, which can only be vivified by our living gold, or by means of our magistery.

De même[107] pour connaître[108] ce que les philosophes entendent par leur mercure; il faut savoir[109] qu'il y en a de 3 espèces. Le 1er est une substance spirituelle, aérienne, participant d'un peu de soufre, il est de la Nature de l'air, qui en est le véhicule. C'est pourquoi[110] il s'en va[111] à la moindre chaleur, il communique la vie et la force générative aux choses sublunaires, il porte un feu fermentatif dans les semences. Il y a un philosophe qui le nomme vulcain[112] lunatique; par le 2me ils entendent une substance homogène formée par l'union de 2 corps qui en se détruisant[113] l'un et l'autre, en agissant l'un sur l'autre comme le mâle[114] et la femelle, ou comme corps et esprit dont il en résulte une substance qui a toutes les dispositions nécessaires pour être[115] procrée par l'art et par la nature, de devenir de perfection en perfection jusqu'au souverain degré. La[116] 3ème[117] espèce est le mercure métallique et commun qui peut devenir le mercure des philosophes, quand il est joint au seul et unique mercure des métaux en forme de sperme cru[118] et non encore mûr.[119] Car il renferme en lui[120] la vertu de teindre et de perfectionner les métaux, parce qu'il était[121] auparavant or et argent en puissance, comme le dit le Cosmopolite;[122] il est appelé[123] hermaphrodite,[124] a cause qu'il contient dans son propre ventre son mâle[125] et sa femelle, lequel étant[126] digéré jusqu'à une blancheur pure et fixe, devient argent, étant[127] poussé jusqu'à la rougeur,[128] et après il devient or.

107. mesme.
108. connoistre.
109. sçavoir.
110. pourquoy.
111. vat.
112. vulquain.
113. detruisants.
114. masle.
115. estre.
116. Le.
117. 3me.
118. crud.
119. mure.
120. luy.
121. estoit.
122. Cosmopolitte.
123. appellé.
124. hermaphroditte.
125. masle.
126. estant.
127. estant.
128. rougeure.

In the same way, to know what the philosophers mean by their mercury; you must know that there are three species. The first is a spiritual substance, aerial, participating a little in sulphur, it is of the nature of the air, which is its vehicle. That is why it leaves at the slightest heat, it communicates life and the generative force to the sublunary things, it carries a fermentative fire into the seeds. There is a philosopher who calls it Lunatic Vulcan.[59] By the second they mean a homogeneous substance formed by the union of two bodies, which destroy each other, acting on one another as the male and the female, or as body and spirit, which results in a substance which has all the necessary dispositions to be procreated by art and nature, to develop from perfection to perfection until the sovereign degree. The third species is the metallic and common mercury, which may become the mercury of the philosophers, when it is joined to the one and only mercury of metals in the form of raw and not-yet-mature sperm. For it contains within it the virtue of tingeing and perfecting metals, because it was formerly gold and silver in potential, as the Cosmopolitan says. It is called hermaphrodite, because it contains its male and its female in its own belly, and having been digested into a pure and fixed whiteness, it becomes silver; and then, having been pushed to redness, it becomes gold.

59   This refers to the anonymous author of the *L'Ancienne Guerre des Chevaliers* (*Ancient War of the Knights*, see note 39), the subtitle of which reads: *Entretien de la Pierre des Philosophes avec l'Or et le Mercure. Touchant la véritable matière, dont ceux qui sont savans dans les Secrets de la Nature, peuvent faire la Pierre Philosophale, suivant les règles d'une pratique convenable, et par le secours de Vulcain Lunatique* (A Dialogue of the Philosopher's Stone with Gold and Mercury, concerning the true matter with which those who are knowledgable in the Secrets of Nature can make the Philosophical Stone, according to the rules of a suitable practice, and by the help of Lunatic Vulcan).

De la séparation et purification des principes de notre[2] mercure en général

JE NE DOUTE POINT QUE LES VÉRITABLES ENFANTS[3] de la science ne reçoivent une grande satisfaction de l'éclaircissement de ces mystères[4] cachés. Cette séparation et cette purification des principes qui composent notre[5] mercure, consiste en général dans une parfaite dissolution et sublimation du corps de la lune dont il prend naissance, et par l'union intime de l'âme avec son corps dont l'esprit est l'unique liens qui fait cette union et cette conjonction dont il en résulte une substance infiniment plus noble que la première.

Je vous ai[6] déjà enseigné les principales[7] opérations de notre[8] divin art ; vous avez[9] vu[10] que ce sont toujours 2 choses qui en produisent une: que de ces 2 choses l'une tient lieu de mâle[11] et l'autre de femelle, l'une est le corps et l'autre est l'esprit; que le mâle[12] et cette femelle ne sont autre chose que le corps et l'esprit, et selon l'expression des philosophes particuliers, le corps est le sang ou le menstruel.[13] Vous avez[14] encore vue que ces 2 choses sont de même[15] nature et tirées[16] d'une même[17] racine;[18] en sorte que la solution du corps dans son propre sang que c'est la solution du corps dans son propre

---

1.	6me.	7.	principalles.	13.	mestruë.
2.	nostre.	8.	nostre.	14.	aves.
3.	Enfans.	9.	aves.	15.	mesme.
4.	misteres.	10.	vuë.	16.	tirée.
5.	nostre.	11.	masle.	17.	mesme.
6.	ais.	12.	masle.	18.	racinne.

SIXTH CHAPTER

Of the separation and purification of the principles of our mercury in general

I DO NOT DOUBT THAT THE TRUE CHILDREN OF Science receive a great satisfaction from the clarification of these hidden mysteries. This separation and purification of the principles which compose our mercury consists, in general, in a perfect dissolution and sublimation of the body of the moon from which it is born, and by the intimate union of the soul with its body, whose spirit is the unique bond which makes this union and conjunction, from which a substance infinitely more noble than the first results.

I have already taught you the principal operations of our divine art: you have seen that it is always two things that produce one: that of these two things one takes the place of the male and the other of the female; one is the body and the other is the spirit; that the male and the female are nothing but the body and the spirit, and, according to the expression of particular philosophers, the body is the blood or the menstruum.[60] You have also seen that these two things are of the same nature and drawn from the same root, so that the solution of the body in its own proper blood is the solution of the body

---

60 *Mestruë* in the manuscript, likely means 'menstruum'.

sang;[19] C'est la solution du corps qui est le corps blanc ou de la lune que les philosophes appellent l'or blanc; C'est la solution du mâle[20] par la femelle, car le corps blanc contient le rouge ou du corps par son esprit.

Or cette solution ne vous réussirait[21] pas ainsi[22] que le marque excellemment[23] l'auteur[24] du triomphe hermétique sans la conjonction de la femelle. C'est, dit-il, dans leurs embrassement réciproques qu'ils se confondent et se changent l'un dans l'autre. En vain vous auriez,[25] dit-il, ouvert et sublimé le corps de la pierre; C'est à dire la terre blanche qui est la terre dont vous avez[26] tiré ce sel précieux,[27] si vous ne lui[28] faisiez[29] épouser la femme que la nature lui[30] a destiné; elle est cet esprit dont le corps ou ce sel tire sa 1ère origine. Ce sel précieux[31] se dissout comme la glace à la moindre chaleur du feu. Or ce précieux[32] sel qu'il appelle corps ce fait par la continuelle effusion de son propre sang qui est son menstruel[33] naturel, avec lequel il s'unit si étroitement[34] et si intimement qu'ils ne font qu'une seule et même[35] substance. C'est cette substance qui est la matière prochaine dont est formé le mercure des philosophes, ainsi[36] que nous le dirons au chapitre suivant.

Tout le secret donc consiste, après avoir lavé cette terre morte et noire et coupé[37] la tête[38] du Corbeau, ainsi[39] que nous l'avons enseigne;[40] il ne faut pas jeter[41] cette terre, car le feu et le soufre sont cachés dans cette terre qu'il faut laver, dit l'Auteur[42] du triomphe Hermétique, avec son esprit pour en extraire le Baume, le sel fixe qui est le sang de notre[43] pierre.

19.	Repeated in MS.	28.	luy.	37.	couppé.
20.	masle.	29.	faisies.	38.	teste.
21.	reussirat.	30.	luy.	39.	ainsy.
22.	ainsy.	31.	pretieux.	40.	enseignes.
23.	excellament.	32.	pretieux.	41.	jetter.
24.	l'autheur.	33.	menstruë.	42.	l'Autheur.
25.	auries.	34.	estroittement.	43.	nostre.
26.	aves.	35.	mesme.		
27.	pretieux.	36.	ainsy.		

which is the white body or the moon which philosophers call white gold. This is the solution of the male by the female, for the white body contains the red, or the body its [female red] spirit.

But this solution would not succeed as well, as the author of the *Hermetic Triumph* excellently indicates, without the conjunction of the female. It is, he says, in their reciprocal embracements that they merge and change into one another. In vain would you have, he said, opened and sublimed the body of the stone; that is to say, the white earth which is the earth from which you have drawn this precious salt, if you did not make him marry the woman whom nature has destined for him; she is that spirit from which the body or salt derives its first origin. This precious salt dissolves like ice at the slightest heat from the fire. Now this precious salt, which he calls body, is made by the continual effusion of its own blood, which is its natural menstruum, with which it unites so closely and intimately that they are but one and the same substance. It is that substance which is the proximate matter from which the mercury of the philosophers is formed, as we shall say in the next chapter.

The whole secret therefore consists after having washed this dead and black earth and cutting off the head of the Raven, as we have taught; this earth must not be thrown away, for fire and sulphur are hidden in this earth which must be washed, says the author of the *Hermetic Triumph*, with its spirit to extract the Balm, the fixed salt which is the blood of our stone.

Laquelle opération ne s'accomplit qu'après une digestion convenable et par une lente distillation; C'est ce qui est confirmé par Hermès, il faut que par le moyen de l'âme aqueuse que nous ayons la forme sulfureuse[44] ce qui se fait par notre[45] vinaigre en la mêlant[46] avec ce dit vinaigre, car elle s'y dissout en la composant, et il devient très clair et très souverain.

Le Cosmopolite en a enseigné le moyen en peu de mots et il dit après avoir purgé vos éléments, faites-en[47] sorte que le feu et l'eau deviennent amis;[48] ce que vous ferez[49] ainsi,[50] en versant sur la terre, l'esprit qui en a été[51] tiré, et l'auteur[52] du triomphe Hermétique ajoute, page 134 ce que vous ferez[53] en abreuvant[54] la terre de son eau, car il faut que le corps soit dissout par l'eau et que la terre soit pénétrée de son humidité pour engendrer notre[55] fils du soleil qui est notre[56] mercure.

Ce mercure est formé de l'union de ces 2 substances dont l'un est l'esprit et le sel est le corps. C'est le volatil et le fixe qui joints ensemble qui sont néanmoins de même[57] nature et s'embrassent comme mâle[58] et la femelle et qui s'élèvent[59] ensemble insensiblement, paraissent[60] au haut du vaisseau[61] en manière de sel cristallin[62] qui se fond et se réduit en eau de lui-même,[63] et pour lors est aussi[64] different[65] de la 1ère[66] forme liquide; ainsi[67] que le remarque le triomphe Hermétique, page 135, que l'esprit de vin exactement rectifié et acué de son sel, est différent du vin dont il a été[68] tiré. Hermès dit que c'est cette eau dont nous avons plus de besoin dans notre[69] œuvre et qui sort de cette pierre, les philosophes cachent ces[70] opérations

44. surphureuse.	54. abbreuvant.	64. aussy.
45. noste.	55. nostre.	65. differente.
46. meslant.	56. nostre.	66. 1re.
47. faite en.	57. mesme.	67. ainsy.
48. amys.	58. masle.	68. este.
49. feres.	59. s'élevant.	69. nostre.
50. ainsy.	60. parroissent.	70. cette.
51. este.	61. vesseau.	
52. l'autheur.	62. cristalin.	
53. feres.	63. luy mesme.	

This operation is accomplished only after a suitable digestion, and by a slow distillation. This is confirmed by Hermes.
It is necessary that by means of the aqueous soul we have the
sulphurous form, which is done by our vinegar by mixing it
with this said vinegar, because it dissolves in the component,
and it becomes very clear and very sovereign.

The Cosmopolitan has taught the means in a few words,
and he says, after having purged your elements, make it so
that fire and water become friends, which you will do thus,
by pouring on the earth the spirit that has been drawn from
it. And the author of the *Hermetic Triumph* adds, page 134,
that you will do it by watering the earth with its water, for it
is necessary that the body be dissolved by water and the earth
be penetrated by its humidity to generate our son from the
sun which is our mercury.

This mercury is formed from the union of these two substances, one of which is the spirit, and the salt is the body. It
is the volatile and the fixed which join together, which are
nevertheless of the same nature and embrace as male and
female, and which rise together imperceptibly, appearing at
the top of the vessel in the manner of a crystalline salt that
melts and is reduced into water by itself, and for that reason
is also different from the first liquid form. As the *Hermetic
Triumph* remarks, page 135, the spirit of wine precisely rectified and sharpened[61] by its salt is different from the wine
from which it has been derived. Hermes says that it is this water that we need more in our work, which comes out of this
stone. The philosophers hide these operations by mixing it

---

61   *Acué* in the manuscript. In the *Hermetic Triumph*, the word has been
        translated as 'sharpened'.

en la mêlant[71] avec les précédentes. C'est pourquoi[72] il faut
que le sage Artiste y prenne garde, et je m'y serais[73] trompé
moi-même,[74] si je n'y avais[75] bien pris garde. L'Auteur[76] du
triomphe hermétique qui est le plus claire sur ces opérations,
joint celle dont nous venons de parler avec celle où l'on tire
l'esprit blanc et l'esprit rouge.

Le triomphe décrit[77] encore cette opération en ces termes; si vous ne blanchissez[78] ces fèces[79] féculentes[80] et noires
pour en séparer le soufre blanc, le sel armoniac des sages qui
est leur chaste Diane qui se lave dans le bain. Tout ce mystère[81]
n'est que l'extraction du sel fixe dans lequel consiste toute la
force de notre[82] mercure, l'eau qui s'élève[83] par distillation emporte avec elle une partie de ce sel igné,[84] de sorte que l'infusion de l'eau sur le corps réitérée plusieurs fois imprègne,
engraisse et féconde notre[85] mercure et le rend propre à être[86]
fixé, c'est à dire qu'il produit le mercure et l'eau qui compose
cette eau sèche.[87] C'est de ce sel que se forme le mercure des
philosophes, lorsqu'il est joint avec l'eau sèche[88] et humide
radicale des corps du soleil et de la lune. C'est le sel nitre[89]
du Cosmopolite[90] qui se réduit en eau qui compose cet admirable sel nitre qui étant[91] joint à l'humide radical,[92] forme
notre[93] mercure qui est appelé[94] l'eau de nitre [*aqua salis nitri
de terra nostra inquia est unda viva*]. Comme enseignent les
philosophes particulièrement dans le chapitre suivant.

71.	meslant.	80.	fæculentes.	89.	nistre.
72.	pourquoy.	81.	mistere.	90.	Cosmopolitte.
73.	serois.	82.	nostre.	91.	estant.
74.	moy mesme.	83.	s'esleve.	92.	radicale.
75.	avois.	84.	ignée.	93.	nostre.
76.	L'Autheur.	85.	nostre.	94.	appelle.
77.	d'escrit.	86.	estre.		
78.	blanchisses.	87.	seiche.		
79.	fæces.	88.	seiche.		

with the preceding ones. That is why the wise artist must be on guard, and I would have been deceived myself had I not been very careful. The author of the *Hermetic Triumph*, who is the clearest on these operations, joins that of which we have just spoken with that in which the white spirit and the red spirit are drawn.

The *Triumph* still describes this operation in these terms: if you do not whiten these feculent and black feces, you will not separate the white sulphur, the sal armoniac of the sages which is their chaste Diana who bathes herself in the bath. All this mystery is but the extraction of the fixed salt in which all the force of our mercury consists, the water which is elevated by distillation, carries with it a portion of this igneous salt, so that the infusion of the water on the body repeated several times impregnates, fattens, and fertilises our mercury and makes it proper to be fixed, i.e., that it produces the mercury and the water that compose this dry water. It is from this salt that the mercury of the philosophers is formed when it is joined with the dry water and radical humidity of the bodies of the sun and the moon. It is the nitre salt of the Cosmopolitan which is reduced to the water which composes this admirable nitre salt, which, being joined to the humid radical, forms our mercury, which is called the water of nitre (*aqua salis nitri de terra nostra in qua est unda viva*),[62] as the philosophers teach, especially in the next chapter.

---

62 Latin: 'water of salt-nitre from our earth, in which is a living wave [or stream]'. Cf. *De Lapide Philosophorum Tractatus Duodecim* (Twelve Treatises on the Philosopher's Stone) also known as *Novum Lumen Chymicum* (New Chemical Light), 1604, tractate XI: *Rx. Aqua salis nitri de terra nostra in qua est riuulus et vnda viua, si ad genuam foderis foveā*: 'Take the water of sal-niter from our earth in which there is a rivulet, living and undulating, if you dig a pit to the knees'.

De la Composition du grand dissolvant et du mercure des philosophes

PUISQUE JE NE PARLE QU'A VOUS VRAIS DISCIPLES[2] d'Hermès, je veux vous révéler un secret que vous ne trouverez[3] point entièrement dans les livres des philosophes; les uns se[4] sont contentes de dire que de leurs liqueurs, on en fait 2 mercures, ainsi[5] que le remarque le triomphe Hermétique page 141. L'un blanc et l'autre rouge dont Flamel remarque particulièrement l'usage disant qu'il faut se servir du mercure citrin pour les imbibitions au rouge; par conséquent du mercure blanc, comme disent d'autres philosophes e mercure blanc est le bain de la lune, et le mercure rouge le bain du soleil. Le mercure blanc est la lunaire et le mercure rouge est le vinaigre très aigre, comme dit le triomphe Hermétique.

Cette opération est précisément marquée par l'auteur[6] du triomphe Hermétique, page 14. Nourrissez,[7] dit-il, ces 2 mercures d'une chair[8] de leur[9] espèce,[10] le sang des innocents égorgés, c'est à dire, les esprits des corps sont le bain où l'or et la lune se vont baigner.

Le Cosmopolite[11] dit la même[12] chose en d'autres termes, notre[13] vieillard engloutira l'or et l'argent et seront tous les

---

1. 7me.
2. dissiples.
3. trouveres.
4. ce.
5. ainsy.
6. l'autheur.
7. Nourisses.
8. chaire.
9. leurs.
10. especes.
11. Cosmopolitte.
12. mesme.
13. nostre.

SEVENTH CHAPTER

Of the composition of the great solvent and the mercury of the philosophers

SINCE I SPEAK ONLY TO YOU, TRUE DISCIPLES OF Hermes, I wish to reveal to you a secret which you will not find entirely in the books of the philosophers. Some are content to say that of their liquors are made of two mercuries, as the *Hermetic Triumph* remarks on page 141, the one white and the other red. Flamel in particular notes the usage, saying that one must use the citrine mercury for the ablutions to the red; consequently for the white mercury, as other philosophers say, the white mercury is the bath of the moon, and the red mercury the bath of the sun; the white mercury is the Lunaria and the red mercury is the sharpest vinegar, as the *Hermetic Triumph* says.

This operation is precisely marked by the author of the *Hermetic Triumph*, page 14.[63] Nourish, he says, these two mercuries with a flesh of their species, the blood of the slaughtered innocents, that is to say, the spirits of the bodies are the bath where the gold and the moon go to bathe.

The Cosmopolitan says the same thing, in other words: our old man will devour gold and silver and both will be

---

63   The reference is on page 142 of *Le Triomphe Hermetique* (1699), not page 14.

deux consommés après leur mort.[14] Le vieillard comme l'explique le triomphe Hermétique, est notre[15] mercure, puis qu'il est la 1ère[16] matière des métaux qui est l'eau sèche[17] de Geber et l'humide onctueux qui est la matière prochaine de notre[18] pierre qui contient le soufre et le mercure des sages tant le soufre blanc qui est extrait du corps de la lune que le soufre qui renferme le corps rouge qui contient tout ce qui est nécessaire a l'œuvre et qui est appelé[19] le mercure animé et le mercure double et d'autres rebis qui ne perd jamais sa vertu, étant[20] enfermé dans une bouteille de verre bien blanche, ainsi[21] que le dit le triomphe Hermétique page 144.

Vous voyez[22] par là, le mérite de cette précieuse[23] liqueur à laquelle les philosophes donnent[24] mille différents noms, elle est l'eau de vie des sages, l'eau de diane, la grande lunaire, elle est notre[25] mercure, notre[26] huile incombustible qui au froid se congèle et se liquéfie à la chaleur. Hermès l'appelle la terre des feuilles,[27] C'est la fontaine du Comte de Trévisan, C'est le grande alkaest,[28] dit le triomphe, qui dissout radicalement[29] les métaux, elle est la véritable eau permanente qui dissout les corps parfaits et les unit inséparablement à eux, et en augmente le poids et la teinture.

Philalèthe[30] décrit[31] cette opération un peu autrement. Notre[32] mercure, dit-il, animé, quoi[33] qu'épuré n'est pas encore coagulé, mais est encore volatil, il n'est point encore parfait jusqu'à ce qu'il ne laisse aucune fèces,[34] ni[35] résidence dans le vaisseau;[36] pour lors ce sel philosophique s'appelle un soleil indigeste qui n'est pas encore mûr.[37] C'est leur lune vive, C'est

14. morts.	22. voyes.	30. Philalette.
15. nostre.	23. pretieuse.	31. d'escrit.
16. 1re.	24. donnes.	32. Nostre.
17. seiche.	25. nostre.	33. quoy
18. nostre.	26. nostre.	34. fæces.
19. appellé.	27. fæuilles.	35. ny.
20. estant.	28. alkaet.	36. vesseau.
21. ainsy.	29. radicallement.	37. mure.

consumed after their deaths.[64] The old man, as the *Hermetic Triumph* explains, is our mercury, since it is the first matter of metals, which is the dry water of Geber, and the unctuous humidity which is the proximate matter of our stone, which contains the sulphur and the mercury of the sages, both the white sulphur which is extracted from the body of the moon, and the sulphur which contains the red body, which contains all that is necessary to the work, and which is called animated mercury and double mercury, and by others, *rebis*, which never loses its virtue, being enclosed in a bottle of glass, well-sealed,[65] as the *Hermetic Triumph* says on page 144.

By this you see the merit of that precious liquor to which the philosophers give a thousand different names: it is the water of life of the sages, the water of Diana, the great Lunaria, it is our mercury, our incombustible oil which congeals in the cold and liquefies in the heat. Hermes calls it the earth of the leaves, it is the fountain of Count Trevisan, it is the great Alkahest, says the *Triumph*, which radically dissolves the metals, it is the true permanent water which dissolves the perfect bodies and unites inseparably with them, increasing the weight and tincture.

Philalethes describes this operation a little differently. Our animated mercury, he says, although purified, is not yet coagulated, but is still volatile, it is not yet perfect until it leaves no feces or sediment[66] in the vessel; for at that time the philosophic salt is called an undigested sun, which is not yet mature. It is their living moon, it is the true and first being of

---

64   *De Lapide Philosophorum Tractatus Duodecim*, 1604, tractate XI.

65   While the text uses the expression *bien blanche* (i.e., *bien blanché*, 'well whitened'), this appears to be an error, since the passage from *The Hermetic Triumph* that he quotes actually says *bien bouché* ('well sealed').

66   *Résidence*, 'residuum'.

le véritable et premier être[38] de l'or, étant[39] encore volatil et le champ dans lequel le soleil est semé. C'est pourquoi[40] les 1er[41] philosophes dit-il, par ce moyen, le fixe fut fait volatil, le dur rendu mou,[42] le coagulé fut dissout, C'est pourquoi[43] ils mirent les 2 choses ensemble, les enfermèrent dans un vaisseau[44] de verre et les mirent sur le feu, et un autre endroit, il dit encore, vous devez[45] savoir[46] que notre[47] œuvre demande[48] un véritable changement de Nature; ce qui ne se peut faire si la dernière union de 2 natures, C'est à dire du fixe et du volatil ne se fait et ne peuvent finir qu'en forme d'eau, car il ne se fait point d'union des corps, mais c'est seulement un broiement;[49] Car il n'y a que les esprits qui se pourraient[50] bien unir ensemble. C'est pourquoi[51] pour l'union de nos mercures, il faut une eau métallique, homogène à laquelle on prépare la voie[52] par la calcination qui à précédé et qui se fait auparavant par un dessèchement[53] qui est proprement une dissolution ou réduction en atomes[54] de l'eau avec la terre par le crible de la Nature, c'est-à-dire, et les atomes[55] de l'eau sont plus déliés[56] et plus subtilisés[57] que l'eau ne requiert[58] et qu'il n'est nécessaire, afin que la terre reçoive le fermentatif de l'eau.

Le Triomphe le dit encore plus positivement; réduisez,[59] dit-il, tout le composé en eau, et faites[60] une parfaite union du volatil et du fixe, l'eau qui s'élève[61] par distillation emporte avec elle, une partie de ce sel igné, de sorte[62] que l'effusion de l'eau sur le corps réitérée plusieurs fois, imprègne,[63] engraisse

38.	estre.	47.	nostre.	56.	déliées.
39.	estant.	48.	demende.	57.	subtilisées.
40.	pourquoy.	49.	broyement.	58.	requiere.
41.	irs.	50.	pourront.	59.	reduises.
42.	mol.	51.	pourquoy.	60.	faite.
43.	pourquoy.	52.	voye.	61.	s'esleve.
44.	vesseau.	53.	deseichement.	62.	sort.
45.	deves.	54.	atosme.	63.	impreigne.
46.	sçavoir.	55.	atosmes.		

gold, being still volatile; [it is] the field in which the sun is sown. That is why the first philosophers, he says, by this means, made the fixed volatile, the hard soft, the coagulated dissolved; that is why they put the two things together, enclosed them in a glass vessel, and put them on the fire. And in another place, he says again, you must know that our work demands a true change of Nature; which cannot be done if the last union of two natures, that is to say, of the fixed and the volatile, is not done, and can only end in the form of water; because there is no union of the bodies, but it is only a grinding; because only the spirits can unite well together. This is why, for the union of our mercuries, a metallic, homogeneous water is required, for which the way is prepared by calcination, which is a prerequisite, and which is previously made by a drying out which is properly a dissolution or reduction into atoms of the water with the earth, through the sieve of nature, that is to say. And the atoms of water are more loosened and more subtilised than water requires and which is necessary, so that the earth receives the fermentative from the water.

The *Triumph* says it even more positively; reduce, says he, the whole compound to water, and make a perfect union of the volatile and the fixed, the water which rises by distillation carries with it a part of this igneous salt, so that the effusion of the water on the body, repeated several times, permeates,

et féconde[64] notre[65] mercure et le rend propre à être[66] fixé qui est le but et le terme du 2ème[67] œuvre.

[Ce qu'il faut fait après que le soleil a esté[68] dissous par le mercure].[69] Cette opération quoique[70] déjà assez[71] parfaite n'a pas encore acquis sa dernière et parfaite dépuration; C'est pourquoi[72] mettez[73] la dans un matras proportionné; en sorte que les 3 quarts de celui-ci[74] soit vides[75] et duquel le col doit avoir pour le moins 8 pouces[76] de hauteur.[77] Cela fait, bouchez[78] l'orifice du matras et le mettez[79] aux cendres qui surpassent au moins la matière d'un doigt;[80] en cet état vous ferez[81] circuler vos matières pendant un mois philosophique, afin[82] qu'elles s'unissent bien ensemble et dans la conjonction de ces 2 substances, il se fera[83] un combat et vous apercevrez[84] dans ce vaisseau,[85] monter et descendre[86] des fumées des nuées et des brouillards qui procèdent du soufre et de l'écume[87] de ces 2 Dragons qui combattent et se dévorent l'un et l'autre, jusqu'à ce que de ces deux, il ne s'en fasse qu'un,[88] alors le calme et la sérénité[89] paraissent[90] dans le vaisseau[91] et la mer des philosophes est toute tranquille par la cessation des vents et des orages que la fureur de nos 2 combattants[92] y avait[93] excité, et après que la mer a tué le serpent Python[94] qui voulait[95] la dévorer.

Chermeze nous marque cette opération en ces termes. Quand je verrais[96] toute la grosseur de l'eau se durcir et que je les verrais[97] sensiblement commencer à devenir à cet état,

64. fæconde.	76. poulces.	87. l'escume.
65. nostre.	77. d'authur or	88. qu'une.
66. estre.	d'auteur.	89. cerenité.
67. 2me.	78. bouché.	90. parroist.
68. eté.	79. mettes.	91. vesseau.
69. Marginal note.	80. doit.	92. combatants.
70. Quoyque.	81. feres.	93. avoit.
71. assée.	82. affin.	94. Pithon.
72. pourquoy.	83. ferat.	95. vouloit.
73. mettes.	84. apperceveres.	96. voires.
74. d'iceluy.	85. vesseau.	97. verres.
75. vuides.	86. dessendre.	

fattens, and fertilises our mercury and makes it proper to be fixed, which is the purpose and the end of the second work.

[That which must be done after the sun has been dissolved by the mercury].[67] This operation, although already quite perfect, has not yet acquired its last and perfect depuration. That is why [you] put it in an adequate matrass, so that three quarters of it is empty, and the neck must be at least eight-inches high.[68] This done, plug the orifice of the matrass and put it in ashes which surpass the matter by at least a finger. In this state, circulate your matters for a philosophical month so that they will unite well together and in the conjunction of these two substances, there will be a fight and you will see in this vessel ascending and descending fumes, clouds and mists which proceed from the sulphur and foam of these two Dragons, who fight and devour each other, until these two become one. Then calmness and serenity appears in the vessel, and the sea of the philosophers is completely tranquil due to the cessation of the winds and storms which the fury of our two fighters had excited there, after that the sea has killed the serpent Python that wanted to devour it.

Hermes[69] marks this operation in these terms. When I see the fullness of the water harden and I see them noticeably begin to develop into this state, then I will rejoice, for then I

---

67   Marginal note in manuscript.

68   The manuscript has *d'authur* or *d'auteur*, but the intention appears to be *de hauteur* (of height).

69   The manuscript has 'Chermeze', a probable scribal error for 'Hermes'. Variant versions of this passage (about the 'water' gradually solidifying being a sure sign that the operator is on the right track) were variously attributed to Khalid and Hermes in Arabic and Latin sources. For an example from an Arabic source attributing it to Khalid, see: H. E. Stapleton, G. L. Lewis, and F. Sherwood Taylor, 'The Sayings of Hermes quoted in the Mā' Al-Waraqī of Ibn Umail', in *Ambix*, vol. 3, (April, 1949), nos. 3–4, p. 77. For an example from a Latin source attributing it to Hermes see: *Gloria Mundi*, reprinted in *Musæum Hermeticum Reformatum et Amplificatum* (Frankfurt, 1678), p. 301.

alors je me réjouirai,[98] pour lors je serai[99] sûr[100] d'avoir trouvé ce que je cherchais.[101] Étant[102] en cet état, tirez[103] l'eau du matras sans brouiller le fond par inclination ou par une languette de draps et la mettez[104] dans une retorte proportionnée pour la rectifier pour la dernière fois à feu de sable par degrés;[105] que si toutefois il restait[106] quelques fèces[107] dans la retorte, après la distillation, il faudrait[108] cohober et distiller tant de fois qu'il n'y reste plus rien et que tout passe dans le récipient. Alors vous aurez[109] le mercure parfait de l'or, vous en ferez[110] de même[111] du mercure parfait de la lune.

C'est la fin du 1ère[112] œuvre que beaucoup d'Auteurs[113] confondent avec le 2ème,[114] mêlant[115] les opérations qui regardent la 1ère[116] ou passant la 1ère[117] font de la seconde leur première, ce qui donne beaucoup d'embarras[118] aux novices et commençants.[119]

Enfin vous étés[120] présentement persuadé de que d'un sujet vil, nous en tirons une précieuse[121] liqueur formée d'un esprit très subtile et le volatil et d'une[122] huile très fixe qui étant[123] réunis[124] l'un à l'autre, s'embrassent pour ne se quitter jamais; ainsi[125] le corps reprenant son esprit, devient immortel et glorieux[126] comme lui.[127]

Les Sages nous ont exprimé[128] tout ceci[129] par un serpent qui se mord la queue et dont ils ont orné[130] le caducée de mercure.

98. rejouyres.	109. aures.	120. este.
99. seray.	110. enferes.	121. pretieux.
100. sçure.	111. mesme.	122. d'un.
101. chercois.	112. 1r.	123. estant.
102. Estant.	113. d'Autheurs.	124. réunie.
103. tires.	114. 2me.	125. ainsy.
104. mettes.	115. meslant.	126. glorieuse.
105. degré.	116. 1re.	127. luy.
106. restoit.	117. 1re.	128. exprimes.
107. fæces.	118. dembaras.	129. cecy.
108. faudra.	119. commen-sants.	130. ornes.

will be sure to have found what I was looking for. While it is in this condition, draw the water from the matrass without disturbing the bottom, by inclination, or by a strip of cloth, and put it in an adequate retort to rectify it for the last time on a sand fire by degrees. If, however, some feces remain in the retort after the distillation, it should be cohobated and distilled so often until nothing remains, and everything passes into the receiver. Then you will have the perfect mercury of gold; do the same with the perfect mercury of the moon.

This is the end of the first work that many authors confuse with the second, mingling the operations which concern the first, or passing the first to make the second their first, which brings a great deal of embarrassment to novices and beginners.

Finally, you have now been persuaded that from a vile subject we derive a precious liquor formed of a very subtle and volatile spirit and a very fixed oil, which being united to each other, embrace, never to leave each other. Thus the body, recovering its spirit, becomes immortal and glorious like the spirit.

The Sages have expressed all this to us by a serpent which bites its tail, which they adorn with the caduceus of mercury.

Flamel nous représente la même[131] chose par 2 Dragons
qui se dévorent par ses figures hiéroglyphiques,[132] ils nous veulent faire entendre que leur mercure est tiré de 2 substances
d'une même[133] racine, l'une des quelles est fixe et l'autre volatile,[134] une corporelle et l'autre spirituelle; quelques philosophes l'appellent le lait[135] de la vierge et l'enfant que l'on tire du
ventre de sa mère, l'esprit que nous tirons, est le lait[136] ou le fils
de cette vierge mère et le sel ou l'huile fixe est la mère de ce
même[137] fils; et d'autres disent qu'il faut que le fils rentre dans
le ventre de sa mère, ce qui nous marque l'union et la mariage
philosophique de ces 2 substances. C'est pourquoi[138] après
avoir tiré par l'esprit le sel fixe dont nous avons parlé[139] et que
nous les avons suffisamment[140] purifié,[141] nous les unissons
ensemble, afin que la conjonction de ce corps avec cet esprit
étant[142] faite, il en résulte le dissolvant universel et le mercure
des philosophes.

Quant à son origine, je vous ai[143] fait[144] remarquer au
commencement de cet ouvrage qu'il[145] venait[146] du Ciel et
des influences des astres; que c'était[147] un esprit qui descend[148]
imperceptiblement du Ciel en terre et qu'il était[149] cet esprit
universel qui régénère dans les entrailles virginales[150] de la
terre que les philosophes mettent au jour et qu'ils font re-
naître[151] ce phœnix dans ces cendres. Nous avons dit encore
qu'il tire toute sa force et sa vertu de cet esprit invisible que
l'air porte en son ventre pour en grossir la terre qui est la femelle qui se joint au soufre qui est le mâle;[152] et du concours[153]
de ces deux substances, il en résulte la semence prolifique, de

131. mesme.	140. suffisament.	149. estoit.
132. hieroglifiques.	141. purifies.	150. virginalles.
133. mesme.	142. estant.	151. renaistre.
134. volatille.	143. ais.	152. masle.
135. laiet.	144. fais.	153. concour.
136. laiet.	145. quelle.	
137. mesme.	146. venoit.	
138. pourquoy.	147. C'estoit.	
139. parles.	148. dessendoit.	

Flamel represents for us the same thing in his *Hieroglyph-ic Figures* by two dragons that devour themselves; they [i.e., the philosophers] want us to understand that their mercury is drawn from two substances of the same root, one of which is fixed and the other volatile, one corporeal and the other spiritual; some philosophers call it the milk of the virgin and the child drawn from the belly of its mother; the spirit which we draw is the milk or the son of this virgin mother, and the salt or fixed oil is the mother of this same son. Others say that the son must return to the womb of its mother, which marks for us the union and philosophical marriage of these two substances. That is why after having drawn out the fixed salt of which we have spoken by means of the spirit, and hav-ing sufficiently purified it, we unite them together so that the conjunction of this body with this spirit is accomplished. This results in the universal solvent and the mercury of the philosophers.

As to its origin, I have pointed out to you at the begin-ning of this work that it came from Heaven and the influ-ences of the stars; that it was a spirit which descended im-perceptibly from Heaven to earth. It was this universal spirit, which regenerates in the virginal entrails[70] of the earth, that the philosophers bring to light, whose rebirth they bring about like the phœnix from the ashes. We have also said again that it derives all its strength and virtue from that invisible spirit which the air carries in its belly to enlarge the earth, which is the female that joins herself to the sulphur which is the male. The concurrence of these two substances results in the prolific seed, of which the earth is the matrix and

70 *Les entrailles*, 'entrails, innards', but also 'depths, womb', thus the 'vir-ginal depths' or 'virginal womb' of the earth.

laquelle la terre est la matrice et l'aimant,[154] ainsi[155] que le dit
le grand Hermès dans sa table d'émeraude[156] qui fût trouvée
dans son sépulcre après le Déluge en la vallée d'Ebron, le
soleil en est le père, dit-il, et la lune la mère et est porté[157] par
les vents dans le sein de la terre, comme entre les bras mater-
nels[158] de sa nourrice pour s'y cacher à nos yeux jusqu'à ce que
l'industrie du sage le fasse paraître[159] en le faisant sortir par
le secours[160] du feu du sujet où il est caché, ainsi[161] que nous
l'avons enseigné.[162]

   C'est donc ce même[163] esprit qui descend[164] d'en haut du
ciel dans le centre de la terre où il commence à se coaguler par
la vertu de son sel hermaphrodite[165] qui est son aimant[166] que
les philosophes appellent leur acier, parce qu'il attire continuellement cet esprit et le retient en le coagulant. C'est ce sel im-
prégné de la vertu céleste qu'il faut tirer avec grande industrie,
comme dit Hermès, vous séparerez[167] subtilement[168] et adroitement la terre du feu secret et avec grand esprit et doucement
de l'épais;[169] mais prenez[170] garde de ne pas étouffer[171] le feu
de cette terre par les eaux du déluge. C'est ce Roi[172] qui descend[173] du Ciel, c'est l'âme qu'il faut rendre à son corps qui
doit le ressusciter. Ce sont ses paroles, c'est l'eau divine est
le Roi[174] descendu[175] du Ciel qui rappelle l'âme à son corps
et qui derechef lui[176] rend la vie de mort qu'il était.[177] Par là,
vous voyez[178] que cette quintessence spirituelle et invisible est
maintenant rendue visible et corporelle. C'est ce fils du lys
qui renaît du ventre de sa mère par distillation. C'est ce fils

154. l'ayman.	163. mesme.	172. Roy.
155. ainsy.	164. dessend.	173. dessend.
156. d'hemeraude.	165. hermaphroditte.	174. Roy.
157. portée.	166. aymant.	175. dessendu.
158. maternelle.	167. seapares.	176. luy.
159. parroistre.	168. subtillement.	177. estoit.
160. secour.	169. l'espais.	178. voyes.
161. ainsy.	170. prenes.	
162. enseignes.	171. ettouffer.	

the magnet, as the great Hermes says in his *Emerald Tablet,* which was found in his sepulchre after the Deluge in the valley of Hebron. The sun is its father, he says, and the moon the mother, and it is carried by the winds in the bosom of the earth, as in the maternal embrace of its wet nurse. This is to hide it from our eyes until the industry of the sage makes it appear, releasing it with the help of the fire which comes from the subject in which it is hidden, as we have taught.

It is therefore this same spirit which descends from above the heavens into the center of the earth, where it begins to coagulate itself by the virtue of its hermaphroditic salt, which is its magnet, which the philosophers call their steel because it continually attracts this spirit and retains it by coagulating it. It is this salt, impregnated with the celestial virtue, which must be drawn with great industry, as Hermes says. You must subtly and skillfully separate the earth from the secret fire, gently and with great spirit [separating it] from its density; but be careful not to smother the fire of this earth by the waters of the flood. It is this King who descends from Heaven. It is the soul, which must be restored to its body, that must resurrect him. These are his words: it is the divine water, [it] is the King descended from Heaven who recalls the soul to its body and who again restores life to that which was dead. By this you see that this invisible, spiritual quintessence is now made visible and corporeal. It is this son of the lily who is reborn from his mother's womb by distillation. It is this son, too, whom the industrious artist knows how to draw from his mother's

aussi[179] que l'industrieux Artiste sait[180] tirer du ventre de sa mère et qui après rend féconde[181] sa mère, et par ce moyen elle engendre des enfants à l'infini.[182] C'est pourquoi les sages font dire au Mercure, la mère qui m'a engendré par moi[184] a été[185] engendrée[186] et par ce fils spirituel, elle est aussi[187] sans cesse en état de régénérer ce fils et le reproduire. Vous avez[188] pour lors tous les éléments fixes et dans leur repos propre à souffrir la grande digestion. Faute de ce, plusieurs n'ayant pas fait cette paix et voulant commencer une longue digestion, les éléments se sont divisés, raréfiés, leurs[189] vaisseaux[190] ce sont cassés et ont perdus tous leur ouvrage; quoi[191] qu'ils travaillassent sur la vraie[192] matière.

Fin de cet
œuvre

179. aussy.	185. este.	191. quoy.
180. sçait.	186. engendré.	192. vrais.
181. fæconde.	187. aussy.	
182. l'infiny.	188. aves.	
183. pourquoy.	189. leur.	
184. moy.	190. vesseaux.	

womb, and who afterwards renders his mother fertile, and by this means engenders children infinitely. This is why the sages make Mercury say: the mother who has engendered me, has been engendered by me, and by this spiritual son she is also ceaslessly in a state of regenerating this son and reproducing him. You therefore have all the elements [you need], fixed and in their own proper repose, to suffer the great digestion. Lacking this, many who have not attained this peace have wanted to begin a long digestion: the elements have divided and rarefied, their vessels have shattered, and they have lost all their work—even if they were working on the true matter.

End of this
work

Table de ce qui est contenu dans ce manuscrit, qui peut servir d'instruction abrégée[1]

CHAPITRE IER[2]

L'Ecriture Sainte[3] compare la couleur verte[4] avec l'or.

Dieu a caché aux hommes la connaissance[5] de la matière.

La matière est unique dans son principe et la nature agit dans les mêmes principes.

Les philosophes se[6] sont servis de deux différentes voies[7] pour l'œuvre; la 1ère[8] qui coûte beaucoup regarde de l'art, la 2éme,[9] regarde la nature et qui est de peu de dépences.

Ces voies[10] quoique[11] différentes dans leurs operations etc.

Les philosophes disent que l'alchimie en a trouvé encore d'autres qu'ils rapportent pour exemples.

La matiere en generale est renfermée dans des corps impurs.

CHAPITRE 2ÈME[12]

La matière en particulier est une humidité onctueuse,[13] elle se cache dans le centre des éléments,[14] le feu n'a aucun pouvoir sur elle

1.	abregé.	5.	connoissance.	10.	voyes.
2.	1r.	6.	ce.	11.	quoyque.
3.	Ste.	7.	voyes.	12.	2me.
4.	Likely meant verre.	8.	1re.	13.	honctueuse.
		9.	2me.	14.	elemens.

Table of what is contained in this manuscript, which can serve as an abridged instruction

FIRST CHAPTER

The Holy Scripture likens the green[71] colouration with gold.
God has hidden from men the knowledge of the matter.
The matter is unique in its principle and nature works according to the same principles.
The philosophers have made use of two different ways for the work: the first costs much and concerns art; the second concerns nature and costs little.
These different ways differ however in the operations, etc.
The philosophers say how alchemy came to be discovered and still others who report by examples.
The matter is generally enclosed within impure bodies.

SECOND CHAPTER

The matter in particular is an unctuous humidity, it hides in the center of the elements, fire does not have any power over it

---

71   This appears at first to be a typographic or scribal error, since the biblical context implies *verre* (glass) and not *verte* (green). In the Book of Revelation 21:21, the streets of the new Jerusalem are of pure gold and transparent like glass. However, our text also speaks about 'colouration', and so the author must have undoubtedly meant the colour green, not 'glass'.

Cette matière, quoique[15] fixe, se volatilise par les elements.[16]

Cette matière renferme le feu des sages.

Le temps[17] de la cueillir.[18] Et de deux spermes la matière du mercure est formée.

Le philosophe doit imiter la nature que Dieu a formé pour le commerce du ciel et de la terre, en imitant Dieu dans la création du ☉ [monde].

Le philosophe[19] tire de ces 2 luminaires et de ces éléments[20] toutes les terrestres;[21] ils en font un composé ou un Elixir.

Dieu donne cette science à qui il lui[22] plait.

Il n'est pas difficile à l'homme d'avoir la pierre, mais il lui est impossible de déterminer la matière.

La matière se trouve partout.

La dépence de l'œuvre est modique et le sujet de la matière est vil quoique précieux.[23]

CHAPITRE 3ÈME[24]

De la préparation des élements[25] et de leur séparation en général

On ne change rien de la matière et ce qui parait[26] impur, on le change en un plus pur, qui est le feu de Pontanus. Remarquez[27] bien le reste.

Espèce de séparation de substance dans le 1er[28] et le 2ème[29] œuvre.

Dieu a tout créé par nombre, poids, et mesure.

Dans le 1er[30] œuvre, il y a quelque séparation, c'est la nature qui fait et dans la 2ème[31] c'est l'Artiste qui le sépare.

15. quoyque.	21. terrestreites.	27. Remarqué.
16. elemens.	22. luy.	28. 1r.
17. tems.	23. pretieux.	29. 2me.
18. ceüillir.	24. 3me.	30. 1r.
19. pphe.	25. elemens.	31. 2me.
20. elemens.	26. paroit.	

This matter, though fixed, is volatilised by the elements.

This matter encloses the fire of the sages.

The time of collection. And from two sperms the matter of the mercury is formed.

The philosopher should imitate the nature that God has formed via the commerce of heaven and earth, imitating God in the creation of the ☉ [world].[72]

The philosopher draws from these two luminaries and from these elements all of the grossest parts; they make from them a compound or an Elixir.

God gives this science to whoever he pleases.

It is not difficult for man to have the stone, but it is impossible for him to determine the matter.

The matter is found everywhere.

The expense of the work is modest and the subject or matter is vile, though precious.

THIRD CHAPTER

*Of the preparation of the elements and their
separation in general*

One doesn't change anything of the matter and what appears to be impure, one changes into [something] purer, which is the fire of Pontanus. Take good notice of the residue.

The type of separation of the substance in the first and second work.

God created everything through number, weight, & measure.

In the first work there is some separation, which is made by nature, and in the second it is the Artist that separates.

72   The cruciferous globe used here symbolises earth or antimony.

198 LA CLEF DU CABINET HERMÉTIQUE

Les substances unies ensemble forment une eau appellée argent vif.

Cette eau est très cachée, son origine vient de l'air, il la faut
prendre à l'heure de sa naissance.

C'est l'eau et le feu des philosophes,[32] c'est dans cette eau qu'ils
introduisent leur feu, lequel s'accorde avec l'eau et qui est
la clé[33] de l'œuvre.

CHAPITRE 4ÈME[34]

Des elements[35] en particulier
et de leurs préparations

La matière se trouve partout, mais les philosophes[36] ont un
sujet particulier.

Il faut prendre le sujet dans le moment et dans le lieu de sa
naissance par méditation.

Il faut les dépouiller des corps impurs.

Il ne faut pas s'attacher aux paroles mais au sens de la chose et
a ce qu'elles signifient.

Il ne faut pas s'attacher à l'extérieur des principes, mais à leur
intérieur, et joindre l'humide avec le sec, le feu avec l'eau,
le chaud avec le froid.

Ce travaille ne passe pas les forces de l'homme.

CHAPITRE 5ÈME[37]

Des opérations en général

Il y a 12 opérations génerales qui sont autant de clés[38] pour
ouvrir les portes du cabinet hermetique.

La calcination de l'œuvre ne se fait pas par le feu, la matière se
calcine elle-même.

32. pphes.	35. elemens.	38. clefs.
33. clef.	36. pphes.	
34. 4me.	37. 5me.	

The substances unite together and form a water which is
  called *argent vive.*
This water is very hidden, and its origin is from the air; one
  must take it in its hour of nativity.
It is the water and the fire of the philosophers, it is in this
  water that they introduce their fire, which accords with
  the water and is the key to the work.

FOURTH CHAPTER

Of the elements in particular and their preparations

The matter is found everywhere, but the philosophers have a
  particular subject [in mind for use].
One must take the matter in the moment and place of its
  birth by meditation.
One must strip them [the elements] from the impure bodies.
One must not be attached to words but rather the sense of
  the thing and what they signify.
One must not be attached to the exterior of the principles,
  but their interior, and join the humid to the dry, fire to
  water, the warm to the cold.
This work does not go beyond the capacities of man.

FIFTH CHAPTER

Of the operations in general

There are twelve general operations which are as many as the
  keys for unlocking the gates of the hermetic sanctum.[73]
The calcination of the work is not made through fire, the matter calcines itself.

---

73   *Cabinet* (see Preface).

La rubification est comprise sous la calcination; la trituration précède presque toujours la calcination; broyer la
matière, c'est la nature qui le fait et qui la met en poudre.

Cette trituration se[39] fait lorsque la terre commence à se sublimer, qui est la 3ème[40] préparation donnée au sujet.

La dissolution est la réduction d'un corps en eau par réitérée
lotion, toute la matière se réduit en eau, c'est ce feu qui se
convertit en eau.

C'est dans cette operation, que la pierre se dissout elle-même,
la main de l'artiste est nécessaire à cette dissolution.

Cette operation est la clé[41] des 7 portes, la 1ère[42] donne entrée
à la 2ème[43], la 2ème[44] la donne à la 3ème,[45] ainsi[46] jusqu'à
la 7ème.[47] Cette dissolution précède la calcination, qui
est la plus essentielle de l'œuvre.

La sublimation est une purification du sujet qui rejette les
impuretés maternelles où le corps se crible et par ce moy-
en, l'eau devenant plus subtile,[48] elle attire à elle l'âme du
soleil.

On a pas besoin detant de vaisseaux,[49] les vaisseaux[50] sont les
elements.[51]

La distillation est souvent confonduë par le terme de sublimation.

Remarquez[52] le reste.

L'esprit blanc et l'esprit solaire[53] de notre corps, qui sont les 2
premiers luminaires, le mercure blanc et lemercure rouge.

L'inhumation, est une opération essentielle dans l'oeuvre;
c'est de rendre la terre spirituelle et de spirituelle la rendre corporelle, le volatil le rendre fixe et rendre le fixe
plus parfait.

---

39. ce.
40. 3me.
41. clef.
42. 1re.
43. 2 me.
44. 2me.
45. 3me.
46. ainsy.
47. 7me.
48. subtille.
49. vesseaux.
50. vesseaux.
51. elemens.
52. Remarqués.
53. solaires.

The rubification is included under the calcination; the trituration almost always precedes the calcination; the trituration of the matter is done by nature who turns it into powder.

This trituration is made when the earth starts to sublimate, which is the third preparation given to the subject.

The dissolution is the reduction of a body into water by repeated washing, the whole matter is reduced to water, it is this fire that converts itself into water.

It is in this operation that the stone dissolves itself, the hand of the artist is necessary in this dissolution.

This operation is the key to the seven gates: the first gives the entry to the second, the second [gives entry] to the third, and so on until the seventh [gate]. This dissolution precedes the calcination, which is the most essential [operation] of the work.

Sublimation is a purification of the subject which gets rid of the maternal impurities, or the body is sieved in this way, the water becomes more subtle and attracts to it the soul of the sun.

One doesn't need so many vessels, the vessels are the elements.

The distillation is often confused with the term sublimation.

Take notice of the residue.

The white spirit and the solar spirit of our body are the two first luminaries, the white mercury and the red mercury.

Inhumation is an essential operation in the work; it is to make the earth spiritual and from the spiritual make it corporeal, make the volatile fixed and make the fixed more perfect.

C'est par cette opération qu'on blanchit le noir et qu'on coupe la tête[54] au corbeau.

Voire, par un feu continuel, une rozée monter dans le vaisseau[55] et un espèce de brouillard qui retombent incessamment nuit et jour.

Le corps communique sa fixité à l'eau et l'eau communique sa volatilité au corps.

La lotion est de blanchir le corps noire par réitérée imbibition de son eau dont il a été tiré pour le 1er[56] et le 2ème[57] œuvre.

L'union des 2 mercures blanc et rouge qui sont 2 substances pour faire le mercure animé et le mercure citrin de la 1ère[58] operation.

Cette opération se[59] fait encore pour joinder la lune au corps du soleil, c'est l'union du mâle[60] et de la femelle du derniere oeuvre de la 1ère[61] partie.

La putréfaction est la génération des substances lunaires et solaires d'où procèdent les luminaires. Ce sont les petits Corbeaux qui sortent de leurs nids et qu'il faut empêcher[62] qu'ils n'y entrent.

C'est le temps[63] qu'il faut bien gouverner le feu et ne pas laisser dessécher[64] la matière tout à fait et empêcher que les petits corbeaux ne retournent dans leurs nids qui sont des petits atomes.[65]

La coagulation, la fixation, et la nutrition regardent la 2ème[66] partie de l'œuvre qui est multiplication.

54. teste.	59. ce.	64. deseicher.
55. vesseau.	60. masle.	65. atosmes.
56. 1re.	61. 1re.	66. 2me.
57. 2me.	62. empescher.	
58. 1re.	63. tems.	

It is by this operation that one whitens the black and cuts the head off the raven.

Look, by a continual fire a dew arises in the vessel and a sort of fog settles incessantly night and day.

The body communicates its fixity to the water and the water communicates its volatility to the body.

Washing is to make the black body white through repeated ablutions of its water, from which it has been drawn during the first and second work.

The union of the two mercuries, white and red, which are the two substances for making the animated mercury and the citrine mercury of the first operation.

This operation is again made for joining the moon to the body of the sun, it is the union of the male and female of the last work of the first part.

Putrefaction is the generation of the lunar and solar substances from which the luminaries proceed. These are the little ravens that fly out of their nests and which one must hinder from entering.

It is the moment when one must carefully govern the fire and not allow it to dry out the matter completely, and to prevent the little ravens from returning to their nests, which are the little atoms.

Coagulation, fixation, and nutrition concerns the second part of the work which is multiplication.

DEUXIÈME PARTIE
SES OPÉRATIONS EN PARTICULIER,
NÉCESSAIRES POUR LA PRATIQUE

Se donner de garde les philosophes[67] écrivent,[68] car ils confondent et mettent dans les operations; ce qui doit être au commencement, ils le mettent à la fin; et la fin au commencement.

La pierre se[69] fait de 2 sortes de façons.

L'auteur de ce livre dit qu'il entend parler de l'oeuvre des anciens et il défend[70] la lecture de certains manuscrits[71] appelés[72] procédés.

Il avertit qu'il ne dira pas les choses de point en point; qu'il ne se sert pas de supposition ni de similitude—mais de quelques expressions figurées et de quelques petits voiles—aisé à developer.

L'auteur divise l'ouvrage en 2 parties, la 1ère[73] regarde la composition de la pierre et sa perfection jusqu'à la fermentation.

La 2ème[74] comprend toutes les opérations qu'il est nécessaire de faire pour la 2ème[75] et dernière perfection de la pierre. Remarque à faire sur cette division.

CHAPITRE 1ER[76]

De l'extraction de l'œuvre

Après avoir tiré la matière de la minière; il faut nécessairement faire une bonne provision de cette eau, parce qu'elle contient beaucoup de matière, mais peu d'esprit.

67. pphes.
68. escrivent.
69. ce.
70. deffend.
71. manuscris.
72. appelles.
73. 1re.
74. 2me.
75. 2me.
76. 1r.

SECOND PART
OF THE OPERATIONS PARTICULARLY
NECESSARY FOR THE PRACTICE

Be on guard how the philosophers write, because they con-
    found their operations: that which must be at the begin-
    ning they put it at the end; and the end [they put] at the
    beginning.

The stone is made in two different ways.

The author of this book says that he intends to speak about
    the work of the ancients and he defends the reading of
    certain manuscripts called 'processes'.

He warns that he does not describe the things point by point;
    that he does not use supposition or similitude—except
    for a few figurative expressions and some small veils—
    easy to develop.

The author divides the work into two parts: the first concerns
    the composition of the stone and its perfection until the
    fermentation.

The second [part] comprises all the operations which are nec-
    essary to do for the second and final perfection of the
    stone. Make note of this division.

FIRST CHAPTER

Of the extraction of the work

After having drawn the matter from the mine; it is necessary
    to make a good supply of this water, because it contains
    much of the matter but little of the spirit.

Remarquez[77] les articles suivants.

Les réiterées ablutions sur la terre de cette eau qui se change en un lait onctueux[78] devient la vie de la matière de la pierre.

Cette eau renferme toutes les vertus du ciel et de la terre, elle est le dissolvant de la nature ou le Roi[79] et la Reine se beignent.

Le temps[80] de ramasser cette eau est au printemps,[81] aux 3 signes des Bélier,[82] Taureau[83] et Gémeaux.[84]

Cette eau est un aimant[85] qui attire à elle toutes les influences du ciel, du soleil, de la lune et des astres, pour les communiquer à la terre.

On ne peut avoir cette eau que par le moyen de la terre.

Cette eau après plusieurs et réitérées lotions sur la terre, la purifie, et la terre donne toute la vertu à l'eau non pas à la 1ère[86] mais à la 7ème[87] lotion.

CHAPITRE 2ÈME[88]

De la séparation des elements[89]

La nature se dépouille de toutes ses impuretés par l'opération qui se fait dans la séparation des éleménts,[90] à cause de beaucoup de superfluitiés et de differentes natures qui sont dans les principes, ce qui ce fait par la putréfaction.

Le grain de froment jeté[91] dans la terre qui s'y pourrit,[92] est rapporté par[93] exemple.

C'est ce feu de fumier qu'il faut purifier et introduire dans la matrice, qui est aqueux, aérien, igné[94] et terrestre.

77.	Remarqués.	83.	toreaux.	89.	elemens.
78.	honctueux.	84.	jumeaux.	90.	elemens.
79.	Roy.	85.	ayman.	91.	jetté.
80.	tems.	86.	1re.	92.	pourry.
81.	printems.	87.	7me.	93.	Pour ('par').
82.	Bellier.	88.	2me.	94.	ignée.

Notice the following articles.

The repeated washings on the earth of this water, which changes into an unctuous milk that becomes the life of the matter of the stone.

This water contains all the virtues of heaven and earth, it is the solvent of nature where the king and the queen bathe.

The time to collect this water is during spring, in the three signs of Aries, Taurus, and Gemini.

This water is a magnet that attracts all the influences of the sky, the sun, the moon, and the stars, to communicate them to the earth.

We can only have this water by means of the earth.

This water, after several and repeated washings on the earth, purifies it, and the earth gives all [of its] virtue to the water, not at the first [washing] but after the seventh washing.

SECOND CHAPTER

The separation of the elements

Nature is stripped of all its impurities by the operation which is made during the separation of the elements, due to many superfluities and different natures which are in the principles, which is made through putrefaction.

The grain of wheat cast unto the earth [and] which rots, is reported for example.

It is the fire of manure that must be [used for] purifying and which must be introduced into the matrix, which is aqueous, airy, igneous, and terrestrial.

Ce feu participe des 4 qualitiés du froid [du chaud, de l'humide et du sec, et du][95] soufre aussi et il est un argent vif.

Ce feu qui ne vient pas de la matière, achèvera tout l'ouvrage et perfectionne ce qui est impur et imparfait, qui fait apparâitre[96] les 3 couleurs: le noir,[97] le blanc et le rouge.

Ce feu ce trouve dans le fumier qui corrompt, putréfie les semences et qui donne la fécondité à la terre.

Ce feu est cette eau qui sort de la fontaine qui est dans un chêne[98] creux, ce vieux chêne[99] creux c'est le vaisseau[100] qui doit être de chêne,[101] dans lequel il faut corrompre l'eau qu'il réserve.

Il y a d'autres feux.

Le secret de l'opération de ce feu est de de savoir[102] le temps[103] fixe de cette putrefaction.

On ne peut extraire les éléments[104] ni[105] les principes, sans que la matière n'ait été aussi corrompue auparavant.

La putréfaction parait[106] bonne, quand il se trouve dans ce feu aqueux quelque acidité, une odeur de sépulchre.

Philalèthe dit que faire que paraisse sur la superficie de l'eau des petites[107] bouteilles semblables aux yeux de poisson.

Cette eau qui est le feu secret et l'agent qui bout et se fermente dans la putrefaction.

Secret mistérieux des philosophes[108] caché touchant le vaisseau.[109]

Faites bien vos remarques sur les articles ci[110] devant et après.

Le vaisseau[111] qui enferme celui[112] de la matière doit être de bois de chêne.[113]

---

95. MS illegible.
96. apparoitre.
97. noire.
98. chesne.
99. chesne.
100. vesseau.
101. chesne.
102. scavoir.
103. tems.
104. elemens.
105. ny.
106. paroit.
107. petittes.
108. pphes.
109. vesseau.
110. cy.
111. vesseau.
112. celuy.
113. chesne.

This fire participates in the four qualities, the cold [and warm, the humid and the dry],[74] and of Sulphur also, and it is an *argent vive*.

This fire which does not come from the matter completes the whole work and perfects that which is impure and imperfect [and] makes the three colours appear, the black, the white, and the red.

This fire is found in the manure, which corrupts and putrefies the seeds and gives fecundity to the earth.

This fire is this water which comes out of a spring which is in a hollow oak, this old hollow oak is the vessel which must be made of oak, in which one must corrupt the reserved water.

There are other fires.

The secret of the operation of this fire is to know the fixed time of this putrefaction.

One cannot extract the elements or the principles without the matter having also been corrupted before.

Putrefaction seems good when one finds some acidity in this watery fire [and] an odor of the sepulchre.

Philalethes says that there must appear small bubbles on the surface of the water that resemble fish eyes.

This water is the secret fire and the agent that boils and ferments in the putrefaction.

The secret and hidden mystery of the philosophers concerning the vessel.

Take good notice of the articles before and after:

The vessel which encloses the matter must be of wood from an oak.

74   Reconstructed from context. Manuscript illegible.

Le vieux chêne[114] est pris[115] là pour la matière universelle duquel[116] il sort du tronc, 2 fleurs, l'une blanche, l'autre rouge, qui sont les 2 substances des quelles nous tirons notre feu.

De l'extraction des 2 luminaries or et mercure,
c'est-à-dire l'opération de ces 2 substances
qu'ils appellant vinaigre
mercuriel[117]

Manière de faire le sel des philosophes[118] par le moyen de l'opération ci-dessus[119] qui est appelé[120] corps de la lune qui sert pour l'ouvrage au blanc et à la composition du mercure des philosophes.[121]

Joindrez[122] les 2 mercures blanc et rouge ensemble, appelé[123] Elixir, esprit. Ne vous arrêtez[124] pas aux paroles des philosophes,[125] mais au sens de leurs paroles.

La distinction qu'il faut faire et savoir[126] connaître;[127] des vraies[128] opérations et des fausses, et ne pas mettre un matière pour l'autre.

L'auteur conseille de s'attacher plutôt[129] aux philosophes[130] qui ont peu écrit et aux règles certains des principes.

Cet ouvrage peut être facilement fait par les mains d'une femme.

On peut trouver la matière en une impure et en une semaine.

Dieu la réservée pour les pauvres.

114. chesne.
115. prit.
116. du quel.
117. mercurialle.
118. pphes.
119. cy-dessus.
120. appellé.
121. pphes.
122. Joindre.
123. appelles.
124. arrestes.
125. pphes.
126. scavoir.
127. connoitre.
128. vrais.
129. plustot.
130. pphes.

The old oak is taken here for the universal matter from whose
    trunk two flowers emerge, one white and the other
    red, which are the two substances from which we draw
    our fire.

Of the extraction of the two luminaries gold and mercury,
    that is to say the operation of these two substances
    that they call the mercurial
    vinegar

The manner of making the philosophers' salt through the
    above operation, which is called the body of the moon
    and which serves for the white work and the composi-
    tion of the philosophers' mercury.
Join the two mercuries, white and red, together, called elixir,
    spirit. Do not limit yourself to the words of the philoso-
    phers but to the meaning of their words.
The distinction which must be made and known; of the true
    operations and false ones, and not to replace one matter
    with the other.
The author advises to focus instead on the philosophers who
    have written little, and on certain rules of the principles.
This work could be easily made by the hands of a woman.
One can find the matter in an impure [matter], and after a
    single week, which God has reserved for the poor.

Les 2 voies[131] sont véirtables, néanmoins[132] celle des pauvres est la plus excellente. L'une se[133] fait en 7 mois et l'autre en 18 mois.

Prenez[134] garde au change que les philosophes[135] donnent dans le régime de l'une et l'autre pratiques.

CHAPITRE 3ÈME[136]

De l'extraction des corps de 2
luminaires, soleil et lune

Rien n'est si caché que l'opération de l'extraction des 2 luminaires soleil et lune, il est impossible de la deviner sans une inspiration divine ou un ami[137] qui vous le dise.

Ces opérations consistent a bien dissoudre et purifier la matière par l'union de l'âme avec le corps, dont l'Esprit est l'unique lien qui opère cette conjunction.

La séparation du corps de la lune, de celui du soleil qui est renfermé dans la teinture rouge. En y ajoutant 2 fois autant d'esprit blanc.

La séparation de la terre qui contient le feu et l'air; se[138] fait en ôtant l'eau de la terre.

Une cendre noire qui est comme une terre subtile qui nage sur la superficie de l'eau, qu'il faut cueillir, qui est comme la crème sur le lait, qui est un soufre fixe, qui est aussi une racine avec son suc rempli[139] de force, que l'on purifie jusqu'à ce que son esprit [et sel][140] paraisse.

Il faut encore rectifier et clarifier la 1ère[141] teinture; et de la dernière qui est l'esprit, en séparer les fèces.[142]

131. voyes.

132. neantmoins.

133. ce.

134. Prenes.

135. pphes.

136. 3me.

137. amy.

138. ce.

139. remplit.

140. MS unclear.

141. 1re.

142. fæces.

The two ways [to the stone] are true, however that of the poor
is the most excellent. One [way] is made in seven months
and the other in eighteen months.
Be careful of the exchange that the philosophers make in the
regimen of the two practices.

THIRD CHAPTER

*On the extraction of the bodies of the two
luminaries, sun and moon*

Nothing is so hidden as the operation of the extraction of the
two luminaries, sun and moon; it is impossible to guess it
without divine inspiration or from a friend who tells you.
These operations consist in dissolving and purifying the matter well, through the union of the soul to the body, and
in which the Spirit is the only link which performs this
conjunction.
The separation of the body of the moon, from that of the
sun, which is enclosed in the red tincture. By adding two
times as much of the white spirit.
The separation of the earth that contains the fire and the air;
which is made by removing the water from the earth.
A black ash that is like a subtle earth swims on the surface
of the water, which must be collected, which is like the
cream of milk, which is a fixed sulphur, which is also a
root with its juice filled with force, and which is purified
until its spirit [and salt][75] appears.
One must again rectify and clarify the first tincture; and the
last one which is the spirit, by separating the feces.

75   Assumed. Manuscript illegible.

Quand la terre noire sera dissoute, il la faut prendre, pour la faire digérer, putréfier[143] et la cuire jusqu'à ce qu'elle se subtilise.

Cette terre ou pierre se dissout dans l'eau mercurielle[144] lunaire que l'on ne peut avoir sans la séparer de la terre noire.

Dans les principales opérations, ce sont toujours 2 choses qui en produisent une autre et qui de ces 2 choses, l'une tient lieu de mâle[145] et l'autre de femelle (les 3 principes).[146]

Cette opération n'est proprement qu'une séparation.

Si l'on pousse trop le feu du 1er[147] degré chaud, la noirceur se convertira en rouge et sera brûlée.

Il faut continuer de mettre à part la cendre noire jusqu'à ce qu'il ne vienne plus de rouge, qui arrivera quand l'eau deviendra blanche.

[Prenez ce qui est dissous, et versez dessus la][148] poudre noire, pour la faire corrompre et putréfier.[149]

CHAPITRE 4ÈME[150]

De la conversion des éléments et la conjonction
des 2 luminaires, la lune et le soleil

Il faut distiller, 8 mois durant à petit feu, les teintures qui feraient[151] changer le corps noire en un rouge brûlé.

Manière de faire distiller cette terre noire avec son eau au B.M. pour la blancher.

On tire le sel de la terre qui sera blanc après la 7ème[152] distillation par la 2 ème[153] opération, avec l'esprit lunaire pour extraire le mercure des philosophes.[154]

143. putrifier.
144. mercurialle.
145. masle.
146. Marginal note.
147. 1r.
148. MS illegible.
149. putrifier.
150. 4me.
151. feroient.
152. 7me.
153. 2me.
154. pphes.

When the black earth dissolves, it must be taken, in order to further digest, putrefy, and cook it until it is subtilised.

This earth or stone dissolves in the lunar mercurial water which cannot be had unless one separates the black earth.

In the principal operations, there are always two things that produce another, and of these two things one is the male and the other the female [The three principles].[76]

This operation is nothing but a separation.

If one pushes the fire of the first degree until it is too hot, the black is converted to red and will be burnt.

One must continue to set aside the black ash until there is no longer any redness, which arrives when the water becomes white.

[Take what is dissolved, and pour over it][77] the black powder in order to make it corrupt and putrify.

FOURTH CHAPTER

Of the conversion of the elements and the conjunction of the two luminaries, the moon and the sun

One must distill for eight months[78] on a slow heat, the tinctures that will make the black body change into a burnt red.

The manner of distilling this black earth with its water on a bain-marie, for the whitening.

One draws the salt of the earth which will be white after the seventh distillation by the second operation, with the lunar spirit for extracting the mercury of the philosophers.

76   Marginal note in manuscript.

77   Assumed. Manuscript illegible.

78   Eight months seems excessive for a 'distillation' operation. The main text of the manuscript says 'eight philosophical months'.

Le 1er[155] élément qui sort est l'eau pure froide et humide qu'il
  faut distiller 7 fois.
Gardez- vous[156] bien de ne pas mêler[157] les terres et les fêces,[158]
  et l'eau de la 1ère[159] operation avec celle de la 2ème.[160]
Remarques sur l'auteur du Combat des chevaliers.
La liqueur qui sort du creux du chêne qui est une substance
  homogène et qui [cette liqueur, lorsqu'elle est sé-][161]
  -parée du noir, elle contient 3 differentes substances et 3
  principes naturels; sel, soufre et mercure.
Le feu et le soufre sont cachés dans le centre de la terre noire,
  qu'il faut laver pour en extraire le sel fixe qui forme le
  mercure des philosophes.[162]
Cette eau qui a été distillée 7 fois, il en faut mettre une des
  7 sur ce sel fixe et observer la même méthode[163] que l'on
  a fait pour l'eau rouge comme vous avez[164] fait de l'eau
  blanche.

CHAPITRE 5ÈME[165]

De la purification et séparation des principes
du mercure des philosophes

Cette eau est la clé[166] et le chef d'oeuvre hermétique, parce
  qu'elle le commence et elle le finit.
Les philosophes[167] ont tous cachés la préparation de cette eau.
Le triomphe hermétique dit que cette eau est le feu sacré des
  sages et l'unique instrument pour la sublimation.
[Il a décrit toute les merveilles du][168] feu et de l'eau.
Si vous ne comprenez[169] pas ces choses, priez[170] Dieu qu'il
  vous éclair.

155. 1r.
156. Gardes vous.
157. mesler.
158. fæces.
159. 1re.
160. 2me.
161. MS illegible.
162. pphes.
163. metode.
164. aves.
165. 5me.
166. clef.
167. pphes.
168. MS illegible.
169. comprenes.
170. pries.

The first element that comes [out], is the pure water, cold and
humid, which must be distilled seven times.

Beware of not mixing the earths and the feces, and the water
of the first operation with that of the second.

Remarks on the author of the *War of the Knights*.[79]

The liquid that comes out of the hollow oak is a homogenous
substance and which [this liquor, when it is separated][80]
from the black, contains three different substances and
three natural principles: salt, sulphur, and mercury.

The fire and the Sulphur are hidden in the center of the black
earth, which one must wash in order to extract the fixed
salt which forms the philosophers' mercury.

This water which has been distilled seven times; one must put
one of the seven on the fixed salt and observe the same
method that one would use for the red water as [the one]
you have made for the white water.

FIFTH CHAPTER

*On the purification and separation of the principles
of the mercury of the philosophers*

This water is the key and the master of the hermetic work because it begins it and ends it.

The philosophers have all hidden the preparation of this
water.

The *Hermetic Triumph* says that this water is the sacred fire
of the sages and the only instrument for the sublimation.

[It has described all the marvels of the][81] fire and of the water.

If you do not understand these things, pray to God that he
may enlighten you.

79   Anonyme, *L'Ancienne guerre des Chevaliers*, in Limojon de St Didier,
     Le Triomph hermétique, 1699. See note 39.
80   Assumed. Manuscript illegible.
81   Assumed. Manuscript illegible.

C'est ce feu qui est renfermé dans cette eau qui est notre mercure qu'elle dissout la pierre naturellement et sans violence.

Les différents[171] noms que les philosophes[172] ont donnés à
   cette eau si précieuse.[173]

La vertu qu'il faut donner à l'or de se[174] multiplier pour en
   faire la médicine universelle.

Le soufre vif de l'or qui donne la vie même à l'or commun qui
   fait végéter et multiplier.

Le terme de la pierre est donné en plusieurs sens différents,[175]
   comme en 3 sortes d'ordre.

3 sortes d'or des philosophes.

3 espèces de mercure.

Remarque à faire sur les 3 ordres de la pierre, sur les 3 sortes
   d'or et sur les 3 espèces de mercure.

CHAPITRE 6ÈME[176]

De la séparation et purification

[Les principes de separation et la purification des][177] philosophes,[178] qui consiste dans une parfait dissolution et sublimation.

La solution du corps blanc ou de la lune appellée or blanc.

La solution ne s'en peut faire, sans la conjonction de la femelle
   avec le mâle[179] qui est le sel précieux.[180]

Ce précieux[181] sel appellé corps se[182] fait par une continuelle
   effusion de son proper sang qui est un menstrue naturel.

Il ne faut pas jeter[183] la terre morte dans laquelle le feu et le
   soufre sont cachés et qu'il faut laver.

---

171. differens.	176. 6me.	181. pretieux.
172. pphes.	177. MS illegible.	182. ce.
173. pretieuse.	178. pphes.	183. jetter.
174. ce.	179. masle.	
175. differens.	180. pretieux.	

It is this fire that is enclosed in this water which is our mercury and which dissolves the stone naturally and without violence.

The different names that the philosophers have given to this so precious water.

The virtue which one must give to gold in order to multiply it and make the universal medicine.

The living sulphur of gold which gives life even to common gold which makes it vegetate [i.e. grow] and multiply.

The term stone is given in many different senses, as in three kinds of orders.[82]

Three kinds of philosophers' gold.[83]

Three species of mercury.

Remark to be made on the three orders of the stone, three sorts of gold, and three species of mercury.

SIXTH CHAPTER

On the separation and purification

[The separation and purification principles of the][84] philosophers, which consists of a perfect dissolution and sublimation.

The solution of the white body or the moon called white gold.

The solution cannot be made without the conjunction of the female with the male which is the precious salt.

This precious salt is called a body and is made by a continual effusion of its own blood, which is a natural menstruum.

One must not discard the dead earth in which the fire and the sulphur are hidden and which must be washed.

82   See the Latin Geber's 'triple difference of medicines'; William R. Newman, *The Summa Perfectionis of Pseudo-Geber: A Critical Edition, Translation, and Study* (Leiden, 1991), pp. 749–769.

83   Drawn from the *Hermetic Triumph* of Limojon de St Didier.

84   Assumed. Manuscript illegible.

Tâchez[184] d'avoir, par le moyen de l'âme aqueuse, la forme sulfureuse,[185] ce qui se[186] fait par notre vinaigre.

Abreuver la terre de son eau et qu'elle soit pénetrée de son
humidité pour engendrer le mercure.

Le mercure est formé de l'union de ces 2 substances, dont l'un
est l'esprit et le sel est le corps.

Remarque à faire pour ne pas se [tromper par ces opéra-
tions][187] car les philosophes[188] la cachent.

Tout ce mystère[189] n'est que l'extraction du sel fixe[190] qui produit le mercure, et l'eau qui compose cette eau sèche.[191]

CHAPITRE 7ÈME[192]

*La composition du grand dissolvent et du mercure des
philosophes,[193] est faite de leurs liqueurs, ils en font
2 mercures, le blanc pour le Bain de la lune
et le rouge pour le bain du soleil*

Le Cosmopolite[194] dit la même chose en disant, notre vieillard[195] engloutira l'or et l'argent.

Plusieurs différents[196] noms que les philosophes[197] donnent à
cette précieuse[198] liqueur.

Cette précieuse[199] liqueur est le 1er[200] Être de l'or. Le champ
dans lequel soleil est semé, que le fixe fût fait volatile.

Il faut donc une eau métallique homogène, à laquelle on
prépare la voie,[201] par la calcination qui a [precede et
qui se fait par un dessèchement][202] qui est proprement
une réduction de la matière en atomes par le crible de
la nature.

---

184. Tacher.
185. sulphureuse.
186. ce.
187. MS illegible.
188. pphes.
189. mistere.
190. fix.

191. seiche.
192. 7me.
193. pphes.
194. Cosmopolitte.
195. viellard.
196. differens.
197. pphes.

198. pretieuse.
199. pretieuse.
200. 1r.
201. voye.
202. MS illegible.

To try to have by means of of the aqueous soul, the sulphurous form, which is done by our vinegar.
To water the earth from its water and be penetrated by its
 humidity to engender the mercury.
The mercury is formed from the union of two substances, of
 which one is the spirit and the salt is the body.
A remark to make to not [be mistaken by these operations][85]
 because the philosophers hide that.
The whole of this mystery is the extraction of the fixed salt
 which produces the mercury and the water that composes this dry water.

SEVENTH CHAPTER

*The composition of the great solvent and of the mercury
of the philosophers is made from their liquors,
they make two mercuries; the white for the
bath of the moon and the red for
the bath of the sun*

The Cosmopolitan said the same thing, in saying that our old
 man devours gold and silver etc.
Many different names that the philosophers have given to
 this precious liquor.
This precious liquor is the first being of gold. The fields in
 which the sun is sown, that the fixed was made volatile.
One must therefore have a homogeneous metallic water, for
 which we prepare the way, by calcination, which is [a prerequisite, and which is made by a drying out],[86] which is
 properly a reduction of the matter into atoms through
 the sieve of nature.

85   Assumed. Manuscript illegible.
86   Assumed. Manuscript illegible.

Ce qu'il faut faire après que le soleil a été dissout par le mercure:

Le combat des 2 dragons qui se dévorent jusqu'à se[203] que de ces 2 il ne s'en fasse plus qu'un.

Hermes[204] dit qu'il faut voir la grosseur de l'eau se durcir pour se réjouir.

Prendre garde à la fin du 1er[205] œuvre pour parfaire le mercure.

Le mercure est tiré de deux substances qui viennent[206] d'une seule et unique racine, l'une est fixe et l'autre volatile.

Beaucoup de noms donnés a ce mercure.

Après avoir tiré ces 2 substances par le moyen[207] du sel fixe, il en résulte le Dissovent universel et le mercure des philosophes.[208]

[Il tire toute sa force et sa virtu de][209] l'esprit invisible pour en grossir la terre qui est la femelle qui se joint au mâle[210] qui est le soufre. Et du concours de ces 2 substances, il en vient la semence profilique.

La table d'emeraude[211] du grand Hermès, qui fût trouvée dans son séphulchre, dans la vallée d'Ebron, après le Deluge.

Ce même esprit descend[212] du Ciel dans le centre de la terre où il commence à se[213] coaguler par la vertu de son sel hermaphrodite qui est son aimant.[214]

Fin de la table

❧

203. ce.
204. Chermeze.
205. 1r.
206. vient.
207. moyens.
208. pphes.
209. MS illegible.
210. masle.
211. d'hemeraude.
212. dessend.
213. ce.
214. ayman.

What one must do after the sun has been dissolved by mercury:

The combat of the two dragons that devour each other until these two become only one.

Hermes[87] said that one must see the mass of the water harden [coagulate] to rejoice.

Take care at the end of the first work to perfect the mercury.

The mercury is drawn from two substances that come from one single root; one is fixed and the other volatile.

Many names [are] given to this mercury.

After having drawn these two substances by means of the fixed salt, it results in the universal solvent and the mercury of the philosophers.

[It derives all its strength and virtue from][88] the invisible spirit in order to grow the earth, which is female, who is united to the male, which is sulphur. And from the struggle between these two substances comes the prolific seed.

The *Emerald Tablet* of the great Hermes was found in his sepulchre in the valley of Hebron after the deluge.

This same spirit descends from Heaven into the centre of the earth where it begins to coagulate by the virtue of its hermaphroditic salt, which is its magnet.

End of the table

87   'Chermeze' in the manuscript. Amended to 'Hermes'.
88   Assumed. Manuscript illegible.

THE MANUSCRIPT bears a final side note that reads: *Mrs. B. H. Tyler 13 June 1977*. This is the yet-unidentified name of the person who donated the manuscript to the New York Library, probably along with the other related material from Albert H. Gallatin. We found a reference to a 'Mrs. B. H. Tyler' as a member, for several years, of the Yonkers Art Association in New York, which met and exhibited at the Yonkers Public Library. She served as an executive of the association at one point. At that time (circa 1923) she was a part of the 'Young Woman's Christian Association' (of the Yonkers Art Association). If she was a 'young woman' in 1923 (about 20–25 years of age), then she could have been around 74–79 years old when she donated the manuscript in 1977, which makes logistic sense. Being an artist or collector, she may have been related to the famous artist, also with the initials B. H., i.e., Bayard Henry Tyler (1855–1931), although we could not verify if this was the case (he was also a member of the very same Yonkers Association). We doubt if she was his wife because of the huge age difference (he would have been 68 in 1923, and already had a wife in 1889 or 1899). The Tylers seem to have been an important family in the USA, and included the tenth President.

APPENDIX

HOW MANY HERMETIC *CABINETS*?

As inferred in the introduction, our first task, after having acquired a copy of the manuscript from the New York Public
Library, was to try to establish whether this text was in fact
the same *Cabinet hermétique* that we had already found three
separate references to in three different sources. In connection with this, we had to find out if any of these texts had
anything to do with the mysterious and elusive source that
Fulcanelli had quoted from. What follows is a summary of
our findings from the three different texts that mention a
'Hermetic Cabinet' (*Cabinet hermétique*):

1. JACOB TOLL'S *GUIDE TO THE CHYMICAL HEAVEN*

Being already familiar with the French translation of Jacobus
Tollius' *Manuductio ad Cœlum Chemicum* (1688),[1] we were
also familiar with the reference it makes to a text it calls *Le
Cabinet hermétique*. (The italicised text in the following ci-
tation denotes important passages that will help clarify some
issues when compared to the Latin original):

---

[1] Jacobus Tollius, *Manuductio ad cælum chemicum*, Amstelædami:
Apud Janssonio-Waesbergios, 1688. The French edition (Jacques Tol,
Le Chemin du ciel chymique) appeared with no publishing information on the title page, but dates from 1690–1710 according to the Bibliothèque nationale de France.

LA MÉTHODE que je me suis
proposée pour faire un Ouvrage
si excellent et si beau, est toute
différente de celle que les autres
ont suivie. Dans chemin si
glissant et qui conduit tant de
personnes au précipice, *j'ai pour
guide le sçavant Paracelse, et le
fameux Basile Valentin*, encore
mille fois plus docte et plus
instructif que luy.

J'avois déjà résolu de
disposer des vaisseaux; j'avois
commencé la préparation du
Mercure, suivant la doctrine de
Philalete, par plusieurs lotions et
triturations; je dissolvois et pur-
geois des Métaux avec des Vinaigres et des Eaux fortes, *lorsque
par un bonheur inopiné, il me
tomba entre les mains un Livre
intitulé: Le Cabinet hermétique.*
Je lus ce Livre avec une avidité
extraordinaire, sans y rien
comprendre: *mais après avoir
reconnu que Paracelse* ne s'estoit
point ressouvenu des choses que
l'on avoit confié à sa bonne foy,
je commencé d'examiner avec
plus d'exactitude la nature des
Métaux, et de la conférer avec
les expériences que les autres en
avaient déjà fait. Enfin l'esprit
plus éclairé qu'auparavant, je
m'apperçu que personne ne suiv-
ait le vray chemin, et que tout
le monde perdait son temps et
son argent: Je resolus de prendre
une route toute différente, *et de
suivre celle que cét Adepte avait
inutilement recommandé à nôtre
Paracelse.* Laissant donc à part
tous les sentimens différents,
je me suis proposé cette règle

THE METHOD which I have
proposed to make a work so
excellent and so beautiful, is
quite different from that which
the others followed. In a path
so slippery and which leads so
many people to the precipice,
*my guide is Paracelsus, and the fa-
mous Basil Valentine*, a thousand
times more learned and more
instructive than him.

I had already resolved to
dispose the vessels; I had begun
the preparation of the Mercury, following the doctrine of
Philalethes, by several washings
and triturations; I dissolved and
purged Metals with Vinegars
and Strong Waters, *when by
unexpected good luck, it fell into my
hands a Book entitled The Hermetic
Cabinet.* I read this book with
extraordinary avidity, without
understanding anything about
it; *but having recognised that
Paracelsus* was not aware of the
things which had been entrusted
to his good faith, I began to examine with more exactitude the
nature of Metals, and to confer
it with the experiences that others had already made. Finally,
the spirit more enlightened than
before, I realised that nobody
was following the real path, and
that everyone was wasting time
and money: I resolved to take
a different route, *and to follow
that which this Adept had useless-
ly recommended to our Paracelsus.* Thus leaving aside all the
different sentiments, I proposed
to myself this certain rule with
which I could happily reach the

certaine avec laquelle je puisse heureusement parvenir à la fin de ma carrière.

Que la Pierre des Philosophes doit être faite en trois ou quatre jours.

Que la dépense ne doit point excéder la somme de trois ou quatre florins.

Et qu'enfin un seul creuset ou vaisseau de terre suffit.

Et j'estime qu'il faut rejetter toutes les propositions qui ne s'accorderont pas avec ces trois Aphorismes. *Prévenu de la sorte, Basile Valentin m'a esté d'un grand secours*, car après avoir fait représenter un creuset dans ses premiers clefs, il ordonne de continuer par cette voye, et de laisser là tous autres vaisseaux, le feu de lampe, de fien de Cheval, de cendre, de sable, et de flâmes; et d'appliquer son esprit aux plus profonds mystères de l'Art.

end of my career.

That the Stone of the Philosophers' must be made in three or four days.

That the expense must not exceed the sum of three or four florins.

And finally, a single crucible or earthen vessel suffices.

And I think we must reject all proposals that do not agree with these three Aphorisms. *Warned in this way, Basil Valentine was very helpful to me*, because after having a crucible represented in his first keys, he orders to continue by this way, and to leave aside all other vessels, the lamp fire, Horse dung, ashes, sand, and flames; and to apply his spirit to the deepest mysteries of Art.

However, a comparison with the Latin original quickly revealed a couple of details which helped clarify the actual nature of the *Cabinet hermétique* that Toll was referring to. It is obviously the Latin collection of alchemical texts entitled *Musæum Hermeticum*:[2]

Nam mea quidem diversissima ab ceterorum methodo conficiendi pulcherrimi operis ratio est: quam mihi, lubricam hanc plerosque in exitium præcipitantem viam ingresso, duo suppeditavere præceptores, *hospes scilicet ille Helvetianus, et instructior illo, multisque partibus eruditior, Basilius Valentinus.* Jam de vitris

---

2 The first edition was published in Frankfurt, 1625. A second 're-formed & expanded' edition was published in 1678.

parandis cogitabam; Jam Mercurium, ad Philalethæ
doctrinam, lavando terendoque purgabam: jam acetis
et aquis, ut vocant, fortibus metalla dissolvebam, dis-
cerpebamque; quum nescio, quo bono fato, *sors mihi
Fortuna Musæum Hermeticum in manus tradidit*. Hoc
avidissime perlecto, quamvis non intellecto, *ubi ea cog-
novi, quae Helvetius* optima sibi fide commissa non
revocavit ad animum; perpendere accuratius naturam
coepi metallorum, eamque cum aliorum hominum
conatibus conferre. Tandem aliqua inde luce clario-
re illustratus, quod nemini usitatam viam procedere
viderem, omnemque illis operam frustra positam im-
pensamque diversam plane et insolitam illam semitam
ingredi statui, *quam Helvetio Adeptus ille incassum
commendaverat.*

Damnatis igitur omnibus aliter sentientium opin-
ionibus, illam mihi certissimam proposui cynosuram,
ad quam iter hoc meum chemicum dirigerem.

*Conficiendum opus philosophicum unico triduo, vel
quatriduo, trium quatuorve florenorum impendio, et
in testula, sive catillo fusorio.* Quicquid ab hisce tribus
dissentiret aphorismis, rejidendum existimavi. *Sic ani-
mato Basilius Valentinus suppetias tulit*, et in ipsis clavi-
bus suis, catilli apposita effigie, pergere hac via jussit,
vitraque et ignes lampadum, fimi equini, cinerum, are-
narum, flammaeque ordinarios negligere, mentemque
in penitiora artis adyta immittere.[3]

From the equivalent passages in the Latin text, it is easy
to see that what the anonymous French translator has rendered as *Le Cabinet hermétique*[4] is the title of the collection
known as the *Musæum Hermeticum.* Moreover, the particular

3   *Manuductio ad Caelum Chemicum* (Amsterdam, 1688), pp. 3–4.
4   The word *cabinet* is apparently being used here in the archaic sense of
     a room or chamber for studying. See Guillaume Le Brun, *Dictionnaire
     universel François et Latin, tiré des meilleurs auteurs. Troisième edition,
     revue, corrigée et augmentée* (1770), p. 184.

text Toll has in mind is obviously the Helvetius[5] account entitled *Vitulus Aureus* (*The Golden Calf*). Although he never
specifically mentions the title, he does mention Helvetius several times. The French translator has also very obviously misunderstood this reference to literally mean 'Swiss', and that's
why he keeps incorrectly rendering 'Helvetius' as 'Paracelsus'.
Apparently the French translator could not think of any other Swiss authority on the subject and concluded that Toll was
referring to the famous sixteenth-century Swiss physician. He
evidently had not read the seventeenth-century Dutch physician's account, so the reference totally eluded him.

The claim that the 'philosophical work' (i.e., the con-
fection of the Philosophers' Stone) can be carried out
in three or four days inside a crucible using a strong fire,
with the whole operation costing only three or four florins, is
something very peculiar to the Helvetius account. In all the
Greek, Arabic, Latin, and European vernacular sources composed before Helvetius' account that we have read so far, we
have never encountered this exact claim. At least as far back
as the Jabirian corpus it is possible to encounter claims regarding procedures for reducing the time it takes to make the
elixir/stone, but it is not specifically stated that the whole
work is carried out in a crucible from beginning to end, or
using strong fires only.[6] This not only further confirms the

5   Johann Friedrich Schweitzer. 'Helvetius' being a Latinisation of the
     German surname Schweitzer

6   For an example of a Jabirian text making such 'abbreviating' claims see
     Le livre de la Royauté, published in M. Berthelot and M. O. Houdas,
     La chimie au moyen âge, volume 3 (Paris, 1893), pp. 126–132. The
     author claims that the confection of the elixir/stone can vary as much
     as 70 years to just 15 days, and that there's even one process using 'the
     way of the Balance' which only lasts 'a blink of an eye'. He also claims
     that the process which is the main object of this book 'is performed
     without distillation, without purification, without either dissolution
     or coagulation', statements that he then proceeds to contradict later
     on by in fact letting us know that 'the fundamental principle is that
     the elements of the Stone are well purified and freed from the oils

text Toll is referring to, but, together with the references to Basil Valentine, it will also be pertinent to our discussion of the next source.

In conclusion regarding Toll: it is obvious that the *Cabinet hermétique* reference is certainly not to our anonymous manuscript but to the *Vitulus Aureus* of Helvetius, reprinted in the second edition of the *Musæum Hermeticum*.

which corrupt it and which prevent it from producing completely its effect: this is what requires long and short operations. Certainly, dear friend, the real substance, when it is clean of those oils which vitiate it, is a thing which tinges, and if it were not so, the operations could not give it this virtue'. For another Arabic text making 'abbreviating' claims, consult the dialogue between Maria and Aras, or 'Aros' or 'Ares', as the Latin and vernacular translations render his name (the reference is obviously to Aras al-Hakim, i.e., Aras the Sage, one of the interlocutors in the *Mushaf al-Hayät*, i.e. *The Book of Life*, a long alchemical dialogue with a Byzantine emperor named Theodorus, a much-quoted and referenced text in the Arabic literature on alchemy, as seen for example in the numerous references to it in the works of Ibn Umail and al-Iraqi), with commentaries by a certain 'Abbād', in Bağdatlı Vehbi MS. 2273, ff. 136–150. A microfilm copy of this manuscript exists in the Martin Levey microfilm collection of Arabic scientific manuscripts at the University of Utah, Marriott Library, Levey Original Reel 9 Title 1. A shorter and somewhat different version of the Maria and Aras dialogue, without the comments by Abbād, was translated into Latin and several vernaculars, the translators having obviously misunderstood some parts of the Arabic original (for example, they have misunderstood the trash-heaps or dunghills of cities and towns in the Arabic original, where two of the four substances used for making the stone are said to be found, for actual 'hills' or 'mountains'). See, for example, the English translation said to have been made from an Arabic manuscript at the 'Royal Library at Paris', published in *The Lives of the Alchemystical Philosophers* (London, 1815), pp. 363–366. The author of the Maria and Aras dialogue claims that the stone can be 'whitened' in a day or less, but there is no claim in it that this is supposedly performed exclusively in crucibles and using strong fires.

II. THE *PETIT ALBERT*'S BOOK ON THE WONDERFUL
SECRETS OF NATURE

The next source we must examine is a 'book of secrets'[7] known
as the *Petit Albert* (Little Albert), apparently printed for the
first time in Bellegrade in 1658.[8] Claiming to have been translated from a Latin original,[9] it contains the following process
for making gold, which the author claims to have found in a
book entitled the *Cabinet hermétique*:

7   *Le Solide Tresor des Merveilleux Secrets de la Magie Naturelle & Caba-*
      listique du Petit Albert, Traduit exactement sur l'Original Latin, qui a
      pour Titre, Alberti Parvi Lucii libellus de mirabilibus Naturae Arcanis.
      We used the 1704 Geneva edition, pp. 135–136, which is considered to
      be the second edition. An English paraphrase of this process was pub-
      lished in A. E. Waite's *A Lexicon of Alchemy or Alchemical Dictionary*
      (London, 1892), pp. 365–366, but without identifying the source.
      We present here a more literal translation.

8   The existence of this reputed 1658 edition has been recorded by Sar-
      ah Nègre, *Un travail de compilation sur les superstitions populaires des*
      XVIIE et XVIIIE siècles : L'histoire des imaginations extravagantes de
      Monsieur Oufle, par l'abbé Laurent Bordelon, Mémoire de Master 1
      Cultures de l'écrit et de l'image. dir. Philippe Martin, ENSSIB (2014),
      p. 103, and Caroline Sanchez, *Entre jeu et magie, une littérature*
      ludique : Étude de livres de jeux divinatoires et du Grand et Petit Albert,
      Mémoire du Master 2 Cultures de l'écrit et de l'image, dir. Philippe
      Martin, ENSSIB (2015), pp. 71–72, 77–78. Thanks to Lawrence M.
      Principe, we have been able to consult a copy of this rare 1658 edition
      in order to compare it with the 1704 edition.

9   Nobody so far seems to have found this elusive alleged Latin original.
      Both Sarah Nègre (*op. cit.*, p. 103) and Caroline Sanchez (*op. cit.*, p.
      71) conclude it never existed.

POUR FAIRE L'OR
ARTIFICIELLEMENT.

Ce n'es pas feulement en
creusant & fouillant dans les
entrailles de la terre que l'on
trouve l'or. L'art peut bien imiter
la nature en ce point, puisqu'elle
la perfectionne en bien d'autres
choses; je dirai donc icy ce qui a
été éprouvé une infinité de fois,
& qui est devenu fort commun
entre ceux qui travaillent au
grand oeuvre. Vous aurez donc
un grand creuset qui foit à
l'épreuve du plus violent feu, &
l'ayant mis sur un fourneau bien
ardent, vous mettrez au fond
dudit creuset de la poudre de
colofone, de l'épaisseur du petit
doigt , & vous sapoudrerez sur
cette colofone l'épaisseur d'un
doigt de fine poudre de limaille
de fer, vous couvrirez cette limaille d'un peu de soufre rouge,
vous pousserez le feu du fourneau jufqu'à faire fondre liquide-
ment la limaille de fer, puis Vous
y jetterez du Borax dont usent
les Orfèvres pour souder l'or;
vous y jetterez pareille quantité
d'arsenic rouge & autant pesant
d'argent qu'on y a mis de limaille
de fer, & laissez cuire cette
composition en poustant le feu
du fourneau, & prenez garde
de respirer la vapeur du creuset
à caufe de l'arsenic. Vous aurez
un autre creuset, dans lequel
vous verserez par inclination la
matiere recuite que vous aurez
auparavant bien melangé avec
une spatule de fer, & vous fairez
en sorte qu'elle coule dans ce

TO MAKE GOLD
ARTIFICIALLY.

It's not just by digging &
searching in the bowels of the
earth that we find gold. Art can
imitate nature in this respect,
since it perfects it in many other
things; I will therefore state
here what has been experienced
an infinite number of times,
and which has become very
common among those who
work in the great work. You will
therefore take a great crucible,
which will resist the fiercest
fire, and having put it on a very
ardent furnace, you will put
in the bottom of the crucible
some powder of colophony, of
the thickness of the little finger,
and on this colophony you will
sprinkle the thickness of a finger
of fine powder of iron filings,
you will cover these filings with
a little red sulphur, then you will
push the fire of the furnace until
the iron filings are melted fluid-
ly; then you will throw in of the
Borax that Goldsmiths use for
soldering gold; you will throw in
it a quantity of red arsenic and
as much silver as you put in of
iron filings, and let it be cooked
by firing the furnace, and take
care not to breathe the vapors
[emanating] from the crucible
because of the arsenic. You will
take another crucible, in which
you will pour by inclination
the cocted matter, which you
have previously mixed well with
an iron spatula, and you will
make it flow into this second

second creuset purifié & sans ordures, & par le moyen de l'eau de separation l'or se precipitera au fond; & quand vous l'aurez recueilli vous e fairez fondre dans un creuset & vous aurez de bel or qui vous dedomagera de vos peines & depenses. J'ay tiré ce secret d'un livre qui a pour titre le Cabinet Hermetique, & la facilité avec laquelle on y peut réussir, n'a invité à en faire plusieurs fois l'experience, d'autant plus volontiers que je l'ay trouvé conforme dans son exécution à ce que dit le trés savant Basile Valentin, que l'épreuve du grand oeuvre des Philosophes fe peut faire en moins de trois ou quatre jours, que la depense ne doit point exceder la somme de trois ou quatre florins, & que trois ou quatre vaissaux de terre peuvent suffire.[10]

crucible, purified and without its recrements, & by means of the water of separation the gold will precipitate at the bottom; and when you have collected it, you will melt it in a crucible, and you will have fine gold which will compensate you for your troubles and expenses. I have drawn this secret from a book entitled the Hermetic Cabinet, and the facility with which one can succeed, has invited to perform several times the experiment, all the more willingly because I have found conforming to its execution what the very wise Basil Valentine says, that the trial of the great work of the Philosophers can be done in less than three or four days, that the expense should not exceed the sum of three or four florins, and that three or four earthen vessels may suffice.

With the only exception of the identity of the 'red sulphur',[11] the process is described with sufficient clarity and all

10   Op. cit., pp. 135–136. The exact same entry is found in the Bellegrade edition, pp. 169–170, therefore we have to put into doubt the authenticity or accuracy of its alleged '1658' date, since it means it would predate the publication of Helvetius' account (1667), the text that forms the basis of the claims made in Toll's book (1688), which is easy to suspect is the source that the 'Little Albert' is relying on.

11   Regarding what could the identity of this substance be, one might be tempted at first to think it is 'red arsenic' (i.e., realgar, the red sulfide of arsenic), since 'red sulphur' was in fact a common *Deckname* for arsenic. See, for example, Martinus Rulandus, *Lexicon Alchemiæ* (1612), p. 459 ('Sulphur rubeum, id est, Arsenicus'). However, this substance is already mentioned by its common name further on, when it is introduced into the hot crucible alongside silver. It doesn't seem to serve much purpose to give this well-known substance another name

the substances involved are cited by their commonly known names. The process is presented as having been tested many times by many people, insinuating that it will afford a 'proof' of the reality of transmutation to seekers after the 'great work' (i.e., the making of the Philosophers' Stone.) It should also be noticed that the author points out very similar things we have seen Toll claim based on the statements found in the Helvetius account, namely: that the making of the Stone can be performed in a matter of a few days for the sum of three or four florins, that all can be performed in crucibles, and that such claims are attributed to 'the very wise Basil Valentine'.

It is true that the brass-founder of Helvetius' account recommends Basil Valentine as a source, but he does not place much importance on him, but rather on Sendivogius.[12] But Toll, on the other hand, reverses the order and makes Basil Valentine to be the important source, while he relegates Sendivogius to a place of lesser importance.[13] The *Petit Albert*

when there does not appear to be any intention whatsoever from the part of the author to try to hide its identity, and also to use it twice in a process which is actually mostly just a straightforward melting operation. Accordingly, another possibility is that by 'red sulphur' the author might in fact mean another substance, like one of the several preparations that passed under such a name in the chymical literature of the 17th–18th centuries. For an example of these, see Hans Christoph von Ettner, *Rosetum Chymicum* (1724), p. 422. The 'rothen Schwefel' is described as the product of grinding equal parts of yellow sulphur and 'crocus' of iron ('well-reverberated and open'), imbibing this mixture with 'oil of vitriol' several times and then subliming it.

12　The brass-founder mentions Basil Valentine once, but places more emphasis on Sendivogius, about whom he says that 'in his obscure words the truth is latent'; John Frederick Helvetius, *The Golden Calf, which the World Adores, and Desires*, London: John Starkey, 1670, p. 118.

13　Toll only mentions Sendivogius once, and in a rather passing manner, where even a non-alchemical author like Cicero is given more attention: 'car il y a un feu céleste, et un feu terrestre, celui-ci est de l'esprit volatil, celui-là du corps fixe ; l'un du Soleil supérieur, l'autre du Soleil inférieur, comme parle Sendivogius, et comme dit Ciceron, tel est celui qui se trouve renfermé dans le corps des Animaux, et qu'on

does not mention Sendivogius at all, but points to Basil Valentine. This argues for reliance on Toll's statements, rather than directly on Helvetius' account. The fact that the French translation of Toll's text also refers to *Le Cabinet hermétique* might also have something to do with this, and would suggest not only reliance on Toll's statements, but more specifically on the anonymous French translation of Toll's book. The process attributed to *Le Cabinet hermétique* by the *Petit Albert* does not seem to be contained in the *Musæum Hermeticum*, so it is possible that perhaps the *Petit Albert* actually got the process from some other source which he rebaptised as *Le Cabinet hermétique* in order to fit with Toll's reference (in its French version), without realising what book Toll was actually referring to.

As for the process itself, it bears a very close resemblance to the one that had already been published in the sixteenth century by Giambattista della Porta in the 'expanded' edition of his *Magia Naturalis*:[14]

GOLD OUT OF SILVER. And so little but it will pay your cost, and afford you much gain. The way is this. Put the fine filings of Iron into a Crucible that will endure fire, until it grows red hot, and melts. Then take artificial Chrysocolla, such as Goldsmiths use to Solder with, and red Arsenic, and by degrees strew them in. When you have done this, cast in an equal part of Silver, and let it be exquisitely purged by a strong vessel made of ashes.[15] All the dregs of the Gold[16] being now

appelle feu vital et salutaire, lequel conserve toutes choses, les nourrit, augmente, soûtient, et les rend capables de sentiment'; *op. cit.*, p. 29.

14   First published in 1584. We use the English translation, *Natural Magick*, London, 1658, p. 172.

15   Obviously a reference to a cupel.

16   We think that a mistake has been made here. It seems like it should be 'of the silver', since this is the metal under treatment, the gold being the desirable byproduct of the process, whereas the 'dregs' formed during the process are an undesirable byproduct to be eliminated

removed, cast it into water of separation, and the Gold
will fall to the bottom of the vessel, take it. There is
nothing of many things that I have found more true,
more gainful, or more hard. Spare no labor, and do it as
you should, lest you lose your labor.

As can be readily seen, the process is very close to the one
prescribed by the *Petit Albert*, which is said to be taken from
Le Cabinet hermétique. We tabulate side-by-side here the list
of substances employed in order to further show the similarities and differences between both processes:

DELLA PORTA'S PROCESS	LE CABINET HERMÉTIQUE'S PROCESS
—	Powder of colophony
Filings of iron	Fine powder of iron filings
—	Red sulphur
Artificial chrysocolla[17] used by goldsmiths for soldering	Borax used by goldsmiths for soldering

through cupellation or scorification with lead. The Latin text does in
fact say 'of the gold' (*iam exclusis sordibus omnibus auri*), so the mistake was not by the English translator.

17   That Porta does understand borax, or a kind of borax, by this 'artificial Chrysocolla' is supported by what is stated in a cosmetic recipe
on page 246: 'artificial Chrysocolla, called Borax'; for more details
about how 'chrysocolla' and borax were made, see *Materia Medica:
Or, A New Description of the Virtues and Effects of all Drugs, or Simple
Medicines Now in Use*, London, 1727, volume 2, p. 214. The difference between the two substances is explained as being basically one
of purity. 'Chrysocolla' seems to have had a mixture of 'saltish' and
'urinous' substances from its first solution and crystallisation in a mixture of urine and water, whereas borax was crystallised from water a
second time.

DELLA PORTA'S PROCESS	LE CABINET HERMÉTIQUE'S PROCESS
Red arsenic	Red arsenic
Silver	Silver
Lead[18]	—
Water of separation[19]	Water of Separation

The difference between the two processes can therefore be said to be that the one reproduced by Porta does not use colophony and 'red sulphur'.[20] Colophony is easily identified, but it is not clear what the process taken from the *Cabinet hermétique* means by 'red sulphur'. Also, in Porta's process the treated silver is cupelled or scorified in order to get rid of any residual 'dregs' produced in the process that might become attached to the silver, whereas the process taken from the *Cabinet hermétique* separates the treated silver from the 'recrements' formed during the process by means of a high-temperature 'decantation' (i.e., the liquid silver is carefully poured out into another crucible, while the 'recrements' remain behind in the crucible that was used to carry out the operation). Finally, both processes use the well-known assaying operation of 'parting' with *aqua fortis*, in order to isolate the formed gold from the leftover unaltered silver.

18 Not specifically mentioned, but obviously implied by Porta's instructions. See notes 15 and 16.

19 That is, *aqua fortis*, which dissolves silver but not gold, thus its use in separating the artificial gold produced by the process from the remaining parts of silver that have not been altered.

20 See note 11.

III. CAGLIOSTRO

According to François Ribadeau Dumas, Count Alessandro di Cagliostro (1743–1795) had access to a text called the *Clef du cabinet hermétique*:

> With the most authentic adepts, Cagliostro set to work at the athanor furnace; he began to cook the mercurial substance, he operated the dissolution, coagulation, Prime Matter, according to the true recipes of the Key to the 'Hermetic *Cabinet*'. Some witnesses claim that he made gold, that he managed to grow pearls.[21]

Unfortunately, the author does not give any further information regarding this subject, and gives no references where he obtained this information. Whether this text used by Cagliostro was our *Clef du cabinet hermétique*, or the elusive *Cabinet hermétique* referred to by the *Petit Albert*, or some other text with a similar title, we have not been able to find out. However, if Dumas' remark that Cagliostro was following 'recipes' from this text is accurate, it would seem to suggest that this was a different text than the one we are presenting to the public. Our text is not written in the style of 'recipes'. Such a characterisation certainly fits better with the style of the descriptive process reproduced by the *Petit Albert* rather than our text, which adopts the more enigmatic style characteristic of alchemical texts and never identifies any of the substances involved in the operations it describes in a totally clear manner. On the other hand, the remark that Ca-

---

21 'Avec les plus authentiques adeptes, Cagliostro se mit au travail du four de l'athanor ; il se prit à cuire la substance mercurielle, il opéra dissolution, coagulation, Matière Première, selon les vraies recettes de la Clef du « Cabinet Hermétique ». Certains témoins assurent qu'il fit de l'or, qu'il parvint à grossir des perles'. *Cagliostro: homme de lumière*, Paris: Éditions Philosophiques, 1981, p. 45.

gliostro was 'cooking' the 'mercurial substance' and operating 'the dissolution, coagulation, Prime Matter', would indeed fit with the contents of our *Cabinet hermétique*, which deals exclusively with the making of the Philosophers' Stone. But since we have no idea of the entire contents of the *Cabinet hermétique* referred to by the *Petit Albert*, we cannot discount the possibility that it also dealt with the subject of making the Stone, so it still remains a possible candidate for the identity of the text that was used by Cagliostro.

In conclusion regarding the *Petit Albert* and Cagliostro: the issue of which exact text or texts these sources are referring to remains unresolved, at least until such a time as more information comes to the surface. The *Petit Albert* seems to be referring to a different text than our *Cabinet hermétique*, but the one used by Cagliostro could be either one, or even yet a third *Cabinet hermétique* still not identified, one that contains both apparently clear, recipe-style instructions, as well as the more enigmatic 'hints and clues' of our present *Clef du cabinet hermétique*.

BIBLIOGRAPHY

ALBERT, LE PETIT. *Le Solide trésor des merveilleux secrets de la magie naturelle et cabalistique du Petit Albert.* Bellegrade: [s.n.], 1658.

_____. *Le Solide Tresor des Merveilleux Secrets de la Magie Naturelle & Cabalistique du Petit Albert, Traduit exactement sur l'Original Latin, qui a pour Titre, Alberti Parvi Lucii libellus de mirabilibus Naturae Arcanis.* A Genève: Aux dépens de la Compagnie, c. 1710.

ANON. *Dialogue between Āras and Māriyah, with interpolated commentary by 'Abbād, entitled Sharḥ risālat Māriyah al-ḥakīmah (Explanation of the epistle of Maria the Sage)*, in Baǧdatlı Vehbi Efendi Kütüphanesi MS. 2273, ff. 136–150. Microfilm copy at the Martin Levey microfilm collection of Arabic scientific manuscripts, University of Utah, Marriott Library, Levey Original Reel 9 Title 1.

_____. *De Alchimia Opuscula Complura Veterum Philosophorum.* Francoforti : Ex officina Cyriaci Iacobi, 1550.

_____. *L'Ancienne guerre des Chevaliers*, in Limojon de St Didier, *Le Triomphe Hermétique ou la pierre philosophale victorieuse.* Amsterdam: Henry Wetstein, 1699.

_____. *Lettre aux vrais disciples d'Hermès*, in Limojon de St Didier, *Le Triomphe Hermétique ou la pierre philosophale victorieuse.* Amsterdam: Henry Wetstein, 1699.

_____., ed. *Musæum Hermeticum Reformatum et amplificatum, Omnes Sopho-Spagyricæ Artis Discipulos fidelissime erudiens, quo pacto Summa illa veraque Lapidis Philosophici Medicina, qua res omnes qualemcunque defectum patientes, instaurantur, inveniri et haberi queat: Continens Tractatus Chimicos XXI.*

Præstantissimos, quorum Nomina et Seriem versa pagella indicabit. Francofurti: Hermannus à Sande, 1678.

————. *La Clef du cabinet hermétique.* MSS Col36. New York Public Library Manuscripts and Archives Division. N.D. (eighteenth century).

————. *La Clef du cabinet hermétique.* S.L.: Lulu/Editions Philemon, 2018.

ARTERO, JEAN. *Julien Champagne: Apôtre de la Science Hermétique.* Paris: Grenoble Le Mercure dauphinois, 2014.

BERTHELOT, MARCELLIN, & M. OCTAVE HOUDAS. *La chimie au moyen âge.* Paris: Imprimerie Nationale, 1893.

BÖKE, CHRISTER, JOHN KOOPMANS, STANISLAS KLOSSOWSKI DE ROLA, & AARON CHEAK, trans., eds. *The Hermetic Recreations: Including the Scholium.* Auckland: Rubedo Press, 2017.

CANSELIET, EUGÈNE. 'Quelques réflexions alchimiques sur les drogues', in *Les Cahiers de la Tour Saint-Jacques,* n°1, 1er trim. Paris: H. Roudil, 1960.

CHAMPAGNE, JULIEN. *La Vie Minérale: Étude de Philosophie Hermétique et d'Esotérisme Alchimique.* Manuscript, 1908. Amboise: Éditions Les Trois R, 2011.

————., & FREDERICK HOCKLEY. *Procédé de Mr Yardley: Communiqué par lui à Mr Garden, de Londres en 1716, transcrit d'une lettre autographe de Sigismond Bacstrom de 1804.* Manuscript, 1913. Amboise: Éditions Les Trois R, 2015.

CHEAK, AARON. *Light Broken through the Prism of Life: René Schwaller de Lubicz and the Hermetic Problem of Salt.* Dissertation, University of Queensland, 2011.

COENDERS VAN HELPEN, BEREND. *Escalier des sages ou la philosophie des anciens.* Groningen: Charles Pieman, 1686.

D'ESPAGNET, JEAN. *Enchiridion physicæ restitutae, in quo verus naturæ concentus exponitur, plurimique antiquæ philosophiæ errores per canones et certas demonstrationes dilucide aperiuntur. Tractatus alter inscriptus. Arcanum hermeticæ philosophiæ opus: in quo occulta naturæ et artis circa lapidis philosophorum materiam et operandi modum canonice et ordinate fiunt manifesta.* Parisiis apud Nicolaum Buon, sub signo D. Claudij & hominis syluestris, 1623.

DUBOIS, GENEVIÈVE. *Fulcanelli devoilé.* Paris: Dervy, 1996.

————. *Fulcanelli and the Alchemical Revival: The Man Behind the*

Mystery of the Cathedrals. Translated by Jack Cain. Rochester, Vermont: Destiny, 2006.

DUMAS, FRANÇOIS RIBADEAU. *Cagliostro: homme de lumière.* Paris: Éditions philosophiques, 1981.

DUNGAN, NICHOLAS. *Gallatin: America's Swiss Founding Father* (New York: NYU Press, 2010).

ETTNER VON EITERITZ, JOHANN CHRISTOPH. *Rosetum chymicum oder: Chymischer Rosen-Garten, aus welchem der vorsichtige Kunst-Beflissene voll-blühende Rosen, der unvorsichtige Laborant aber Dornen und verfaulte Knospen abbrechen wird.* Frankfurt: Rohrlach 1724.

FERGUSON, JOHN. *Bibliotheca Chemica: A Catalogue of the Alchemical, Chemical, and Pharmaceutical Books in the Collection of the Late James Young of Kelly and Durris ESQ., LL.D., F.R.S., F.R.S.* Two volumes. Glasgow: Maclehose, 1906.

FULCANELLI. *Le Mystère des cathédrales et l'interprétation ésotérique des symbols hermétiques du grand œuvre.* Paris: Jean Schmidt, 1926;

———. *Les Demeures philosophales et le symbolisme hermétique dans ses rapports avec l'art sacré et l'ésotérisme du grand-oeuvre.* Paris: Jean Schmidt, 1930.

———. *Le Mystère des cathédrales.* Translated by Mary Sworder. London: Neville Spearman. 1971

———. *The Dwellings of the Philosophers.* Translated by Brigitte Donvez and Lionel Perrin. Boulder, Colorado: Archive Press, 1999.

GALLATIN, ALBERT H. *Albert H. Gallatin Letters, 1864.* Northfield, Vermont: Norwich University Archives, Kreitzberg Library, 1864.

GIBERT, JEAN-FRANÇOIS. *Propos sur la Chrysopée, suivi de 'Manuscrit de Pierre Dujols-Fulcanelli traitant de la pratique alchimique'.* Paris: Dervy, 1995.

GRIMES, SHANNON. *Becoming Gold: Zosimos of Panopolis and the Alchemical Arts in Roman Egypt.* Auckland: Rubedo Press, 2018.

HELMONT, FRANCISCUS MERCURIUS VAN. *C.LIII. aphorismes chymiques : ausquels on peut facilement rapporter tout ce qui regarde la chymie / mis en ordre par les soins & et travail de l'Hermite du Fauxbourg ; nouvellement traduit du Latin en françois,*

par m.s.d.r. Paris : Chez Laurent d'Houry, 1692.

HELVETIUS, JOHN FREDERICK. *The Golden Calf, which the World Adores, and Desires.* London: John Starkey, 1670.

HERMANN, PAUL. *Materia Medica: Or, A New Description of the Virtues and Effects of all Drugs, or Simple Medicines Now in Use.* London: Charles Rivington, 1727.

LE BRUN, GUILLAUME. *Dictionnaire universel François et Latin, tiré des meilleurs auteurs. Troisième edition, revue, corrigée et augmentée.* Paris: Libr. associés, 1770.

LIMOJON DE ST DIDIER, ALEXANDRE-TOUSSAINT DE. *Le Triomphe Hermétique ou la pierre philosophale victorieuse. Traitté plus complet & plus intelligible, qu'il y en ait eû jusques ici, touchant le magistere hermetique.* Amsterdam: Henry Wetstein, 1699.

MAY, GREGORY. *Jefferson's Treasure: How Albert Gallatin Saved the New Nation from Debt.* Regnery History, 2018.

NÈGRE, SARAH. *Un travail de compilation sur les superstitions populaires des XVIIe et XVIIIe siècles : L'histoire des imaginations extravagantes de Monsieur Oufle, par l'abbé Laurent Bordelon.* Mémoire de Master 1 Cultures de l'écrit et de l'image. Dir. Philippe Martin. ENSSIB, 2014.

NEWMAN, WILLIAM R. *The Summa Perfectionis of Pseudo-Geber: A Critical Edition, Translation, and Study.* Leiden: Brill, 1991.

NORWICH UNIVERSITY ARCHIVES. *Guide to the Albert H. Gallatin Letters, 1864.* Northfield, Vermont: Norwich University Archives and Special Collections, 2010.

PARACELSUS, THEOPHRASTUS BOMBASTUS VON HOHEN-HEIM, & BERNARD GEORGES PENOT. *Philippi Aureoli Theophrasti Paracelsi Utriusque Medicinae doctoris celeberrimi, centum quindecim curationes experime[n]taque: e Germanico idiomate in Latinu[m] versa. Accesserunt Quaedam præclara atque utilissima a B. G. a Portu Aquitano annexa.* Lyon: Lertout, 1582.

———. *A hundred and fouretene experiments and cures of the famous physitian Philippus Aureolus Theophrastus Paracelsus; translated out of the Germane tongue into the Latin. Whereunto is added certaine excellent and profitable workes by B.G. a Portu Aquitano. Also certaine secrets of Isacke Hollandus concerning the vegetall and animall worke. Also the spagericke antidotarie for gunne-shot of Iosephus Quirsitanus. Collected by Iohn Hes-*

ter—Centum quindecim curationes experimentaque è German-
ico idiomate in Latinum versa. London: Vallentine Sims dwell-
ing on Adling hill at the signe of the white Swanne, 1596.

PORTA, GIAMBATTISTA DELLA. *Natural magick by John Baptis-*
ta Porta, a Neapolitane; in twenty books ... wherein are set forth
all the riches and delights of the natural sciences. London: Printed for Thomas Young and Samuel Speed, 1658.

RULANDUS, MARTINUS. *Lexicon Alchemiae Sive Dictionarium*
Alchemisticum: Cum obscuriorum Verborum, & Rerum Her-
meticarum, tum Theophrast-Paracelsicarum Phrasium, Planam
Explicationem continens. Francofurti Palthenius, 1612.

_____. *A Lexicon of Alchemy or Alchemical Dictionary.* Translated
by A. E. Waite. London: S.N., 1893.

SALMON, WILLIAM, et al., *Bibliothèque des philosophes (chymi-*
ques) par le sieur S.D.E.M. Paris: Charles Angot, 1672.

_____. *Bibliotheque des philosophes chymiques, Nouvelle édition,*
revûë, corrigée & augmentée de plusieurs philosophes, avec des
figures & des notes pour faciliter l'intelligence de leur doctrine,
par M. J. M. D. R. Cailleau: Paris, 1740–1754.

SANCHEZ, CAROLINE. *Entre jeu et magie, une littérature ludique :*
Étude de livres de jeux divinatoires et du Grand et Petit Albert.
Mémoire du Master 2 Cultures de l'écrit et de l'image. Dir.
Philippe Martin, ENSSIB, 2015)

STAPLETON, H. E., G. L. LEWIS, and F. SHERWOOD TAYLOR,
'The Sayings of Hermes quoted in the Mā' Al-Waraqī of Ibn
Umail', in Ambix, vol. 3, (April, 1949), nos. 3–4, p. 77.

STERNHALS, JOHANN. *Ritter Krieg, das ist. Ein Philosophisch ge-*
dicht, in Form eines Gerichtlichen Process, wie zwey Metallen,
nemlich, Sol und Mars durch Klag, Antwort, und Beweiss, jeg-
liches Natur und Eygenschafft von jrem natürlichen Gott und
Richter Mercurio gehöret, und entlich durch ein wolgegründtes
Urtel, mit ewigwerender Freundtschafft einig zusamen verbun-
den werden ... Gestellet durch J. Schaubert. M. Wittel: Erffordt,
1595.

TOLLIUS, JACOBUS. *Manuductio ad cælum chemicum.* Amstelædami: Apud Janssonio-Waesbergios, 1688.

_____. *Le Chemin du ciel chymique.* S.L: S.N., 1690–1710.

UŽDAVINYS, ALGIS, ed. *The Golden Chain: An Anthology of Py-*
thagorean and Platonic Philosophy. Bloomington, Indiana:
World Wisdom, 2004.

VALENTINUS, BASILIUS. *Ein kurtz Summarischer Tractat Fratris Basilij Valentini von dem grossen Stein der Uralten, daran so viel tausent Meister anfangs der Welt hero gemacht haben.* Eißleben: Bartholomæum Hornigk, 1599.

VANDENBROECK, ANDRÉ. *Al-Kemi: Hermetic, Occult, Political, and Private Aspects of R.A. Schwaller de Lubicz.* Inner Traditions/Lindisfarne Press Uroboros Series v. 1. Rochester, Vermont: Lindisfarne Press, 1987.

VILLANOVA, ARNALDUS DE. *Arnaldi de Villanova, philosophi, medici et chymici excellentissimi, Omnia, quae exstant, opera chymica : videlicet, Thesaurus thesaurorum: seu, Rosarius philosophorum ac omnium secretorum maximum secretum. Lumen novum, Flos florum, & Speculum alchimiae. Quibus nimirum artis huius mysteria etiam secretissima luculenter enodantur, & quam maximalicet, & potest fieri perspicuitate explicantur.* Francofurti: Typis Ioachimi Bratheringij, 1603.

WAITE, ARTHUR EDWARD. *The Lives of the Alchemystical Philosophers.* London: George Redway, 1815.

ABOUT THE CONTRIBUTORS

CHRISTER BÖKE (MA, History and Theology) has been researching the history of alchemy for the past two decades. His major interest lies in reconstructing alchemical theories from an experimental perspective. Christer wrote his Masters thesis (Lund, 2002) on the 'Paracelsus dispute' (1707–1708) between the Swedish chymists, Urban Hjärne and Magnus Gabriel von Block, triggered by the infamous Paykull affair—a topic he further covered during 'On the Fringes of Alchemy', a workshop held with different scholars in Budapest 2010. Christer participated in the Swedish translation and commentary of Fulcanelli's *Le Mystère des cathédrales* (*Katedralernas mysterium*, 2013), was featured in the documentary *Alkemistens År: The Great Work* (2013), and acted as a peer-reviewer on Carl-Michael Edenborg's alchemical fiction drama, *Alkemistens dotter* (2014). Together with John Koopmans, he edited and translated *Hermetic Recreations*, published in 2017 by Rubedo Press.

JOHN KOOPMANS (BA, Hons, Geography) is a retired professional Regional Planner/demographer. Over the years, he has collaborated in, or contributed to, a number of books concerning biblical history, and the historical study of grail lore. He has also co-authored an alchemical book, *Hermetic Recreations*, published in 2017 by Rubedo Press. When he's not intensely studying alchemy, or transcribing numerous old alchemical texts (many in original handwriting), he continues to maintain a very long, active interest in various studies, including recent and ancient history (civilisations, archæology, religions, sciences, philosophies, esoterica, and mythologies).

JUAN DUC PEREZ is a transcriber and translator who over the years has worked with many other fellow enthusiasts (including present coauthors Christer Böke and John Koopmans) in the transcription and translation of numerous English, Spanish, French, Italian, German, Latin, and Arabic alchemical and chymical texts, many of them unpublished manuscripts. A devoted empiricist, he does not only read about alchemy and chymistry, but invests a great amount of his time and efforts in putting their transmutational assertions to the test. A particular area of interest for him are the experiments and processes that have been put forward specifically and explicitly as proofs of the reality of metallic transmutation in the alchemical and chymical literature of the sixteenth, seventeenth and eighteenth centuries, of which he has already found more than thirty examples.

AARON CHEAK (PHD, Religious Studies) is a scholar of comparative religion, philosophy, and esotericism. Straddling the interstices between integral and Hermetic philosophy, he received his doctorate in 2011 for his thesis on René Schwaller de Lubicz, and served as president of the international Jean Gebser Society from 2013–2015. He has appeared in both academic and esoteric publications, including *Light Broken through the Prism of Life* (2011), *Alchemical Traditions* (2013/2021), *Diaphany* (2015), *Octagon* (2016), and *Lux in Tenebris* (2017). As a translator of French, German, and Greek, he is presently bringing a number of important projects to fruition through Rubedo Press.

CPSIA information can be obtained
at www.ICGtesting.com
Printed in the USA
BVHW072314020221
599232BV00011B/356